Between Protest and Power

Between Protest and Power

The Green Party in Germany

E. Gene Frankland
Ball State University

and

Donald Schoonmaker
Wake Forest University

Westview Press
BOULDER • SAN FRANCISCO • OXFORD

Copyright © 1992 by Westview Press, Inc.

Published in 1992 in the United States of America by Westview Press, Inc., 5500 Central Avenue, Boulder, Colorado 80301-2877, and in the United Kingdom by Westview Press, 36 Lonsdale Road, Summertown, Oxford OX2 7EW

Library of Congress Cataloging-in-Publication Data
Frankland, E. Gene.
  Between protest and power : the Green Party in Germany / E. Gene Frankland and Donald Schoonmaker.
    p. cm.
  Includes bibliographical references and index.
  ISBN 0-8133-8069-3 (cloth). — ISBN 0-8133-8070-7 (pb)
  1. Grünen (Political party)—History. I. Schoonmaker, Donald.
JN3972.A98G784 1992
324.243'08—dc20   92-17901
                                                                        CIP

Printed and bound in the United States of America

The paper used in this publication meets the requirements
of the American National Standard for Permanence of Paper
for Printed Library Materials Z39.48-1984.

10   9   8   7   6   5   4   3   2   1

Contents

Tables and Figures

Tables

Figures

Preface

THIS BOOK EXAMINES the development of the Greens (Die Grünen) as a new party phenomenon in Germany. Its purpose is to provide the student of comparative politics with an understanding of the Greens' historical origins, electoral support, organizational structure, programmatic views, governmental role, and future prospects. We attempt to demonstrate why a party that has typically received 5–10 percent of the votes is important from both a broad theoretical perspective and a historical nation-specific perspective. What has been the impact of the new party on the German political system and the system's impact on the new party? Furthermore, we are interested in how the development of the German Greens compares with that of other West and East European Greens. The German Greens have been the most conspicuous member of a growing family of Green parties in Europe and beyond.

Our curiosity about the Greens dates back to their formative years, 1979–1980. At that time, the conventional wisdom was that the Green party would be a transitory protest phenomenon. Little did we know that we would be devoting virtually all of our research time over the next decade to its development. Since the mid-1980s, the academic literature on the Greens and related "new politics" topics has become voluminous. In late August 1989, we agreed to pool our efforts to produce a book that would integrate our own separate field studies with the findings of other authors. Our goal was a book that would be comprehensive but accessible to the upper-level undergraduate student. In contrast to the authors of many of the earlier textbooks on the Greens, we had no ideological ax to grind. What we had in mind was a solid work of political science rather than of political advocacy.

During the writing of this book, a series of political "earthquakes" occurred: the fall of the Berlin Wall, the disintegration of Communist Eastern Europe, the unification of Germany (and the defeat of the West German Greens in the first all-German elections), the failed Soviet coup, and the breakup of the USSR. These unanticipated events changed the world. And they forced us in midstream to rethink, realign, and reupdate every chapter. The Greens have always been a moving target, but, prior to November 1989, the ground had seemed reasonably stable.

Unfortunately, it is impossible to acknowledge here by name the many people who have helped to make this book possible. We must first thank the nearly one hundred Green (and Alliance 90) parliamentarians, staff assistants, party officers and workers, and activists who were willing to talk at length with us from 1980 to 1991. Second, we thank the parliamentary and party archivists and our professional colleagues who shared information. Third, we acknowledge our institutional support. Gene Frankland's field research was supported by the Deutscher Akademischer Austauschdienst (DAAD) and the Ball State University Alumni Association. Donald Schoonmaker's field research was supported by the Archie Foundation of Wake Forest University. Fourth, we thank Donald Kommers, editor of *The Review of Politics*, for his support in publishing our articles relating to the Greens: Frankland's and Schoonmaker's in the Winter 1988 issue and Frankland's in the Summer 1989 issue (from which we have borrowed some information). Frankland has also drawn upon his article "Green Politics and Alternative Economics," *German Studies Review* 11, no. 1 (February 1988):111–132.

Specifically, we thank Ferdinand Müller-Rommel of the University of Lüneburg and Sara Parkin of the British Green party and the European Greens Coordination for their steady streams of information on Green politics through the years. Alfred Krause of Germany was also a source of continual help and encouragement. We thank the following individuals for their critical reactions to draft chapters: Gerard Braunthal, Michael Hughes, Wendy Baucom, Stephanie Mohl, and Erich Frankland. We are indebted to Elide Varges and Paige Konz for their first-class assistance in word processing. We thank Susan McEachern of Westview Press for her early and enthusiastic response to our prospectus and for her patience through the above-mentioned political "earthquakes" that slowed us down. Finally, we deeply appreciate the support of our wives, Diane Frankland and Meyressa Schoonmaker, throughout the two years of writing and rewriting. We dedicate this book to them.

Of course, full responsibility for the findings and conclusions herein is ours. We welcome professional comments and corrections from readers.

E. Gene Frankland
Donald Schoonmaker

Acronyms

AL	Alternative Liste (Alternative List)
APO	Ausserparlamentarische Opposition (Extra-Parliamentary Opposition)
AUD	Aktionsgemeinschaft Unabhängiger Deutscher (Action Community of Independent Germans)
BAGs	Bundesarbeitsgemeinschaften (federal policy working groups)
BBU	Bundesverband Bürgerinitiativen Umweltschultz (federal association of citizen initiatives for environmental protection)
BL	Bunte Liste (Multicolored List)
CDU	Christlich-Demokratische Union (Christian Democratic Union)
CND	Campaign for Nuclear Disarmament (Britain)
CPN	Communistische Partij Nederland (Communist party of the Netherlands)
CSCE	Conference on Security and Cooperation in Europe
CSU	Christlich-Soziale Union (Christian Social Union)
DDR	Deutsche Demokratische Republik (German Democratic Republic)
DJ	Demokratie Jetzt (Democracy Now)
DM	deutsche mark
EC	European Community
EFTA	European Free Trade Association
EMR	Ecological Movement of Romania
EVA	European Free Alliance
EVP	Evangelische Volkspartij (Evangelical People's party)
FDP	Freie Demokratische Partei (Free Democratic party)
GAL	Grün-Alternative Liste (Green Alternative List)
GAZ	Grüne Aktion Zukunft (Green Action Future)
GDR	German Democratic Republic
GLH	Grüne Liste Hessen (Green List Hesse)
GLSH	Grüne Liste Schleswig-Holstein (Green List Schleswig-Holstein)
GLU	Grüne Liste Umweltschutz (Green List [for] Environmental Protection)
GNP	gross national product

GP   Grüne Partei (DDR) (East German Green party)
GPS   Grüne Partei Schweiz (Swiss Green party)
GRAEL   Green Alternative European Link
IFM   Initiative Frieden und Menschenrechte (Initiative for Peace and Human Rights)
JUSOS   Jungesozialisten (Working Group of Young Socialists)
KB   Kommunistischer Bund (Communist League)
KPD   Kommunistische Partei Deutschlands (Communist party of Germany)
MP   member of Parliament
NATO   North Atlantic Treaty Organization
NDP   National-Demokratische Partei Deutschlands (National Democratic party of Germany)
NF   Neues Forum (New Forum)
ÖDP   Ökologisch-Demokratische Partei (Ecological Democratic party)
PDS   Partei Demokratisches Sozialismus (Party of Democratic Socialism [ex-Communists of East Germany])
PPR   Politieke Partij Radikalen (Political party of Radicals [Dutch])
PS   Parti Socialiste (French Socialist party)
PSP   Pacifistisch Socialistische Partij (Pacifist Socialist party)
RPR   Rassemblement pour la République (Rally for the Republic [neo-Gaullist])
SDS   Socialist German Students Union
SED   Sozialistische Einheitspartei Deutschlands (Socialist Unity party of Germany [Communists])
SPD   Sozialdemokratische Partei Deutschlands (Social Democratic party of Germany)
SPV   Sonstige Politische Vereinigung (Alternative Political Alliance)
UFV   Unabhängiger Frauenverband (Independent Women's Association)
USP   Umweltschutzpartei (Environmental Protection party)
USSR   Union of Soviet Socialist Republics
VGÖ   Vereinte Grüne Österreichs (United Greens of Austria)

Introduction

THIS BOOK FOCUSES ON THE GREENS (Die Grünen) as a new party phenomenon within the Federal Republic of Germany. After 1949 the Christian Democratic party (CDU/CSU), the Social Democratic party (SPD), and the Free Democratic party (FDP) quickly established themselves as the dominant parties of West Germany. After 1961 they were the only parties represented in the Bundestag (federal parliament). This "Bonn system" withstood the dual challenge of the right-wing National Democratic party (NDP) and the left-wing Extra-Parliamentary Opposition (APO) in the late 1960s. However, over the next decade the Federal Republic experienced the proliferation of nonpartisan citizen action groups (Bürgerinitiativen) focused on local problems and the emergence of new social movements concerned with national problems also neglected by the major parties. During the late 1970s, new electoral alliances began to spring up to contest local, state, and the 1979 European Parliament elections. On January 13, 1980, a heterogeneous alliance of activists from diverse political backgrounds, but who shared a deep discontent with the "party cartel," launched the Greens as a new national party.

The Newcomers

The young "antiparty" party managed to survive its early infighting over the federal program, its dismal results in the October 1980 federal elections, and the departure of most of its conservative wing by 1981. By forcefully and creatively raising the issues of ecology, peace, and human rights, which had been largely neglected by the major parties, the Greens soon overcame the Federal Republic's formidable barriers to the success of new parties. During the 1980s, they won parliamentary seats at local, state, and federal levels of West German government as well as in the European Parliament. Green deputies added a streak of color to a somewhat gray West German partisan landscape. They set new issues on the policy agenda, they ignored parliamentary codes of dress and behavior, and they participated in extraparliamentary protest actions. The social profile of these unruly newcomers diverged significantly from that of the established parties: Green parliamentary groups included more young people, women, and teachers and students and reflected unconventional political backgrounds.

The Greens' federal program of 1980 was radical. It advocated nothing less than the transformation of West German society and economy, albeit through nonviolent means. From the outset, the new party challenged the postwar consensus of West German elites that the established political order of representative institutions and passive citizenship should be preserved, that economic growth and consumptive life-styles should be encouraged, and that engagement in the Western Alliance, including its policy of nuclear deterrence, should be maintained. In contrast, the Greens called for the democratization of the political system through grass-roots activism, decentralization, self-administration, and referenda. They rejected the view that progress is synonymous with soaring gross national products (GNPs) and instead emphasized the ecological and social costs of rapid industrial growth. They favored disengagement from NATO and campaigned for unilateral disarmament. Furthermore, the new party took up the causes of women, minorities, and disadvantaged groups at home and abroad. In the early 1980s, the Greens saw themselves discounted by the generally hostile press both as a one-issue (environmentalist) party *and* as a hodgepodge of protest groups.

The Greens represent an organizational experiment in combining features of the fluid cause-focused movement with those of the more rigid election-focused party apparatus.[1] The founders of the Greens embraced the notion of *Basisdemokratie* (grass-roots democracy) to differentiate the new party, as a decentralized participatory democracy, from the formalistic democracy of the established parties, which they perceived as centralized bureaucratic oligarchies. The Greens limited the tenure and the resources of their leaders and banned the practice of simultaneously holding party office and a parliamentary seat. Furthermore, the Greens required their deputies to give up their seats in Parliament to other party members on the candidate list at midterm (rotation). Although this *basisdemokratische* procedure and some others were soon to be modified, the Green party organization presented during its first decade a profile that was an alternative to that of the major West German parties.

Numerous electoral studies have indicated that the Greens have also been a distinctive party in terms of their core voters. Green voters have tended to be under thirty-five years old, highly educated, new middle class (salaried white collar or professional), urban or university town residents, and secular oriented (low or no church attendance). In terms of political background, Green voters have tended to identify themselves as left of center, to indicate so-called postmaterialist value priorities, and to consider the SPD their second party choice. Despite some inept campaigns and intense factionalism (especially at the federal level), Green voters provided the crucial 5 percent support (necessary for party entry into the Bundestag) in two federal elections, two European elections, most state elections, and numerous local elections during the 1980s. Then in the first all-German elections the Greens (West) failed to win seats in the Bundestag. However, the party's recovery in the state parliamentary elections during 1991 and 1992 indicates the unique circumstances of the December 2, 1990, outcome.

Explaining the Green Phenomenon

The sudden emergence of an antiestablishment party within the Bundestag in March 1983 generally alarmed authoritative observers. Some portrayed the Greens as a recurrence of the romantic, nationalist *Wandervogel* movement of the late nineteenth and early twentieth centuries, which helped pave the way for later Nazi youth groups.[2] Some went to the other extreme, portraying the Green party as a tool of Communists and a "watermelon"— green on the outside but red on the inside. Although alarmed by the supposed totalitarian dark side of the unruly newcomers, most pundits saw the Greens as an unstable protest party that would fall apart within a couple of years.

The small Green party has received a disproportionate amount not only of media and partisan attention but also of scholarly attention. The most popular approach has been to explain the Greens' emergence in terms of changing social structures and shifting value priorities. From this viewpoint, a new educated middle class has been emerging throughout Western Europe that has been socialized under conditions of relative peace and prosperity. Its value orientations no longer neatly fit the traditional left-right continuum. According to Ronald Inglehart's cross-national research, these postmaterialists show greater sensitivity to quality-of-life issues, such as the environment, and value the individual rights of self-expression and participation.[3] According to the value-change perspective, the Greens are a postmaterialist party with a core of positive values that are likely to be shared by a steadily growing proportion of the electorate, assuming economic crises do not generate resurging materialist priorities among future generations. Thus the future of the new party largely depends on how well the SPD (which also includes postmaterialists) can co-opt the new politics agenda without losing its materialists to the CDU. In other words, the Greens as an organized party might not survive, but they represent far more than a diffuse protest phenomenon.

The value-shift hypothesis is challenged by a number of scholars who have interpreted the Greens as a cyclical (or generational) protest phenomenon. From this viewpoint, the core supporters of the Greens constitute a new educated class with its own materialistic self-interest. In rough outline, Jens Alber argues that because of the mismatch between the supply of highly educated graduates and the employment opportunities available in West Germany since the late 1970s, many frustrated young people were drawn to antiestablishment politics.[4] Presumably if they became more integrated into the economy they would tend to vote for more "responsible" parties, particularly the reform-oriented SPD. Wilhelm Bürklin, furthermore, stresses the lack of social integration of the educated young supporters of the Greens: As these individuals marry, raise families, and commit themselves to careers, they will inevitably become more sensitive to materialist values.[5] In short, such scholars see the Greens as having no particular long-term significance (and as destined to fade). They explain the Greens' surge in the 1980s as the result of "period effects" and/or life cycle effects.

A third perspective combines certain features of the previous two. Hans-Joachim Veen argues that the Greens are a "milieu" party—they represent a particular narrow constituency rather than a broad electoral alliance, as both the SPD and the CDU do. Green party supporters are not defined by occupation, region, or religion but by their "freedom and personal development-orientated values."[6] Though the Greens attract protest voters, their core supporters share reinforcing policy views *and* are socially integrated in their daily activities by the networks of left-alternative society (co-ops, publications, and support groups, for example). From this view, then, the Green party exists not so much to transform society as to represent and defend its milieu; therefore it lacks the impetus to broaden its political base and to build coalitions with other parties. Thus the electoral niche of the Greens is likely to be secure (though stagnate), and the more imminent threat to their future comes from intraparty factionalism rather than from the SPD's co-optation of their issues.

A more sympathetic perspective is that there would have been no Green party in West Germany without severe environmental problems. Wolfgang Rüdig posits a new social cleavage between economic/exploitative interests and ecological/preservationist interests as the basis for the worldwide emergence of Green parties.[7] There are, in fact, countries where Green parties have emerged despite the presence of "left-libertarian" parties. The West German Greens have enjoyed more success than others because of the timely overlap of the environmentalist agenda and the new left agenda. Robyn Eckersley ventures a more comprehensive explanation: The new educated middle class is most likely to be aware of environmental degradations and to be "the least constrained from pursuing remedial action" because of "its relative structural autonomy from the production process" and "its adherence to the culture of critical discourse."[8] As long as the major parties demonstrate a lack of political will in confronting the causes of the environmental crisis, the Greens will have an electoral base in the new educated class.

Already it should be apparent that new problems and social cleavages by themselves do not explain the rise of Green parties. One must also consider various institutional and political facilitators that constitute the political opportunity structure. Electoral laws are obvious institutional facilitators (or barriers). Since 1953, no party in West Germany other than the three major parties had independently cleared the 5 percent threshold for entry into the Bundestag. In the late 1970s, electoral experiences demonstrated to the environmentalists that to gain parliamentary representation they had to have allies. Subsequently the threshold requirement for continuing success became a vital ingredient of the glue that managed to hold together the Greens' heterogeneous alliance of activists during the 1980s. Another institutional facilitator is public funding for political parties. West German parties that win at least 0.5 percent of the votes receive public funds for campaign expenses. After 1979, the prospects for the generous influx of public funds helped to ensure the national formation of the Green party. The openness of legislative, administrative, and judicial systems to the input from outsider groups and their institutional capabilities to produce innovative outputs constitute a dimension of the political opportunity structure. If legislators, administrators, and judges are somewhat responsive to new demands, then the motivation for new party formation is reduced. Herbert Kitschelt's comparative study of antinuclear movements concludes that the relatively closed political input structures and relatively weak output structures of the Federal Republic encouraged its antinuclear movement to follow a confrontational strategy, which set the stage for the emergence of the Green party.[9]

The vertical division of institutional powers is another possible facilitator for new parties. West Germany's federal system provides opportunities for a new party to win seats in the Landtage (state parliaments), which are more significant than the local councils of unitary systems. The Greens were able to build up resources, experience, and credibility in six Landtage prior to their 1983 breakthrough into the Bundestag. After the December 1990 surprise "eviction" of the Greens (West) from the Bundestag, they still held seats in nine of eleven original Landtage and their Eastern allies held seats in four of five new Landtage.

Finally, there are possible political facilitators relating to the party system itself. Peter Pulzer emphasizes the importance of a major party's "adaptability in policy, in organizational structure, [and] in social appeal."[10] Soon after Helmut Schmidt replaced Willy Brandt as chancellor in 1974, the SPD began retreating from its reform priorities, which alienated many young left-wing party members. Even more, despite evidence of changing public opinion, in the early 1980s the SPD leadership maintained its support for nuclear power plants and its commitment to the deployment of new nuclear missiles by the North Atlantic Treaty Organization (NATO). The Greens were able to move into the vacuum and present themselves as the parliamentary arm of the antinuclear movement and the peace movement and of new social movements in general. However, since the mid-1980s the SPD has endeavored to transform its image by updating its program and promoting a new generation of leaders so as to make the Greens superfluous in the future. Furthermore, the numerical nature of party competition may be a facilitator for new party success. The West German party system had developed with a restricted number of relevant actors. Because the SPD and the CDU/CSU seldom won absolute majorities, a small party receiving over 5 percent of the votes had the opportunity to have a disproportionate policy influence in coalition politics. (The FDP has played this pivotal role through most of the years of the Federal Republic.) During the 1980s, West German Greens as one of four parliamentary parties were better positioned for political revelance than other Green parties in national parliaments where there were several small parties and major parties had multiple alternatives.

Although the fate of new parties is largely determined by external social and political forces, their internal characteristics are also relevant. New parties must cope with problems of factionalism and schisms, gain positive media exposure, and build up organizational capabilities. Obviously a new party's survival is facilitated by having a competent leadership and an active membership. Yet the Greens have distinguished themselves by deep distrust of their leaders and shallow loyalty to their party organization (compared with their faction or issue-constituency). In short, many of the Greens' weak organizational characteristics would seem to be obstacles to the long-term survival of the party unless adapted somewhat to the realities of old politics. Structural reform soared to the top of the Greens' agenda after their setback in the all-German elections.

The Greens and the West German Polity

The stability of the Federal Republic has contrasted significantly with the turmoil of the Weimar Republic between 1919 and 1933. In fact, the Federal Republic was seen in the 1970s by some as *Modell Deutschland*, an example of successful economic and political performance from which other democracies could learn a thing or two. Its militant democracy and economic miracle had marginalized radical left and radical right forces. West Germany's organized labor and management had maintained more of a cooperative than a combative stance toward each other. And the average West German citizen, by historical standards, had enjoyed not only an affluent life-style but also a full set of civil liberties. Participation in its free and competitive elections was high. National governmental power had alternated from right of center to left of center without constitutional crisis. In contrast to Weimar, the party system's dynamics were centripetal with two major parties presenting themselves as *Volksparteien* (people's parties) and the centrist FDP holding the balance of power.

In the early 1980s, the nightmare of the Greens' partisan critics was that the Greens would undermine the democratic stability of the Federal Republic by deadlocking its parliamentary institutions. And in the face of immobility, public opinion might be tempted to authoritarian solutions. The most vocal critics attacked the Greens as agents (or dupes) of totalitarianism. Then, in the mid-1980s, mainstream critics portrayed the Greens as irresponsible because of their aversion to parliamentary compromise, negotiation, and coalition. Yet the Greens were soon backing away from their position of fundamental opposition. Therefore, the next line of criticism was that if the Greens were to participate in government (because of their heterogeneous character) they would introduce a dangerous element of unpredictability as their internal majorities erratically shifted. Outside of Parliament, the Greens were also seen by critics as destabilizing because of their advocacy of protest and civil disobedience and their alleged tacit support for violence. And the policy views of parliamentary and extraparliamentary Greens, if implemented, would undermine the economic prosperity and the national security upon which West German democracy had developed since 1949.

When the idea of forming their own party was being debated in the late 1970s by Green and alternative activists, there were misgivings expressed about utilizing the conventional party format as a vehicle for transforming West German politics. Many recognized the limitations of promotional groups versus economic interests in the neocorporatist style of policymaking that had developed in the Federal Republic. Yet they also saw political parties, even Green ones, as vulnerable to bureaucratic and oligarchical imperatives that would over time elevate their leaders above the grass roots (*Basis*). Accordingly under the Greens' party charter, party leaders and deputies were to be directly accountable and removable by party bodies reflecting the views of the *Basis*. Nevertheless, some activists feared that the electoral success of the Green party would result inevitably in the desiccation of extraparliamentary activism and the accommodation of Green deputies to prevailing parliamentary norms. From this radical viewpoint, unfortunately the Greens have reinforced the system's stability by compensating for the representational shortcomings of the established parties and by channeling counterelites into the parliamentary system, where they have been exposed to its powerful assimilative forces.

Yet from a reformist perspective, the Greens' actions as tribune of outsider groups within parliamentary institutions, though not as exciting as direct actions in the streets, have contributed to political change. The *Volksparteien* had become ineffective in representing new demands because they were "overadapted to existing structures," "overgeneralized," "over-institutionalized," and "overloaded."[11] Almost invariably the bills introduced by Green deputies failed to pass, but they raised numerous questions in Parliament about defense policy, environmental policy, women's equality, civil liberties, and ethnic minorities. Furthermore, Green parliamentary groups channeled financial resources to alternative groups. The major parties soon began responding with programmatic and personnel changes. For example, their programs reflected more sensitivity to women's issues and several of their female members advanced into leadership roles. There were also institutional changes. In 1990, for example, federal and state environmental ministries dotted the governmental landscape, where none could be found in 1980.

Traditionally West German parliamentary oppositions have followed cooperative rather than competitive strategies. The Greens, however, conceived of themselves as the "real" opposition. For example, they pushed inquiries into illegal corporate campaign contributions and voted against increases in parliamentary pay and in public funding for party expenses. In the mid-1980s, the major parties also treated the Bundestag Greens as a real opposition by preventing their deputies from taking up seats on parliamentary boards that oversee the governmental intelligence services. In the Federal Constitutional Court, the Greens challenged (unsuccessfully) not only this but also the generous public subsidies of the major parties' "educational" foundations. In short, Green deputies aggressively used a wide range of instruments to provide the alternative within the system. Peter Merkl concluded (in 1989) that so far the Greens' role has been that of "court jester."[12] One should recall that the jester could play a vital role in the medieval court in speaking the truth to authority.

The impact of the Greens also can be seen in more diffuse terms. Political culture is the concept that political scientists use to refer to the overall pattern of attitudinal and behavioral orientations that citizens have toward their political system. Political culture is important because it is the human context of political institutions. However, untangling the cause-and-effect relationship can be perplexing. Probably the most that we can say is that during the 1980s the Green party reflected and reinforced trends toward a political culture more actively supportive of Western pluralistic democracy. The major parties had become highly institutionalized, professionally led, top-down organizations. The Greens attempted to become the countermodel: a semi-institutionalized, nonprofessionally led, "bottom-up" organization. Furthermore, the Green party has advocated participation throughout society, in contrast to the major parties' more technocratic approach to problem solving.

In cultural terms, the Greens have endeavored to make a clear break with historically troublesome German national characteristics. For example, they have encouraged and reflected a distrust of authority in all realms of life, including their own party organization. They have been opponents of repressive state actions versus dissenters and have been proponents of the human rights of unpopular minorities, such as homosexuals, convicted felons, and Gypsies. During the 1980s, the Green party was alert to infiltrations of neo-Nazis within its own ranks and actively opposed any societal recurrence of imperialism, nationalism, and racism in Germany. In a more everyday sense, John Ardagh credited (in 1988) the Greens with being an important socializing influence upon the young generation of West Germans by contributing to growing informality, nonconformity, and tolerance.[13] Following German reunification, the Greens and their allies have actively opposed the antiforeigner, racist campaigns of right-wing extremists, who have exploited growing socioeconomic anxieties.

The Greens and the New Europe

The Greens were not the first organized Green party in Europe nor the first to win seats in a national parliament. However, it was clearly their successes in the early and mid-1980s that stimulated the formation of new Green parties and encouraged the campaigns of preexisting Green parties throughout Western Europe. By the late 1980s, their "demonstration effect" was also evident in the countries of Eastern Europe and even within the USSR.

The vision of the Greens was of a Europe no longer divided by East-West bloc politics and threatened with nuclear annihilation—a Europe that could turn its resources to addressing the many environmental, economic, and human rights crises at home and abroad. Throughout the decade, the Greens had attempted to reach out to the unofficial peace and environmental groups within the Warsaw Pact countries. At first, the East German Communist leadership welcomed the visits of Greens, but soon it recognized that they could be mischief makers on both sides of the Wall and hindered their entry into the German Democratic Republic (GDR).

From the outset the Greens were distinctive from the major parties in their stance regarding intra-German relations. The overwhelming majority of Greens shared serious misgivings about a reunified Germany. Although not blind to the repressive nature of the Communist regime in East Berlin, they favored two Germanys in a loose confederation or an "Austrian solution" with East Germany as an independent sister state with which friendly relationships would be developed. The Greens were attuned to the views of the critical intelligentsia of East Germany, who sought a third way between Western liberal capitalism and Eastern state socialism. The early aims of the citizen movements, such as New Forum (*Neues Forum*), to bring about a democratized East Germany along the lines of a more humane and less bureaucratic socialism were congruent with those of many Green party activists. However, calls for German reunification soon punctuated the massive peaceful demonstrations of autumn 1989.

In the free national elections of March 1990, the West German Greens provided financial and moral support for not only the small East German Green party but also for the citizen movements. However, by that time the public mood had shifted to favoring rapid reunification and the East German surrogates of West Germany's major parties had drawn mass support away from the grass-roots activists who had spearheaded the first successful democratic revolution in German history. German reunification was on the fast track after the convincing win by the allies of the Christian Democrats in the spring 1990 national and local elections in East Germany. Dire environmental conditions did not generate much support for East German Greens, who won their few seats in the East German Parliament only in alliance with an independent women's association. Green issues were overshadowed by the sudden reemergence of the old politics of material security and nationhood.

As in the writing of the Basic Law of 1949, the party elites were working out the future design of Germany above the heads of the people. The Greens and some SPD activists called unsuccessfully for a slower pace for reunification, a popular referendum, and a new all-German constitution. Reunification was to be quickly arranged before misgivings about the economic and social costs could be mobilized into electoral politics. Despite SPD chancellor candidate Oskar LaFontaine's complaints, his party had joined a de facto grand coalition with the CDU and the FDP on the German question. The Greens were left with little to gain from their singular opposition in the West and not prepared to be stigmatized by associating with the "reborn" Communist party (Party of Democratic Socialism [PDS]), which also opposed rapid reunification, in the East.

Throughout the 1980s, the Greens had advocated the dissolution of both NATO and the Warsaw Pact and their replacement by a new collective security system in Europe. In the early 1990s, political developments appeared to be moving rapidly in that direction. The United States and the USSR had already agreed to remove their medium-range nuclear missiles, the issue that directly stimulated the resurgence of the peace movement in the early 1980s. Both sides were proposing major cuts in conventional and nuclear forces. Soviet troops were being withdrawn unilaterally throughout Eastern Europe and the U.S. Congress was eyeing large cuts in the U.S. defense budget. All German parties, except for the far-right fringe, had suddenly become "peace" parties. The Greens could only quibble about the specific timing and details of defense policy changes.

Since the mid-1980s, the process of European economic integration has been gaining momentum, though member governments still maintain different viewpoints about its final state. The major West German parties have been committed to pushing beyond economic union to political union. The Greens, however, have been ambivalent about European integration. They have favored a departure from the nation-state system of the nineteenth and twentieth centuries, but they have not favored the existing institutional framework of the European Community. The Greens have reacted negatively to its technocratic apparatus, its ineffectual parliamentary institution, and its inherent bias toward monopolistic capitalism. Rather than advocating the Europe of the Twelve, the Greens have advocated a Europe of the Regions. Rather than envisaging Europe as a new superpower in world affairs, they have envisaged Europe as a very loose confederation that does not threaten or exploit anyone at home or abroad.

In the June 1989 European elections, Green parties scored significant gains, confirming poll data that there has been a cross-national surge of public interest in environmental issues. West European party elites have recently learned the importance of "Green-speak." Almost invariably from left to right, however, major party leaders have shared the assumption that environmental protection and industrial growth are totally compatible. Only Green parties have dared to challenge this orthodoxy. With the collapse of Eastern European communism and the self-proclaimed triumph of liberal capitalism over state socialism in all areas, including environmental protection, the policy agenda of the 1990s seems to be transformed. Yet, ecological disasters are likely at the local, regional, national, and global levels in the coming decades. Within the Greens, certain critics are arguing that the future of the party depends upon remastering the politics of ecology and jettisoning much of its ideological baggage from the late 1960s leftist student movement.

The remaking of Europe during the 1990s will involve a fascinating composite of old politics and new politics concerns. The stakes are high and the outcomes are unpredictable. However, if the theorists of social structural change are generally correct, the underlying impetus toward cultural change will resume in Western Europe, despite the "triumph" of liberal capitalism and the citizenry's preoccupation with the economic ramifications of a new Europe. Democracy and ecology are likely to share the post–Cold War political stage with efficacy and equity as "first-order values."[14]

Studying the Greens

More than a decade after its launching, the Green party is electorally and organizationally a small party. Furthermore, it is a party racked by internal controversies. This book argues that the Greens represent a new type of political party. Though they have evolved in ways somewhat counter to the radical democratic aspirations of their founders, the Greens have retained in many regards a distinctive political profile within the German party system. This book also argues that, despite all their moral self-righteousness, ritualized unconventionality, and ferocious factionalism, the Greens have had a positive influence on the political institutions and political culture of the Federal Republic and, as a result, have been a catalyst for the worldwide emergence of Green and alternative parties.

Lastly, we argue that the Greens warrant serious study because of their relevance to the promises and perils of democratic renewal in advanced industrial societies. Robert Dahl has more eloquently suggested that we are approaching the third transformation in the history of democracy, one that deepens its institutional meaning and extends its scope throughout many societal realms.[15] Perhaps the Greens cannot lead us to this promised land, but since 1980 they have struggled to point us in its direction. Thus we maintain that there is much to be learned from their decade-long experience by activist and student alike.

This book attempts to locate the Greens within the historical context of German political traditions. But it is also concerned with the Greens as a manifestation of structural changes that have been occurring during recent decades in advanced industrial societies. To understand the Green phenomenon in West German politics, we selectively review in Chapter 2 developmental patterns in modern German history. Then in Chapter 3 we turn to consider general explanations of political change provided by contemporary political scientists. After contextualizing the Greens, we provide a series of substantive chapters investigating the electoral appeal of the Greens (Chapter 4), their formal and informal structure (Chapter 5), their programmatic development (Chapter 6), and their parliamentary role (Chapter 7). Each of these chapters draws upon multiple streams of data, including primary and secondary sources, and maintains a longitudinal perspective: how and why the Green party has changed since 1980.

The final part of the book consists of chapters devoted to the multiple impacts of the Greens within Germany (Chapter 8), the comparative development of Green parties in other European countries, and the uncertain prospects of this new type of party (Chapter 9). The conclusion, Chapter 10, ponders the larger meaning of the Green phenomenon and provides a reassessment of the Greens' future in view of the results of the historic all-German elections of December 2, 1990.

Notes

1. Robert Harmel, "On the Study of New Parties," *International Political Science Review* 6, no. 4 (1985):410.
2. These young, middle-class "nature lovers" were reacting against bourgeois values, urban industrial life, and established political institutions. Parallels exist with certain components of the Green movement; however, as a party the Greens have maintained a basic commitment to participatory democracy, which was lacking in the earlier *Wandervogel* movement.
3. Ronald Inglehart, *Culture Shift in Advanced Industrial Society* (Princeton, N.J.: Princeton University Press, 1990).
4. Jens Alber, "Modernization, Cleavage Structures, and the Rise of Green Parties and Lists in Europe," in Ferdinand Müller-Rommel, ed., *New Politics in Western Europe: The Rise and Successes of Green Parties and Alternative Lists* (Boulder: Westview Press, 1989), pp. 195–210.
5. Wilhelm P. Bürklin, "Governing Left Parties Frustrating the Radical Non-Established Left: The Rise and Inevitable Decline of the Greens," *European Sociological Review* 3, no. 2 (September 1987):109–126.
6. Hans-Joachim Veen, "The Greens as a Milieu Party," in Eva Kolinsky, ed., *The Greens in West Germany* (Oxford: Berg, 1989), pp. 31–59.
7. Wolfgang Rüdig, "Explaining Green Party Development: Reflections on a Theoretical Framework." Paper presented at the U.K. Political Studies Association conference, Coventry, England, April 4–6, 1989.
8. Robyn Eckersley, "Green Politics and the New Class: Selfishness or Virtue?" *Political Studies* 37, no. 2 (June 1989):221.
9. Herbert P. Kitschelt, "Political Opportunity Structures and Political Protest: Anti-Nuclear Movements in Four Democracies," *British Journal of Political Science* 16, no. 1 (January 1986):57–85.
10. Peter Pulzer, "The Paralysis of the Centre-Left: A Comparative Perspective," in Christian Soe, ed., *Comparative Politics '89/90* (Guilford, Conn.: Dushkin Publishing Group, 1989), p. 90.
11. Joachim Raschke, "Political Parties in Western Democracies," *European Journal of Political Research* 11 (1983):112–113.
12. Peter H. Merkl, "Conclusion: Were the Angry Old Men Wrong?" in Peter H. Merkl, ed., *The Federal Republic of Germany at Forty* (New York: New York University Press, 1989), p. 487.

13. John Ardagh, *Germany and the Germans* (London: Penguin, 1988), pp. 443–444.

14. Robert C. Paehlke, "Environmental Values and Democracy: The Challenge of the Next Century," in Norman J. Vig and Michael E. Kraft, eds., *Environmental Policy in the 1990s* (Washington, D.C.: Congressional Quarterly Press, 1990), pp. 349–368.

15. Robert A. Dahl, *Democracy and Its Critics* (New Haven: Yale University Press, 1989), pp. 322–346.

2

Confronting Modernity:
The Greens and the German
Historical Legacy

IN THE LAST DECADE of the twentieth century, the Germans reunified. In the period after the Berlin Wall was breached on November 1989, Henry Kissinger, German-American historian and statesman, quipped that if unification had not come in his lifetime, he would not have died unfulfilled. Kissinger's sense of irony arises out of a deep knowledge of the complexities of modern German history. The Greens are not only keenly aware of this troubling historical legacy but are also acutely self-conscious about the critical challenge for Germany today: to develop a political culture that confronts a past that has been largely inhospitable to liberal democratic politics. In a sense, that was the Greens' mission in West Germany, and that is the mission in the new Germany for them and their counterparts in the East, Alliance 90/Greens.

It would be simpler to begin with an explanation of the Greens in the post–World War II period, but that would not serve us well at all. Students of political systems have discovered a renewed interest in the uses of history in understanding national political traditions,[1] and it is obvious that Germans in general, and the Greens in particular, are aware that new political traditions are in the making. "Coming to terms with the past" is a fashionable expression that German politicians and intellectuals use today. For the Greens this means an attentiveness to the past in order to shape the political tradition of the future. This is especially true for a party of young, middle-class, and highly educated radical reformers,[2] an intelligentsia sensitive to the transmission of political traditions. It will be equally true for the citizen movements and Greens of eastern Germany, which emerged in 1989.

Sharing Kissinger's fears, the Greens realize that the German confrontation with modernity has been traumatic for the nation and disastrous for Europeans and Americans. We need to examine the German experience with modernity because it has resulted in an inability to achieve a healthy balance among the values of unity, equality, liberty, and security.[3] The German desire for unity and security—especially national security—has often meant that the values of equality and liberty were sacrificed. Because unity was delayed so long in the nineteenth century, when it finally came through military means in 1870 it was fragile and vulnerable.

Bismarck successfully played on the success of national unity as he restricted constitutional liberties and, with the compliance of the middle class, denied equality to the working class. The innovations of the welfare state were another ploy to co-opt working-class support: Security from the dislocations caused by industrialization was offered instead of the equality and liberty of citizenship. The Weimar Republic (1919–1933) was granted liberty and equality in one fell swoop, but its unity was precarious and its sense of national security unstable. In the Third Reich, national unity reached its most perverse extent while all the other competing values were diminished. In the Nazi period, a tribal nationalism set itself against the modern values of constitutional democracy and undermined the security of the global society. In the post–World War II era, West Germany (1949–1990) worked purposefully to implement the values of liberty and equality of citizenship while maintaining domestic and foreign security. In contrast, East Germany (1949–1990) denied liberty, sacrificed equality of citizenship for the promise of equality of material rewards, and offered security behind a wall and a restrictive satellite arrangement.

Unity was absent until the Soviet Empire began unraveling and until dissenters, many of whom became leaders in Alliance 90/Greens, took to the streets and helped mobilize civic courage in their fellow citizens. Now a new Germany has another chance at bringing those modern values into some harmony. Why has it taken so long and why has it been so difficult to achieve a balance of these political values? For the Greens the answer lies in the particular way Germany has met the modern age. Understanding how the Greens view the troubled past and what configuration of these values they propose helps us make sense of their development in the Bonn republic. The ideals of the student movement of the late 1960s are also part of this dialogue with the historical legacy, and the student movement of the 1960s is the energizing force and the crucial catalyst that helps one understand the Green party. But before looking at the elements of change, we need to assess the weight of past tradition.

Reworking Past Traditions

A glance at the historical legacy and the challenge of modernity helps us in answering these questions and in locating the heritage of the Greens. It has been all too easy for critics of the Greens to label them as romantic utopians, flipped-out anarcho-Communists, Nietzchean nihilists or flighty Wandervogel types of the late nineteenth century looking to escape from the realities of a postindustrial society. Similarly, it has been all too easy for the Greens to see themselves as the authentic exponents of the second Enlightenment, the indigenous cadre for a homegrown grass-roots democracy, the true apostles of socialist and feminist ideals and ecological principles, and the modern followers of Gandhi and Martin Luther King, Jr., who have the formula for turning swords into plowshares. Neither explanation is satisfactory. The historical legacy is more complex and the factions within the Greens too diverse to be reduced to a simple explanatory formula.

Quite clearly, no simple paradigm will easily capture these diverse historical and political traditions. The amalgam the Greens have forged in contemporary politics is a result of recovering—and reworking—past political traditions in the context of West German politics, the swing weight of the current Germany. This amalgam is not organically coherent: A part of it does not represent the whole; all the parts must be examined in order to understand the whole. The Greens express their desire to transform past political and cultural traditions in one of their favorite phrases: Concretize utopia. This phrase combines the romantic and idealistic inclination to take utopian designs seriously with the exhortation of the Enlightenment tradition that humans' reason and obligation to civic action encourage them to implement ideals. This new tradition moves beyond both the Kantian admonition to think critically but obey superiors and the German romantic inclination to seek private development over civic action.[4]

Confronting Modernity

There is no simple definition of modernity, but Samuel Beer has cut through much of the conceptual fog by highlighting democracy and science as the key elements of what he calls the political culture of modernity. For Beer, the spirit of democracy implies the concept of equality of citizenship and the tradition of liberalism with the following elements: freedom of political choice, freedom from arbitrary authority, the need to prevent concentration of power (political and economic), the right to dissent, and the necessity for tolerance and pluralism.[5] Moving from subject to citizen is a crucial aspect of modernity.

Many Green activists feel that an authoritarian and totalitarian past calls for not just a representative democracy but a democracy with opportunities for direct participation—a democracy with plebiscitary possibilities. Some also feel that liberalism is an insufficient response to controlling state power and that what Germany needs is a radical democratic tradition with libertarian elements. This pronounced suspicion against state power as well as against organizational hierarchy can be seen as a reaction to the abuse of public power in the German political tradition. In an extreme form, the myth of grass-roots democracy and the inability to tolerate organizational leadership derive their romantic and utopian overtones from the dialogue with the past and the desire—which had a generational imprint to it—to shape an authoritarian-proof polity and a leadership-free organizational vehicle of the future. The values of science not only imply certain attitudes that are questioning, empirical, and rationalist, but they are also part and parcel of the culture of technology and industrialization. As Max Weber has instructed us, they also underpin the structures of bureaucracy and technocracy. The rational and calculating spirit applied to human organization and nature leads to bureaucracy and industrialization. The Greens are especially cognizant of the fact that Weber considered the major conflict of his time to be not between capitalism and socialism but between bureaucracy and democracy: the possibility that technocratic elites could undermine participatory democracy not only on the national level but also, as Roberto Michels has informed us, within the organizational life of parties.

Too Little Enlightenment, Too Much Romanticism, Not Enough Liberalism

The Americans and the French carried out their defining national and democratic revolutions at the end of the eighteenth century, a good hundred years after the English inaugurated the liberal era with the Glorious Revolution of 1688. While these three political systems were promulgating the Rights of Man, extending civil and political rights, and celebrating national unity, the Germans, who were divided into countless principalities, separated by religious differences, and held hostage to the fortunes of larger political units, were languishing in the backwaters of illiberalism. The heritage of provincialism and particularism, the early development of bureaucratic authority, and the strength of clerical power within these principalities made it difficult for subjects to establish the public arenas in which citizenship could be realized. When the intellectual currents of the Enlightenment did come across the Rhine in the late eighteenth century, the conquering armies of Napoleon came along with them—hardly an occurrence to attract popular support for those progressive ideals.

As Peter Gay has noted, "The German *Aufklärer* [Enlightenment figures] were isolated, impotent, and almost wholly unpolitical."[6] Immanuel Kant gave the motto "Sapere aude" ("Dare to know") to those who would be enlightened, and it is no surprise to see the Green political activists some two hundred years later speaking of themselves as *Aufklärer* and of carrying out *Aufklärungsarbeit* (Enlightenment tasks). But while Jefferson and Madison, quintessential Enlightenment figures in America, were designing political institutions and fusing the inevitable links between civil and political rights, the Germans waited in vain for civic roles in the antechambers of many fragmented authoritarian governments.

The Enlightenment generated a countermovement in Germany, a complex set of intellectual and cultural ideas called romanticism. This concept is difficult to describe, but at its core romanticism attempts to right a balance: Against reason it sets feeling, against universal rights it sets particular (often national) traditions, and against personal development through civic action it sets self-development through inward exploration. Both the Enlightenment and romanticism focus on the individual, but the Enlightenment tradition points a clearer way to civic participation. Romanticism, contrary to the thinking of those who take Germany as their only example, does not match up neatly with a corresponding political ideology. Jacques Barzun, a sensitive observer of intellectual currents, makes a vital distinction: "The Romantics wanted for themselves and their people the freedom, diversity, self-reliance, and opportunity for self-development which they praised and used in their works of art and historiography. But they differed as to the means of achieving them."[7]

That may well be true in general, but the political manifestations of romanticism in German politics and history have not complemented the political culture of modernity. Unlike the political ideals associated with the English romantics,[8] the legacy of German romanticism—with some notable exceptions, for example, Heinrich Heine—has not advanced liberal ideas. Historian Koppel Pinson has written that romantics have identified with political reaction and conservative nationalism. Specifically, he states: "Romanticism in Germany always maintained a mark of hostility to democratic and republican ideology and sentiments."[9] Two points should be noted here in quick summary. Romanticism can be associated with liberal or reactionary politics (Hugo in France, Mussolini in Italy), and the element of romanticism in Green politics must be assessed quite carefully, especially in terms of the political means that are promoted. Though most romantics want to decentralize political power, we clearly know of romantic centralizers. To be displeased with the consequences of rapid industrialization and unplanned urban sprawl does not make one an agrarian romantic or a political reactionary. Although the overwhelming majority of the Green political leadership has not sought a preindustrial pastoral idyll, some have imagined and promoted a decentralization of political and economic power that neglects the interdependent parts of a complex industrial society. What is incontestable is that they have made it more difficult for their fellow citizens to ignore serious problems of the postindustrial society.

What is also beyond dispute is that the tradition of liberalism, espoused by an educated middle class, has been an anemic one in most of modern German history. Speaking mainly of the nineteenth century, James Sheehan writes: "Deference to authority and anxiety about disorder, the pull of the state and the fear of the *Volk*, were interrelated and mutually reinforcing parts of the same political vision."[10]

As a party of radical democratic reformers committed to the constitutional rules of the game, the Greens are most aware of these failures of liberalism in the nineteenth and twentieth centuries. Hardly deferential to authority, convinced about the creative possibilities of protest and dissent, suspicious and hostile toward the power of the centralized nation-state, and hopeful about the democratic populus, the Greens see their current mission as reversing the past failures of liberalism. Within the reality of unification, their mission is thus the extension of liberty, equality, and security to all of the new Germany. In commenting on a speech by Antje Vollmer, a Green member of the West German Parliament (1983–1990), journalist-historian Peter Gatter points out that "the lack of a radical democratic and liberal tradition in German politics is for her [Vollmer] the worse defeat in general."[11] The Bundestag speeches of Vollmer and Fischer, two outstanding leaders of the Greens, show obvious signs of creating a dialogue between their generation and party and the older generation of political elites in the traditional parties on the issue of the German political legacy.

Student Politics and Middle-Class Radicalism, 1815–1945

Given the centrality of the middle-class student movement of the 1960s for the formation of the Green party in 1980, it is worthwhile to examine the historical tradition in Germany of student protest and opposition. This tradition has involved generational politics, middle-class radicalism, movement politics, and, in the postwar period, policies critical of capitalism and strong state power with a newfound interest in pacifism, feminism, and ecology. Those public policies, after all, are the hallmarks of the Greens today.

Student participation in the 1830 and 1848 protests for constitutionalism and political rights was not extensive, and the systematic critique that former German student Karl Marx had focused on capitalism caught the attention of few fellow students. Though not relevant to the university students of the late nineteenth and early twentieth centuries, the socialist critique of monopoly capitalism with its utopian and decentralist markings became important for radical students of the 1960s in West Germany. These students, some of whom became activists in the Green party, purposely sought a countertradition to the fascist past. And a minority of these students chose violence and terrorism because they perceived the West German state of the late 1960s as fascist. From 1870 until the end of World War II, student politics had taken place for the most part on the right side of the political spectrum. As Gordon Craig has written, the politics of the student activists during the Second Empire and the Weimar Republic did not advance liberal ideas. Conservative nationalism, anti-Semitism, and antirepublican sentiments prepared the ground for the university students of Weimar, most of whom marched to the Nazi drummer in the late 1920s and early 1930s.[12]

John Maynard Keynes, in *The General Theory of Employment, Interest and Money,* speaks of "madmen in authority, who hear voices in the air, . . . distilling their frenzy from some academic scribbler of a few years back" (p. 383). Keynes is right. New political movements do not spin their ideologies out of thin air. The Greens have distilled their frenzy from a variety of discourses in the political and historical past of Germany. The connection with these historical antecedents is never well defined, but there is sufficient evidence in the writing, speeches, and actions of the Greens to locate the voices from the historical legacy, however complex that task might be. With minor exceptions, the Green tradition is of the Left. This position signifies an optimism about change, even dramatic change, that does not square with cultural pessimism. This leftist tradition is wary of the market as a fair allocator of valued goods, but it does not embrace nationalizing the means of production at all. Ownership of property for most Greens is not an absolute right but a tie to collective responsibility.

As others have pointed out, the Greens are of the New Left, which simply means a commitment to a wider distribution of opportunity through as minimal a national state as possible. Unlike the old traditional Left, they are ambivalent about the securities provided by the welfare state. Their desire for equality of opportunity through expanded educational chances is tempered by their fear that a too-powerful state dispersing entitlements could create dependent and not self-defining personalities.

One solution to the tension between a commitment to egalitarianism and a skepticism of the market and state power is to call for as much decentralized decisionmaking as possible. A fragile political identity, rapid industrialization, and an expanding student intelligentsia produced obvious political conflicts, and the Greens, riding the wave for greater political participation, served as a sort of clearinghouse for some of these groups in the late 1970s and early 1980s.

Industrialization, Bureaucracy, and Technocracy

We noted at the outset that modernity involves democracy and science. One of the truly unique—and disturbing—aspects of the German political tradition has been its ambivalent attitudes toward industrialization, bureaucracy, and technocracy. Gordon Craig has eloquently stated a palpable fact of Germany's rough passage to the modern: Although industrialization brought national and international power, it also brought urbanization, commercialization, industrial economic cartels, and an appetite for ingesting nature's resources while spewing out pollution. Moreover, it also brought fear of a mass society. There is a disconcerting parallel between the political reaction to industrialization, with its large-scale organizations, and some of the critique of the Green party in the 1980s. In analyzing the components of cultural pessimism, Fritz Stern notes reactions to rapid urbanization: "From the 1870s on, the conservative writers in imperial Germany expressed the fear that the German souls would be destroyed by 'Americanization,' that is by mammon, materialism, mechanization and the mass society."[13] If you add militarism to this alliterative flow, you have important elements of the contemporary Green critique. The Greens have had their cultural pessimists, but this continuity with the dark side of romanticism is more than counterbalanced by the solid Green support for constitutional democracy. The strain of cultural pessimism does not overwhelm the dominant Enlightenment tradition of the Greens.

Lastly, we should note that some Green activists feel a historical kinship to the countercultural movements of the late nineteenth and early twentieth centuries. These movements—groups such as Wandervogel, Young Germany, the early stirring of the women's movement, and friends of nature—reacted against both increased urbanization and the authoritarian structures of the bourgeois society. For the most part, these groups made no significant contribution to the muted liberal tradition, and many of them represented the escape into nature and the search for communal experiences of the unpolitical romantic tradition.[14] The roots of the modern politics of ecology are barely discernible here.

The Thousand-Year Third Reich, 1933–1945

It would not be difficult to make the argument that these student political movements of the past offer only a faint resonance to the present-day Greens.[15] In a very particular sense that is true. There is no historical event after the national socialist regime that comes close to explaining the political ideology of the Greens. For the student generation of the 1960s, the Nazi period represented a perverse intensification of the antidemocratic political cultures of earlier German regimes. One could call the Greens a radical democratic movement/party of New Leftists riding the ecological wave, or one could call them a delayed antifascist resistance movement of the middle-class intelligentsia. Both interpretations are fair and call attention to the complex layers of historical forces, some distant, some more proximate, that shaped the Greens. For example, each of the excesses of the Nazi regime finds a corresponding reaction in the Greens' sense of identity. The antipathy to nationalism, the critique of capitalism, the suspicion of centralized power, the concern for tolerance and fair treatment for minorities, the sensitivity toward police and military power— all of these positions are a reflection of the catastrophe of the recent past. Obviously, other parties share these concerns, but it is just as obvious that the Greens feel that not enough has been done to repudiate these traditions in the most aggressive manner. For the Greens, mastering the past is dangerous hyperbole. Coming to grips with this past through democratizing actions that challenge—in their eyes—a stagnant and elite-dominated representative democracy has been more their style.

Fritz Stern has written that the tradition of cultural pessimism in the late nineteenth and early twentieth centuries led to the Nazi debacle. We must make note of this idea because some critics have seen similarities between the Nazi critique of the urbanized bureaucratized mass society, with its reactionary nostalgia for a preindustrial idyll, and the Green critique of the 1970s and 1980s.[16] However, the equation of Green and Brown (the Nazi color) politics results from only superficial connections.

The Nazis successfully mobilized resentments against large-scale organizations, and they did begin their movement with hostility toward capitalism (they were, after all, national socialists), but their basic hostility to any form of democracy, their opportunism with capitalist elites, and their espousal of virulent nationalism and racist politics make them a very implausible forerunner for the Greens. No, the real connection is that the Greens are fiercely antifascist, even though a very small number of their older activists had Brown pasts. The Nazi protest against bureaucratization, urbanization, industrialization, and constitutional democracy was reactionary and their environmental and feminist politics were insignificant or nonexistent themes. The Greens protest against the environmental consequences of industrialization and rapid urbanization within the framework of constitutional democracy and with an interest in expanding the civil and political rights of all citizens. The present-day Greens—even more so with the former East German wing of the party—are unimaginable without their antifascist (or antistalinist) stance. The Greens have been especially vehement in their skepticism of those who speak too glibly of "overcoming the past."[17] And the Greens, with their generational core, have been more prone than the other parties to fears of fascist tendencies in an ever more powerful Germany.

The Second Republic Recovers, 1945–1969

The Second Republic of Bonn promulgated a Basic Law (constitution) in 1949 after a four-year period of military occupation. It is not unfair to suggest that both East and West Germany, as offspring of World War II, have political structures and cultures that were decisively shaped by the political-military blocs in whose orbits they moved in the decades after the war. Claiming a Western allied surrogate paternity for the Federal Republic of Germany is obviously not the same as the Soviet *Diktat* with which East Germany had to deal. And yet we must observe that the political systems of Bonn and Potsdam came after defeat in a world war and that the ensuing bipolar Cold War decisively affected the political cultures of both Germanys.

For the Greens of the West, who came on the scene some three decades later, these events were well known. For them, the Bonn democracy was another "import" model and it came with a series of entangling alliances and contingent conditions, eventually including military obligations. From the standpoint of the student movement of the late 1960s and the Green movement of the late 1970s, very few of the successor generation were interested in exchanging a parliamentary democracy for a one-party socialist satellite dictatorship. What they desired was to put their own stamp of particularity on the democracy currently in place. That meant, in their eyes, moving from a Schumpeterian elite democracy of economic and political cartels dedicated to unrestricted economic growth to a decentralized democracy oriented to grass-roots control with smaller economic units mindful of nature's limited resources.

What occurred between the founding of the Federal Republic in 1949 and the founding of the Green party in 1980 to bring about these differences concerning the proper type of democracy and the right type of economy? Here we need to look at the evolution of the West German party system, the extraparliamentary movements preceding and following the student movement of the late 1960s, and the immediate circumstances—including the issue of nuclear power—that led to the founding of the Green party in 1980. In short, it can be said that in this period of time the West German democracy changed, in a variation of David Riesman's terms, from other-directed to self-directed. The activity of the Greens and unification have only furthered this process of German autonomy.

The Party System: From Dispersion to Concentration, 1949–1980

Three decades after World War II, the political situation of West Germany appeared healthy to those outside of the country. There were two Germanys instead of one with various degrees of *Schadenfreude* (pleasure in someone's pain) among the allies of each Germany. The Cold War alliances seemed reasonably stable, and recognition of the eastern borders of the country had been resolved in the early 1970s. In West Germany, several decades of economic growth had produced a wealthy country. The expansion in public education offered the promise of long-term productivity, the government had successfully assimilated an astounding number of German refugees into society, and the record in employment, social benefits, and educational opportunities for foreign workers was considered good by international standards. The political party system moved from a crowded multiparty competition in 1949 in which the three major parties (Christian Democrats/Christian Socialists, Social Democrats, Free Democrats) gained only 72 percent of the vote to a three-party electoral race in 1980 in which these same parties received 98 percent of the vote. Prior to 1980 there had been stable coalitions to the right and left and—in contrast to the party systems of Italy and Japan, countries with similar political legacies—there had been a turnover in power, suggesting a more competitive type of democracy. Unusually high voting turnouts, changes in the political culture, and an expansion of the repertoire of political actions indicated a more "participant" and less "subject" citizenry.[18] The student disturbances of the 1960s, the terrorism of the 1970s, and the demonstrations against nuclear power of the 1970s and 1980s were seen as minor lapses for the star pupil in the postwar school of democracy.

From the standpoint of a young, female, leftist, middle-class university graduate at the end of the 1970s—a potential voter for the Greens—the reality of West German politics appeared strikingly different. For her, the older generation had passed on a traumatic historical legacy with which it was difficult to come to terms. As a consequence of the war, West Germany was involved in a military alliance that was armed to the teeth with weapons, many of which were nuclear and were stationed in the Federal Republic. When the politicians referred clinically to theater nuclear weapons, the theater was usually Germany. Many of her fellow students, not at all inclined to nationalism, felt that rapprochement between the blocs and the two Germanys would come only with disarmament. Economic development had brought affluence, but in her eyes it was not well distributed. Affluence had created a risk society of pollution, unchecked technology, massive bureaucracies, a too-powerful state, and a publicly financed, male-controlled party system to which there was no really effective opposition. The Social Democrats and the Christian Democrats were Tweedledum and Tweedledee, both with highly oligarchical internal organizations. Both parties, government and opposition, worked hand in glove with the powerful pressure groups and the technocrats of the bureaucracy to hold back needed reforms while they absorbed themselves in rapid economic growth to the detriment of the health of the citizens and the resources of the country. The student protests of a decade earlier, the violence of the terrorists, and the rise of citizen initiatives (Green and alternative parties) were signs of a profound dissatisfaction with "model Germany." This grass-roots activity—without the terrorism—represented this young woman's personal hope to reform the system.[19]

Obviously, the outside observer and the young female not only had different experiences, but, more important, they also had different benchmarks by which they judged the West German party system. The outsider thought about an earlier Germany and saw the present pragmatic parties as a major success of the postwar period. The younger student, sensitive to the fascist past, saw establishment parties and increasingly weak opposition voices.

The Christian Democrats in Power, 1949–1969

From the standpoint of the Greens, the CDU/CSU got things off on the wrong foot by rejecting the Ahlen Program of 1947 in favor of the Social Market economy of Ludwig Erhard, which set the tracks for a more wide open pattern of capitalist growth. The Ahlen Program, often referred to nostalgically by Green leaders, came from the left wing, socially conscious faction of the CDU in North Rhine–Westphalia. The program roundly criticized the capitalist economic system, especially state monopoly capitalism, and "called for a planned economy under the direction of economic councils operating under the control of Parliament."[20]

Aided by spectacular economic growth, this right-of-center coalition rolled up impressive majorities, moving from 31 percent of the vote in 1949 to 50.2 percent of the vote in 1957, the only time in this century that a party has won a majority in a German national election. In a series of bitter parliamentary debates with the Social Democrats in the 1950s, Konrad Adenauer's party committed West Germany to remilitarized status as an active supporter of NATO.[21] The "economic miracle" engineered by Erhard, Adenauer's economics minister, brought a brusque transition to economic affluence, the rapid expansion of the middle class, the widening of educational opportunity on the high school and university level, and a clear sense of international prestige. The campaign slogan in 1957 for the CDU was "No Experiments" and to critically minded West Germans this was a sign that attested to the restoration of a complacent government of authoritarian style increasingly impatient with dissent and opposition.[22]

In this period (1949–1966) the minor parties were absorbed by the Christian Democrats, the Communist party was outlawed by the Federal Constitution, and when the Berlin Wall was built in 1961, there was little critical reaction from Chancellor Adenauer. West Germany was becoming economically powerful, but it seemed, especially to an active segment of the younger generation attending universities in the 1960s, that it had locked in too quickly to a Cold War alliance that was poised on the precarious side of a balance of terror. West Germany seemed incapable of significant reforms in education and women's rights, and rapid reindustrialization and urbanization were creating environmental problems. Looking back at this situation from the perspective of the 1970s, the Greens perceived options thrown away carelessly with the overeager embrace of the Western alliance, which continued to solidify in an increasingly armed bipolar world.

The Social Democrats' Move to the Center, 1959–1990

After a series of three solid electoral defeats in 1949, 1953, and 1957 in which the party could not muster up a third of the vote, the Social Democratic party (SPD) reconsidered its campaign strategy. At Bad Godesberg in 1959 the internal debate was heated. The discussion over opposition to rearmament had created clear factions within the party, and now the leadership suggested a move to the center, an attempt at developing a catch-all Volksparty with a more pragmatic style and with a clear eye to capturing the rapidly expanding new middle class to complement their loyal working-class trade union voters. Their vote increased in 1961 (36.2 percent) and 1965 (39.3 percent), and they emulated some of the media techniques of U.S. politics with their candidate, Willy Brandt. The logic of market rationality seemed unassailable. The pragmatic SPD of the post-Godesberg era would reach for power without the ideological baggage of the pre-Godesberg party of socialist ideas.

The SPD move to the center brought an opening on the left that the activists of the younger generation quickly perceived and that eventually led to the formation of the Green party in 1980. When the SPD aligned itself with the middle-of-the-road politics of West Germany in the late 1950s, it gave a clear boost to the growth of societal critics on the left—especially pacifists—who were the precursors to the extraparliamentary opposition that continued to challenge the mainstream parties through the next several decades. The Easter Marches of the 1960s, modeled on the Campaigns for Nuclear Disarmament in Great Britain, were mobilized against increasing rearmament. Unlike the campaign against rearmament in the 1950s by the Kampf dem Atomtod (Fight Against Atomic Death), which was organized by the Social Democrats and the trade unions, the Easter Marches were a sign of things to come: They were autonomous (not party-controlled) grass-roots organizations that used unconventional protest and demonstration actions to attract public attention.

The Easter Marches had a mixed-aged representation, but an important element of these Marches was the JUSOS (young socialists), the youth organization of the SPD that criticized the SPD in 1963 for "false pragmatism."[23] The Socialist German Students Union (SDS), an SPD-sponsored organization in the postwar period, opposed the SPD on the nuclear arms issue and eventually split from the Social Democrats in 1960.[24] The SDS was a major force in the student protest movement of the late 1960s as well as a staunch supporter of the extraparliamentary opposition, which was a "loose spontaneous amalgamation of pacifist-neutral, radical democratic, Marxist socialist and New Left (SDS) groups."[25] The New Left, which encompassed the hyperactive, undisciplined, radical progeny of the Old Left, was creating a different style of politics than the staid style of the Adenauer years, to which most West Germans had become accustomed.

In its quest for power, the SPD continued to lean toward the center. In 1966, after an economic recession had shaken the confidence of the CDU, the two major parties, CDU/CSU and SPD, formed the Grand Coalition, which left the sole parliamentary opposition, the FDP, with less than 10 percent of the Bundestag seats.

The Grand Coalition confirmed the worst fears of the student activists on the left. That old German passion for unanimity, the distaste for dissent, and the inclination to embrace the state and manage conflict without adversarial politics galvanized the radical and reformers of the student Left. The SPD rode it out, supporting the unpopular Emergency Law of 1968,[26] living with the disorder and disruption of the universities in the 1960s, and managing to obtain governmental power in 1969 in coalition with the Free Democrats. But the feelings of betrayal on the part of the leftist, politically activist student generation were unmistakable.[27] Even the dramatic 1972 electoral victory of the Social Democratic–Free Democratic coalition with the exhortation by Willy Brandt to "risk more democracy" did not erase the suspicions of many of the New Left that the SPD had become the new establishment. The genuine enthusiasm for the signing of the Eastern Treaties with the Soviet Union, a clear sign toward détente, was diminished somewhat by the promulgation of the Radical Decree (1972), which called for tests of political reliability for young university graduates in order to qualify for civil service jobs. The progressiveness of the foreign policy decision was undercut by the conservative nature of the rule to prevent "radicals," a term not clearly defined, from the public service.

By the time that Brandt resigned in 1974 as a result of being compromised by the discovery of an East German agent on his staff, the stage was set for a time of troubles for the SPD. Brandt was replaced by Helmut Schmidt, a technocratic crisis manager who tolerated neither fools nor leftist critics very well. He moved the party to the right while events—rising oil prices, austerity and short-circuited reforms, and demands for nuclear plants and weapons—moved radical reforming students and citizens to the left. The antiauthoritarian extraparliamentary opposition was ready for further confrontations on a hotly contested issue: nuclear power in the form of weapons and domestic energy production.

Extraparliamentary Opposition, 1960–1980

The student protest movement of the late 1960s is the linchpin of the extraparliamentary opposition. According to Roland Roth, a West German political scientist, "Bourgeois enlightenment, radical self-development, and socialist politics formed the poles between which the various public demands of the student movement developed."[28] The student movement for political and societal reform was the most dramatic assertion of the extraparliamentary opposition, a breakthrough in the double crisis of identity and authority for the Federal Republic. There were important precursors as well as followers to this movement. The precursors—the Easter Marches and the campaigns for democracy and disarmament—contributed important techniques in organizational forms and political cultural norms.[29] What began as the antimilitary/disarmament groups of the 1950s ended up as movements for democratic reform and disarmament in the 1960s as the groups became convinced that West German political values had to be changed before policies in the legislature could be altered.

The student protest movement was an eruption of unconventional participatory action and civic assertion by leaders of diverse age groups who believed in peaceful incremental change and who were motivated by the memories of the militarily expansionist National Socialist regime. The SDS must also be included as a precursor, especially in the stage where it was no longer attached to the SPD. Because of the passions aroused, the massiveness of the protest, and the stridency with which the student movement put forth its challenge to the institutional authorities of the late 1960s, it must be considered the center of gravity of the extraparliamentary opposition. For the student generation of that time it was the decisive breakthrough.[30]

There were student protests in almost all of the industrialized democracies in the late 1960s, from Berkeley to Paris to Berlin, but what was unique to the protest action in West Germany—and will no doubt affect the political culture of the new Germany—was the durability of the ideas, the variability of the different political styles that developed, and the long-range influence of the extraparliamentary opposition to German politics. The very idea of what political opposition meant in a democratic society was being tested and stretched. The Green party was most certainly the institutional form of many of the ideals and organizational practices developed in the heady days of the 1950s and 1960s. In addition to analyzing the durability, variability, and influence of the extraparliamentary opposition, we want to assess some of the causes and aims of the forces that asserted a new balance between elite-supporting and elite-challenging participatory politics.

Causes for the Rise of the Extraparliamentary Opposition

In dealing with the complexity of the demands for participation in the political order of West Germany in the 1960s, it is helpful to distinguish between long-term and short-term causes. We have noted earlier that the residues of the authoritarian historical legacy, especially the Third Reich, were more than distant shadows for the younger, educated, middle-class radicals. The crisis of identity and the crisis of authority were tightly linked. Confronting "the immediate innate feeling of an unjustified and dark inheritance"[31] was painful. As Friedrich Tenbruck and other German scholars suggest, by "the cultivation of other identifications, they sought to free themselves from German history."[32] Richard Löwenthal extends this theme. Referring to the Adenauer era (1949–1969), he observes "a catching up on the Enlightenment which took off and finally came to a breakthrough in the vehicle of generational change." This catching up had led to an authority crisis that "was a deep and comprehensive one which is still continuing."[33] In fairness to Löwenthal's full interpretation, we must also add that he perceives the dark romantic currents—the inclination to violence and terrorism—that were also part of the crisis. In an earlier

1970 work, *The Romantic Relapse,* he describes the student movement as a "utopian inspired rebellion," a movement that developed out of a romantic despair that would not accommodate technically conditioned facts of a modern industrial society.[34] The explosive tension between the Enlightenment and romantic strands in the German tradition, heightened by the need for "a conscious counter assault against the idea of National Socialism,"[35] worked itself out in the political actions of the student generation in various ways.[36]

The more proximate causes of the extraparliamentary opposition are easier to identify, though it is difficult to assess their relative influence. We have already made reference to the rapid changes in West German society as being close to a "second industrial revolution"[37] that took place in under fifteen years. The inadequacy of family socialization on difficult political and historical issues produced a generation looking for meaning and answers in a society in which the pragmatic focus of the moment— rapid economic growth—pushed political questions of value to the back burner.[38] The older generation fixated on rebuilding for the future connected poorly with the younger generation concerned about the tragedies of the past.

The rapid expansion of educational opportunities on the *Gymnasium* (advanced high school) and university levels provided the participants for the student protests. As Ronald Inglehart argues persuasively in his work *The Silent Revolution,* the educational expansion created young people with political skills and changed political values.[39] For some of the student generation, these new values were radically critical of the status quo.

Along with these disruptions in the universities, which were exacerbated by overcrowding,[40] we must reemphasize the hostility by the politically active students against what they perceived as overbureaucratized, internally undemocratic, and unresponsive political parties. Consider the analysis of Klaus von Beyme. Von Beyme recognized the issue of a stagnant party system as a problem of the historic legacy—the quest for security and stability: "The party cartel which stood at the end of a concentration process in the party system certainly guaranteed governing stability, which had been one of the chief goals of the constitutional founders in the area of the organization of powers. The price however was a drastic reduction of the political organizational possibilities for alienated outside groups."[41]

Finally, in addition to the value changes, institutional shortcomings, and international events, the Vietnam War blemished the image of the major ally because of the nuclear issue. The nuclear issue involved weapons and the decision by the Social Democrats to press on with the building of nuclear plants. Of all the issues, the nuclear issue was the most responsible for creating the critical mass that led to the formation of the Green party in 1980. The oil crisis of 1973 created a situation where Chancellor Helmut

Schmidt felt it imperative to push ahead on domestic nuclear power. At a later time, he felt it necessary to commit his party to support of Pershing and cruise missiles on West German soil. His decisions generated intense political opposition.

The nuclear issue is crucial in another way. It linked the antiauthoritarian student movement to the ecological and peace movement. When you add the growing forces of many feminists, defecting from a SPD regime that was generous on promises and chary on the delivery of reform, you have the major components of the Greens. From the student movement of the 1960s, these causes propelled a diverse set of responses about how the society and polity should change. The 1970s were a time of testing and experimenting for social change. We need to look at the variability of these responses, the unraveling strands of the student movement.

Extraparliamentary Opposition: Fractured and Dispersed Among the Strands

Obviously, not all university students were set against the status quo. Gerd Langguth reminds us that only a small percentage of the student population was part of the New Left protest of the 1960s and 1970s.[42] Though it is a rough approximation, we can gain a measure of coherence about the protest generation by dividing the groups into dogmatic and nondogmatic leftists (critics of capitalism) and countercultural types, some of whom worked through organizations on the grass-roots level and some of whom simply dropped out. Another distinction of importance has to do with the political means used to achieve the decentralized slow-growth economy with maximum opportunities for self-development. And here we grapple with an issue that had split many of the various leftist factions: the use of violence.

The use of revolutionary violent tactics that would "unmask" the true nature of the "fascist" regime was the path chosen by the terrorists of the Red Army Faction.[43] This plan was romantic utopianism with a nihilist streak, and it wreaked havoc on society in the 1970s. If cultural pessimism and going underground was the way for the Baader-Meinhof gang, then dropping out was an option for many countercultural young people who sought an alternative life-style in urban and rural communes. But by far the largest majority of this politically conscious cohort decided not to drop out but to "drop in" with their own mode of stylized unconventionality. These individuals were the nondogmatic leftists, the pacifists, the feminists, the members of the citizen initiatives, and the idealists who took Willy Brandt seriously when he challenged the citizens to help democratize the system. Some of them cast their lot with political party work on the local level with the Social Democrats or the Free Democrats as the continued economic growth created the usual problems of rapid urbanization and consequent urban blight. Peter Gatter captures this spirit of taking on the status quo in a reform-minded manner quite well: "One day we noted that the world badly needed changing. We put down Don Quixote's armor and mounted the donkey of Sancho Panza."[44] The sectarian debates among fragmented Marxists groups—Maoist, Communist League, Militant, Cell Z—continued, but a larger part of the generation was tempering the knee-jerk dogmatic utopian response with practical grass-roots legwork.

The great increase in organizational activity showed up in the increase of citizen initiatives—coalitions of citizens pushing for public policies, most of which involved collective and not narrowly self-serving goals.[45] The actions of the citizen initiatives and other social movements operated independently from the political parties. They used organizational tactics from the experiences of earlier groups of the extraparliamentary opposition and slowly, by dint of great effort, they posed a substantial problem to the traditional politicians and bureaucrats and their "usual way of business."[46] Of greater political and cultural import was the challenge to the restricted mode of decisionmaking—technocratic expertise wielded by local and state bureaucrats—and, most important, the challenge to the idea that there were no limits to growth.[47] What can we say about the durability of this coalition, which was highly skeptical about unplanned economic growth, against nuclear power and arms buildups, discontent with the traditional political parties, and in favor of more equality of rights for women, minorities, and marginal groups in the society?[48] One way to answer this question is to focus on the influence of these activities on the political culture and structure of the Federal Republic.

The Old Student Slogan: Concretize Utopia

Utopia was still, etymologically and otherwise, no place, but the political institutions of West Germany—again with clear consequences for the new Germany—had shown flexibility. The narrowly top-down, elite-directed, representative democracy had been given more grass-roots shock therapy, which caught the attention of important party leaders. Utopia was not solidly shaped in the sense of fully developed institutional changes, but new norms (political values) and forms (organizational techniques) were in the making. The demands of the late 1960s for more women in positions of power resulted in new female leaders in all of the parties in the early 1990s. There had been a radical questioning about the direction and speed of economic growth. Quantitative indicators to measure progress were being complemented by qualitative measures that took into account the consequences, intended or unintended, of more roads, more cars, more energy use, and more weapons. Citizens were increasingly concerned about the "risk society." Quality of life was not an empty slogan for them.

The critical and aggressive antiauthoritarianism and Marxist seminar sectarianism of the student movement evolved, slowly and painfully, into a participatory ideal with a wide variety of organizational forms. Actions, both conventional (voting) and unconventional (marches, sit-ins), were used to catch the attention of public officials, who were all too used to well-behaved deferential German citizens. As noted by a local activist who later became a Green party official, "We used the streets *and* the law to reach our objectives."[49] Rapid industrialization, unplanned urbanization, and the nuclear issue had helped connect the student generational cohort to a larger number of reform-minded citizens in the society who felt that changes were needed. Would these semi-institutionalized social movements and citizen initiatives be enough to catch the attention of the political party elites? Or was something needed besides movement politics?

The Formation of the Greens: From Movement to Party

As we have noted, the major impetus that energized the coalition that created Green parties and Alternative Lists (other leftist radical and reform groups challenging the traditional party system) on the county and city levels in the late 1970s was the nuclear problem. There were other grievances, but this perceived threat to the environment, both human and natural, stood as a top-down decision from party bureaucrats and public officials—with the encouragement of private power companies—that the citizens on the grass roots strongly resisted. The nuclear issue also brought together an alliance of radical democratic leftists and traditional ecologists and local residents, including farmers and suburbanites. Ecology offered the green umbrella under which a very motley crew gathered to ward off power from afar. As Detlef Murphy and Roland Roth have put it, "Ecology offered itself as a diverse and more flexible concept which allowed various political positions a chance to express political opposition and encouraged wider participation and pragmatic compromise."[50]

The period from 1977 to 1980 was a time of decisive incubation for the Greens. Within these three years, local Green parties were formed, state parties were organized, the Greens as a political union—not yet a party in the German organizational parlance—ran candidates for the European Parliament (1989), and the Green List in Bremen jumped the 5 percent hurdle to win seats in the city-state's parliament. The tracks were set, and after a series of conferences, highly educated political activists met in Karlsruhe on January 12 and 13, 1980, to found a national Green party.

The party barely survived its founding conference. The delegates agreed on the basic principles of the party—grass-roots democracy, social concern, ecology and nonviolence—but they were weak on the specifics of economic policy, confused about whether a Green party member could belong to another party, and heterogeneous in regard to political views. And yet the possibility of this new party serving as an integrating force for radical left groups was present. The Green party would aim to bring together dissatisfied feminists, anxious pacifists, aggressive democratizers, and concerned ecologists. They all agreed that they wanted a party unlike any other, that their antipathy to hierarchy, bureaucracy, and centralization called for a decentralized party structure attentive to the grass roots and, finally, that the sacred cow of economic growth at any cost needed to be led to slaughter. Would those principles be sufficient to enable them to compete in the rough-and-tumble arena of party politics? Could a party of such diverse factions, with members who felt negatively or ambivalently about the organizational imperative, succeed as a fighting machine in competitive electoral politics? In mid-January 1980, hopes were high.

Something Old, Something New, Something Green: Revitalizing Liberalism?

A month or so before the founding conference of the Greens in January 1980, Horst Bieber of *Die Zeit*, who had followed the ecology movement from its earliest political actions, wrote that "to warn of the decline of the industrial West is one matter; to state an alternative is another; and to carry it through, still another. The Greens are most successful with the first matter."[51] Bieber understood the new party's political orientation—a radical democratic movement of socialist and liberal ideals coming together behind a Green (ecological) banner—but few could place the party with any certitude in past political traditions. Rudolf Bahro, the East German critic of "real existing socialism," used his shrewd talent for phrasemaking by saying, "We are not left or right, but forward." That comment was directed toward the internal factions of the Greens as well as toward the media.

We have noted at the beginning of this chapter that Germany's encounter with modernity—science and democracy with their applied derivatives of industrialization and parliamentary government—has been difficult for them and baneful for others. Instead of full citizenship, pluralism, tolerance, and constitutional liberties, the Germans have experienced a failure of liberalism,[52] an ineffective middle class,[53] the weakness of a tradition of opposition politics and acceptable dissent, and the inability to live with disorderly pluralism. There has also been a tragic inclination to a caesarist tradition of military leaders and charismatic Führers. The Enlightenment tradition succumbed to unpolitical romantic ideas that looked askance at reason's possibilities and sought fulfillment in a turning inward. But our theme in this chapter has been that political systems in general, and Germany's in particular, have the potential to reshape past traditions. This reshaping has taken place in West Germany; it has a reasonable chance of continuing in unified Germany.

In the old Federal Republic, the generation in power after the war carried out a significant revitalization of the liberal tradition. By Ralf Dahrendorf's criteria for successful liberalism—equality of citizenship, diversity of elites, acceptance of conflict in political negotiation, and the importance of public virtues[54]—the Bonn Republic's record is noteworthy. However, the first generation of the postwar period—especially the educated middle-class radicals of the New Left—saw incomplete revitalization. They saw catch-all parties strong on patronage and weak on principles; a centralized and bureaucratic state; an economic system that was encouraged by the state to give scant regard for human and natural resources; and a falling back into military alliances that produced an anxious and insecure citizenry.

The Greens are part of this New Left. Unlike parties in German history, they are a unique party of middle-class radical reformers who want to extend and expand—not replace—the constitutional democracy of West Germany. Now they see the challenge of carrying forth a revitalized tradition for the new Germany. In *Structural Change of the Public*, Jürgen Habermas argues that the Greens want to expand the competitive opportunities in the public space without abridging essential liberties in the private space. Their goals are more participation, more direct democracy in controlling the state, and less state power in controlling the citizens. The Greens are not antimodernists at all.[55] Their insistence on small-scale decentralist technique may be ahead of their time. They value equality as strongly as liberty, they have been ambivalent about the security offered by the welfare state, and their indecision on national unity cost them Bundestag representation from the western part of Germany in the 1990 election.[56]

However the Greens have balanced these modern values, liberalism has been doubly revitalized in the postwar period and the Green party has aided in this revitalization. The first achievement by the Bonn Republic's founding generation was to carry out successful "constitutional engineering" and sustained economic growth, which helped create a confident and broadened middle class. The second revitalization, by the children of that middle class, helped develop a wider repertoire of political actions—including practices of opposition and dissent—and a sense that the old-boy network needed to open up to new people and new issues. This second revitalization of liberalism challenged the forms (the traditional parties and the decisionmaking structures they dominated) while asserting new norms of a more participatory political culture. An increasingly stronger and more powerful German state had called forth a stronger pattern of opposition.

As we have noted, the Greens have aided in this dialectical process, and now the third stage of revitalization is at hand: the challenge of economic and political development in the newly unified Germany. But here we move ahead of our analysis. With the past as prologue, we need to inquire in more detail about the developmental pattern of the Greens from 1980 to 1991 in light of various theories explaining their emergence in the Federal Republic.

Notes

1. Joel S. Migdal, "Studying the Politics of Development and Change: The State of the Art," in *Political Science: The State of the Discipline*, Ada W. Finifter, ed. (Washington, D.C.: American Political Science Association, 1983).

2. Alvin Gouldner, *The Future of Intellectuals and the Rise of the New Class*, (New York: Seabury, 1979).

3. Hugh Heclo, "Toward a New Welfare State?" in *The Development of Welfare States in Europe and America*, Peter Flora and Arnold J. Heidenheimer, eds. (New Brunswick, N.J.: Transaction Books, 1981), pp. 383–406.

4. Peter Gay, *The Enlightenment: An Interpretation* (New York: Knopf, 1966); Koppel Pinson, *Modern Germany*, 2nd ed. (New York: Macmillan, 1966); Jacques Barzun, *Classic, Romantic, and Modern*, 2d ed. (Chicago: University of Chicago Press, 1961).

5. For the tradition of liberalism in Germany, see Fritz Stern, *The Failure of Illiberalism* (New York: Knopf, 1972).

6. Gay, *The Enlightenment*, p. 4.

7. Jacques Barzun, "Romanticism and After," in *The Columbia History of the World*, John Garraty and Peter Gay, eds. (New York: Harper and Row, 1972), pp. 859–870; see also James Sheehan, *German History, 1790–1866* (New York: Oxford University Press, 1989), p. 326, in which he says that romanticism is held together by questions and aspirations, not answers and accomplishments.

8. Carl Woodring, *Politics in English Romantic Poetry* (Cambridge: Harvard University Press, 1970).

9. Pinson, *Modern Germany*, p. 40. Both Gordon Craig and Fritz Stern, with some qualification, agree with this assessment, but Jacques Barzun calls forth a more nuanced judgment. He says that the many who turned nationalist "were convinced that without a strong unified political state coextensive with the historic

culture no freedom could survive" and that "some were now willing to accept tyranny rather than helpless disunity." Ibid., p. 868.

10. James Sheehan, *German Liberalism in the Nineteenth Century* (Chicago: University of Chicago Press, 1978), p. 48.

11. Peter Gatter, *Die Aufsteiger: Ein politisches Porträt der Grünen* (Hamburg: Hoffman and Campe, 1989), p. 158.

12. Gordon Craig, *Germany: 1866–1945* (Oxford: Oxford University Press, 1978). A book that adds considerable detail to the broad generalization advanced here is Konrad Jarausch, *Students, Society, and Politics in Imperial Germany: The Rise of Academic Illiberalism* (Princeton: Princeton University Press, 1982).

13. Fritz Stern, *Politics of Cultural Despair* (Garden City, N.Y.: Doubleday, 1965), p. 170.

14. Walter Laqueur, *Young Germany* (New York: Basic Books, 1962). He notes: "The German Youth Movement was an unpolitical form of opposition to a civilization that had little to offer the young generation, a protest against its lack of vitality, warmth, emotion, and ideals," p. 4.

15. Gatter, *Die Aufsteiger*, p. 169; Heiz Hoefl, "Ökologie in Lederhosen," in *Die Grünen*, Joerg Mettke, ed. (Hamburg: Rowolt Verlag, 1982).

16. Anna Bramwell, *Ecology in the 20th Century: A History* (New Haven: Yale University Press, 1989), pp. 219–225.

17. Charles Maier, *The Unmasterable Past* (Cambridge: Harvard University Press, 1989).

18. Samuel Barnes and Max Kaase, *Political Action: Mass Participation in Five Western Democracies* (Beverly Hills: Sage Publications, 1979).

19. For some commentary on "model Germany," see William Paterson and Gordon Smith, eds., *The West German Model: Perspectives on a Stable State* (London: Cass and Company, 1981).

20. Alfred Grosser, *The Federal Republic of Germany* (New York: Praeger, 1964), pp. 61–62.

21. Werner Hülsberg, *The German Greens* (London: Verso, 1988). In the late 1950s there were debates on forming the Bundeswehr on rearmament, including atomic weapons, and on the issue of NATO integration.

22. See the excellent work by Eva Kolinsky, *Parties, Opposition and Society* (London: Croom Helm, 1984); and Eva Kolinsky, ed., *Opposition in Western Europe* (London: Croom Helm, 1987).

23. Gerard Braunthal, *The West German Social Democrats, 1969–1982: Profile of a Party in Power* (Boulder: Westview, 1983).

24. Ibid., p. 87.

25. Ibid.

26. A constitutional amendment that would pass on extraordinary executive power to the government in an emergency situation. It was seen by students and left intellectuals as a further strengthening of authoritarian government.

27. Richard Löwenthal, *Der romantische Rückfall* (Stuttgart: Verlag Kohlhammer, 1970).

28. Roland Roth, "Communications Structure and Nationalism," in *Neue Soziale Bewegungen in der Bundesrepublik* (Frankfurt: Campus, 1987), p. 75.

29. Karl Otto, *Von Ostermarsch zur APD* (Frankfurt: Campus, 1977), p. 23.

30. Gerd Langguth, *Protestbewegungen: Die Neue Linke Seit, 1968* (Köln: Wissenschaft in Politics, 1983), p. 7.

31. Friedrich Tenbruck, "Alltagsnormen und Lebensgefühle in der Bundesrepublik," in *Die Zweite Republik*, Richard Löwenthal and Hans-Peter Schwarz, eds. (Stuttgart: Seewald, 1974), p. 292.

32. Ibid.

33. Richard Löwenthal,"Prolog," in ibid., p. 11.

34. Löwenthal, *Der romantische Rückfall*, p. 5.

35. Ibid., p. 13.

36. The theme of a crisis of authority by political systems after major military defeats with a substantially different political culture is not at all new. See Alexis de Tocqueville, *The Ancient Regime and the French Revolution* (New York: Doubleday, 1955), originally published in 1858; and W. Kornhauser, *The Politics of Mass Society* (Glencoe, Ill.: Free Press, 1959).

37. Ralf Dahrendorf, *Society and Democracy in Germany* (New York: Norton, 1967).

38. Richard Löwenthal, "Why German Stability Is So Insecure," *Encounter* (December 1978):31–37.

39. Ronald Inglehart, *The Silent Revolution* (Princeton: Princeton University Press, 1977); also Barnes and Kaase, *Political Action*.

40. Gordon Craig, *The Germans* (New York: Putnam, 1982).

41. Klaus von Beyme,"Krise des Parteienstaats—Ein internationales Phänomen?" in *Bürger und Parteien*, Joachim Raschke, ed. (Opladen: Westdeutscher Verlag, 1982), pp. 87–100.

42. Gerd Langguth, *Protestbewegungen*.

43. Ibid.

44. Gatter, *Die Aufsteiger*, p. 17.

45. Jutta Helm, "Citizen Lobbies in West Germany," in *West European Party Systems*, Peter Merkl, ed. (New York: Free Press, 1980), pp. 383–397.

46. Ibid. Helm also notes that the power of the business lobby on the local level was clearly challenged.

47. Dennis Meadows, *The Limits to Growth* (New York: Universe Books, 1972); and Claus Offe, "Griff nach dem Bremsen," *Die Zeit*, August 20, 1982.

48. Dorothy Nelkin and Michael Pollah, *The Atom Besieged: Extraparliamentary Dissent in France and Germany* (Cambridge: MIT Press, 1983).

49. Martin Mombaur, "Im Parlament und auf der Strasse," in *Die Grünen: Regierungsparner von morgen?* Jörg Mettke ed. (Hamburg: Rowohlt, 1982), p. 136.

50. Detlef Murphy and Roland Roth, "In Many Directions at the Same Time? The Greens—An Artifact of the 5 Per Cent Clause?" in Roland Roth and Dieter Rucht, eds., *Neue Soziale Bewegungen in der Bundesrepublik Deutschland* (Frankfurt: Campus Verlag, 1987), p. 324.

51. Horst Bieber, *Die Zeit*, October 26, 1979.

52. Thomas Nipperdey, *Deutsche Geschichte, 1800–1866* (Munich: Verlag Beck, 1983), pp. 284–289.

53. Stern, *The Failure of Illiberalism*, pp. 58–76.

54. Dahrendorf, *Society and Democracy in Germany*, p. 29; Donald Schoonmaker, "The Second Bonn Republic at Forty Years, *German Politics and Society* (Center of European Studies: Harvard University) Issue 16 (April 1988):10–22.

55. Claus Offe, "New Social Movements: Challenging the Boundaries of Institutional Politics," *Social Research* 52, no. 4 (Winter 1985):817–868.

56. E. Gene Frankland and Donald Schoonmaker, "Disunited Greens in a United Germany." Paper presented at the American Political Science Association convention, Washington, D.C., September 1991.

3

Several Theories in Search of the West German Greens

Each political system confronts the problems of modernity differently. As we have noted in the previous chapter, the German confrontation with science and democracy has brought tragic consequences for both the Germans and their neighbors. The societal and organizational derivatives of science—technology, industrialization, bureaucracy, and secularization—and of democracy—a mass electorate, competitive politics, and pluralism—resulted in failed experiments in limited constitutional government. Late and rapid industrialization and late and insecure nationhood[1] made it well-nigh impossible to combine in harmonious fashion the modern values of equality, liberty, security, and unity. The Germany that was united from 1870 to 1945 has a history of imbalances among these political values.

In the post–World War II period the two Germanys (1949–1989)—dismembered and divided—developed as offspring of first the World War and then the Cold War. Siblings of one culture and language, their occupier-patrons shaped their political structures and cultures—obviously more in the East than in the West. In the western half a tradition of healthy liberalism came to the fore with an energetic middle class asserting itself politically in a competitive party system and economically through a social market economy. In the East, what some scholars called "Red Prussianism" (the old authoritarian tradition) was put in place, joined to an ideologically rigid single-party dictatorship. The Soviets, in Orwellian style, created a German Democratic Republic that was encouraged to consider itself the antifascist remnant chosen to implement socialist ideals. That failed experiment in social engineering is over now that a new Germany is in place, and our task in this chapter is to understand the rise of a New Left party that could play an important role in the united Germany.[2]

How did it happen in a period of four decades that the Federal Republic of Germany, with its prolonged economic success and hyperstable political system, could spawn middle-class radical reformers such as the Greens who challenged the very basis of this economic and political success? Much of the answer lies with the changes in social structure, political and cultural values, and institutional developments that the sustained economic progress brought forth. Our thesis in this chapter is that the Greens are a product of a complex mix of forces that include (1) the particular historical legacy of Germany, (2) the vast changes in social structure that occurred—and are still occurring—in the transition from an industrial to a postindustrial society, and (3) the shift in cultural and political values brought about by a brusque transition to affluence that produced a sizable middle class with conflicting political values.

The rebuilders and shapers of the economic miracle cut their teeth on rapid economic growth and a cautious representative democracy that assigned considerable powers to dominant Volksparties. A wedge of the younger, educated middle class of radical democrats who became active in politics in dramatic fashion in the late 1960s—a generation with the disposition to create new traditions—looked for reduced or steady-state economic growth through a more decentralized state with plebiscitary opportunities. Obviously the changes in the organizational vehicles and values of this younger generation led to a widening of the repertoire of political actions in West Germany. Overinstitutionalized traditional parties were confronted by quasi-institutional movements representing political cleavages that were not easily captured by the larger parties. These New Left and ecological movements found a parliamentary arm in the Greens, an unconventional, self-styled "antiparty party" prepared to challenge the older political elites in their own legislative arena.

Our task now is to look at the general theories that purport to explain political change in postwar West Germany. We want to assess their validity in illuminating the particular features of the Federal Republic insofar as they shed light on the origins and developmental pattern of the Greens. Our conclusion will be that there is no single theory—be it cultural, structural, or institutional—that adequately explains the appearance and activities of the Greens but that a useful approach is an eclectic one that relies on multivariate analysis to highlight the factors that sustain (or undermine) the Green party.[3]

Postindustrial Society and the Greens

There are theories and generalizations about political change in postwar West Germany that give particular explanatory weight to either values, social structure, institutions, or issues, but they all place special emphasis on the characteristics of the postindustrial society. Before we argue about how well those theories help us understand the Greens, we have a prior task. First we need to sketch out the general features of the postindustrial society and delineate what a postindustrial West Germany looked like. Then we need to reflect on the political implications of the postindustrial society in general, as well as for West Germany in particular, before we see how this political situation affected the Greens. As will become readily apparent, the Green party is very much linked to postindustrialism.

According to Daniel Bell, "Industrial society is the coordination of machines and men for the production of goods. Post-industrial society is organized around knowledge, for the purpose of social control and the diverting of innovation and change; and this in turn gives rise to new social relationships and new structures which have to be managed polit-ically."[4] Bell elaborates on this change from a society of manual workers on farms and in factories to nonmanual workers pushing pencils—or more likely computer keys—in the bureaucratic environment of public and private corporations (or, as Alvin Toffler puts it in the idiom of pop sociology, from the proletariat to the cognotariat). Bell's postindustrial society has five aspects:

1. The economic sector changes from a goods-producing economy to a service economy.[5]
2. The occupational distribution shifts to preeminence for the professional and technical class (jobs that require some college or in Germany at least an *Abitur*).
3. Theoretical knowledge becomes critical as a source of innovation and policy formation.
4. Future planning for technological change is important.
5. Not machine technology but the "technology" of managing complex organizational or ecological problems becomes vital.[6]

The simplest threshold in moving from the industrial to the postindustrial society occurs when there are more people working in the service economy than in manual work (more white-collar than blue-collar workers), but there are other aspects of this type of society that are both cause and effect of this change. There is a rapid decline in the number of those working in the agrarian sector; the size of the working class declines while the size of the middle class expands. The educational sector expands rapidly, as one would expect in a society reliant on knowledge and technology. In fact, as Inglehart notes, some postindustrial societies have more personnel—students, faculty, administration, and staff—in the academic institutions than manual workers.[7] The class structure changes from the traditional pyramid of all societies we know in history with a small upper class at the apex and a mass of toilers at the base to various diamond shapes with a bulge in the middle such as Aristotle idealized in his *Politics*.[8] Not only is this middle-class bulge a new configuration in this body politic and society, but it is an increasingly variegated middle class. The old middle class of property owners and industrial entrepreneurs watch the expansion of a new middle class in which knowledge, not property or wealth, is the crucial resource. Finally, in reference to this new middle class[9] there is also wide differentiation. White-collar tasks run from professional, technical, managerial, scientific jobs to clerical duties with various degrees of responsibility and rewards. It is also worth noting that the new middle-class jobs are usually salaried and often have a greater degree of job security than those of the working class.

There are other characteristics of these postindustrial societies that deserve mention. Postindustrial societies are usually affluent, democratic, protected by social safety nets of various densities, increasingly secular, and the mass media are extensive in their reach. They are societies in which a growing percentage of the students—and the work force—is female, and where family patterns, gender roles, and sexual practices are more in flux than stable.[10] Obviously these societies are not just highly urbanized—some have strong patterns of suburbanization. Economic growth, innovation in technology, marketing, and productivity are the burrs under the saddle of this society. Lastly, the organizational style is bureaucratic with hierarchical and complex line-staff charts directing the energies and ambitions of many in the expanding middle class. This last fact is of critical significance because it points to a tension that plays out in the society and polity. The values of democracy are individualistic and voluntaristic; the organizational imperative calls for discipline and deference. Daniel Bell terms this the rub between an educated populous valuing creativity and independent development in a "social structure which is ruled by an economizing and technocratic mode."[11] At this juncture, we need to speculate about the implications for democratic politics in the postindustrial society. As Samuel Huntington once mused in an essay, How benign will industrial politics be?[12]

Postindustrial Society: The Waning of Class Politics?

S. M. Lipset wrote that "in every order of democracy conflict among groups is expressed through political parties which basically represent a 'democratic translation of the class struggle.'"[13] In the three decades since this was written, significant changes in our understanding of political values and actions have occurred to keep pace with the dramatic changes in the transition from industrial to postindustrial polities. In societies that are urban and suburban, the agrarian sectors have shrunk to less than 5 percent (often 1 or 2 percent), and the political power of the farm block has also diminished. There are more white-collar (nonmanual) employees than blue-collar workers, which has several consequences. The percentage of the working force organized in trade unions is on the decline in most postindustrial societies. The percentage of white-collar employees organized is usually less than that of the manual workers, but the increased number in this sector of the economy, with its high voting rates, makes it a force to which political parties pay close attention. The figures on the expansion of education show startling increases at all levels of education. In most European political systems the percentage of students in university education has gone from less than 2 percent to around 30 percent in three decades.[14] This increase may be the most significant statistic for the development of the postindustrial society. It has had the most decisive, though complex, consequences for political action.[15]

Usually—and there are exceptions—the greater the amount of education, the greater the chances for more political discussion, more organizational membership and activity, more voting, and more knowledge and concern about issues. The postindustrial society has a potential for greater participation in democratic politics. As Inglehart has shown, the spread of political skills such as organizational know-how, awareness of tactics, and the ability to imagine the long-term consequences of public policies have increased at a rapid rate in advanced industrial democracies.[16] Education in general, and higher education in particular, sets the tracks for the politics of reformers, occasionally radical reformers. It does this through students and intellectuals interested in laying bare the gap between the ideals of the polity and the reality of everyday politics, often pointing in all-too-knowing tones to a concern for the principles of the system. Summarizing a wide range of evidence gathered in his study of supporters of the campaign for nuclear disarmament in the 1960s in Great Britain, Frank Parkin states that "higher education has something of a radicalizing effect on many of those who experience it."[17] He adds, "Consequently, when adult society, and especially governments, fail to act in accordance with these ideals, but engage only in compromise and concession, students are prone to exhibit radical reactions."[18]

Obviously not all students become radicalized at the university. Present research attempts to sort out the circumstances that sharpen the conflict between young middle-class students and the political institutions of the society.[19] Many of these students come from the middle class, and upon graduation they continue to swell the ranks of what is called the new middle class. What we need to examine first are the diverse political styles of this expanding middle class in postindustrial societies.

Middle-Class Radicalism: One Option for an Amorphous Middle Class

In the Aristotelian scheme, idealized in his polity, members of the middle class, defined in terms of property ownership, are most likely to listen to reason, suffer least from ambition, not covet the goods of others, and support the rule of law. It is their sense of empathy and their ability to balance the obligations of ruling and being ruled that makes them a crucial balance wheel in a polity. Aristotle realizes that obtaining these conditions is rare. In his inventive update of Aristotle, *Political Man*, S. M. Lipset posits that under certain conditions the middle class (in truth, the marginal middle class) succumbs to extremist politics. Germany is his critical case.[20] Now in the post–World War II period the middle class has become the crucial linchpin of these postindustrial societies. Whereas the traditional middle class of the owners of great wealth and property line up with the right-of-center political parties and practice politics as usual, the new middle class divides its votes across the political spectrum. Especially in the past two decades we have witnessed various examples of middle-class radicalism. Writing in 1968, Parkin speculated: "It could be anticipated in that political protest in affluent societies will tend increasingly to have a middle class rather than a working class base."[21]

He was correct. A wedge of this middle class—the young, educated, secular intelligentsia—has become the core of the New Left. Old Left politics supports the role of large-scale bureaucratic organizational bargaining closely with the dominant economic elites and in agreement on the imperative of extensive economic growth. The New Left has an anti-institutional bias, great skepticism about the benefits of economic growth per se, and an inclination for semi- or quasi-institutionalized politics and unconventional political tactics with some distance from traditional political parties. The issues of economic growth and security for the New Left are secondary to a greater concern about the consequences of growth, especially for the environment. Quality-of-life issues, including more participation and opportunities for self-development, displace security on the public agenda. Whether this group is called New Left, postmaterialists, or Left Libertarians, they provide the personnel for the social movements— peace groups, feminists, ecologists—and new parties in postindustrial societies. This group has become an important agent of change. With declining class-oriented voting, partly a result of a bourgeoisified and more conservative working class, the New Left parties of the new middle class have challenged the political agenda of the traditional parties. This class is made up of the educated younger cohort, who come predominantly from jobs in the social services, not commercial scientific jobs, and who have economic security and distance from the production process.

Finally, the postindustrial society is affluent but has its share of inequalities, which generate political conflict. Women in higher education and in occupations, who are increasing in number, have become mobilized politically, and they have raised a series of gender issues that ranges from discrimination in jobs, authority patterns in families, to the issue of choice in abortion. The size and reach of the welfare state is an issue for the Left and the Right. Here the New Left is caught in a squeeze. Allergic to large-scale bureaucratic intervention, their commitment to egalitarianism— expanding life chances—neutralizes some of their criticism. They resolve this tension by calling for a decentralized state and self-help services. The Old Left is more content with decreased vulnerability in welfare state capitalism regardless of the bureaucratic structures it might entail. And the role of the media in postindustrial societies is a subject of great controversy among scholars. The conservative critics see it as a lever amplifying the message of the democratic radicals,[22] a technology controlled by adversarial types. In contrast, a segment of the critical Left see the media as an Orwellian mind-numbing tool: soap operas, sports, and the Springer boulevard press instead of five-minute hates and cheap gin for the proles in *1984*—techniques to depoliticize citizens, to blur rather than sharpen issues, and to dull the critical senses that citizens need to make valid judgments.[23] At the bottom is a major issue of conflict that the new middle-class intelligentsia, including the West German Greens, take seriously: "In the industrial society more and more people become organized in hierarchically structured and routinized factories or offices with their relationships governed by impersonal bureaucratic rules. This type of organization makes large-scale enterprises possible, may lead to increased productivity, and, as long as economic considerations are paramount, a majority may be willing to accept the accompanying depersonalization and anonymity."[24]

Some members of that large middle class—the younger, educated professionals working in the human service area rather than in the fields of commerce and business—are a resistant minority to the trade-off just sketched. They seek a more participant society in which a decentralized state and economy pays serious attention to the negative consequences of rapid growth. This squabble within the increasingly influential new middle class is affecting the politics of postindustrial society. How have those conflicts manifested themselves in West Germany and what role do the Greens play in those conflicts?

TABLE 3.1   Occupational Composition of the Work Force, 1882–1986
(in percentages)

	1882	1925	1950	1974	1986
Agriculture and self-employed	36	33	28	14	13
Manual workers	57	50	51	45	39
Salaried nonmanual (white collar and service)	7	17	21	41	48

Source: David Conradt, *The German Polity,* 4th ed. (New York: Longman, 1989), p. 23

West German Postindustrial Politics

As in an earlier period of its history, West Germany industrialized and urbanized in extremely rapid fashion from 1949 to 1990. A rapid decline of the agrarian sector and the self-employed class, a gradual rise and then decline of the nonmanual working class, a gradual increase in public employees, and an explosive and dramatic expansion of the service sector took place in a society with a high-density population—one of the densest of the industrial democracies—with very high rates of urbanization. Dahrendorf notes that a veritable "second industrialization revolution" took place in West Germany in the postwar period with a transformation of social classes, increased income and education levels, greater social and geographical mobility, and more differentiated political actions. West Germany's transition to affluence was brusque, so it is no wonder that a questioning of the consequences of the rapid urbanization, industrialization, and economic growth—and an attempt to limit growth—would find its place on the political agenda in the late 1960s and early 1970s.[25] The costs and burdens of rapid economic growth assume very tangible forms when one is reminded that close to sixty million people, many in very densely populated urban areas, were living in a geographic area the size of Oregon in an economy proficient in producing chemicals, automobiles, and energy. The population density of the new Germany is equally high, a sign of problems to come.

The Changing Class Structure in West Germany

West Germany has followed the pattern of other postindustrial societies in several ways. As Table 3.1 shows, the number of people working in the agrarian sector diminished rapidly. Farm pressure groups have less political influence than before and most rely on the politics of nostalgia or compensation instead of the hard currency of votes and money.[26] In West Germany the high coherence of the farm block keeps their political power from rapid abatement. The number of self-employed employers has decreased, a sign of fewer entrepreneurs and increased concentration of economic power. Earlier trends in German society toward a smaller number of very powerful firms—cartelization—have picked up after early attempts at decartelization.[27] Business and industrial elites have been dominant players in postwar West Germany.

Because of extensive educational opportunities and an expanding economy, the salaried middle class and the civil service have grown. As we have noted before, the political implications of this major expansion of the tertiary (service) economy are complicated. Civil servants include postal employees and railroad conductors, teachers and professors, and minor clerks and high civil servants (*leitende Beamte*) working in local, state, and national government. The lower ranks of the civil service tend to be organized more in trade unions and lean toward the Social Democratic Party; the middle and upper echelons are organized into a professional federation that leans toward a right-of-center position. These civil servants vote across the party spectrum, however. The Greens pick up a share of this vote from the younger middle-class intelligentsia, especially those in the fields of teaching, social work, and health care. The salaried middle class (*Angestellte*) is now the largest occupational group in the economy. It is from this group and the civil service—not from the workers or employers—that the Greens have drawn most of their voters and from which they have recruited their leaders. What portion of this large and amorphous middle class inclines toward radical reformism? This question is crucial to understanding the Greens. The expansion of higher education and the unique role of the student movement in the Bonn Republic must be assigned critical influence for the formation of the Greens. It is here that the particularity of West German political development has been defined.

The student rebellion was worldwide and had various effects on industrial democracies, but its impact on West German politics was dramatic, somewhat destabilizing (because of the terrorism of the 1970s), durable in the organizational forms and norms that developed in the 1970s and 1980s, and decisive for the formation of the Green party.[28] It is only in this political system that there were such clear generational markings to the party founded in 1980 that had such obvious links to the student movement, citizen initiatives, and social movements of the 1970s and 1980s. A comment of Inglehart's, spoken in general about the consequences of student protest, applies with particular emphasis to West Germany: Clearly postmaterialism is no longer a student phenomenon. When the postwar generation first became politically relevant in the 1960s, the universities may have been the only major institutions in which there was a dominant influence. This generation's youth, their minority status in society as a whole, and their relative lack of representation at decisionmaking levels dictated a protest strategy.[29]

Inglehart's term, postmaterialism, can be taken as the value code of the New Left or of the new middle-class intelligentsia. Our point here is to repeat what we argued in the chapter on the historical legacy: The double crisis of identity and authority in the postwar Federal Republic galvanized a generational challenge to the political system, its institutions, and its way of doing business. The energies unleashed in the initial confrontation of 1968 were not dissipated as easily or quickly as they were in other political systems. When this angry young middle class—brandishing heated rhetoric and using unorthodox political actions—called for a new political tradition, it clearly meant something quite different from the demands of the young American, British, or French radicals. The student movement has to be seen as a change of direction in the political culture and a direct challenge to traditional political institutions. Again, unlike in the United States, France, or Britain, the leftist West German students were not—in their eyes—challenging indigenously developed democratic forms. For them, the Federal Republic was an "import democracy."

Another unique aspect of the West German brand of postindustrial politics is the way in which the New Left of the late 1960s developed a wide and active range of semi-institutional social movements in the 1970s—peace, feminism, urban reform—that eventually merged via the nuclear issue with the ecology movement. And it is at this juncture that we should note the class composition of the social movements. We have established that a dynamic element of social and political change in postindustrial societies in general and West Germany in particular is a new middle-class intelligentsia composed mainly of the professional sector of the salaried class. The radical reformers are an activist section of this group who challenged the dominant paradigm of "the more economic growth, the better" by stressing the importance of the _quality of life_ instead of the _quantity of things_. It is this group that gave a major thrust to the diversity in the repertory of political actions[30] in West Germany. The organizational structures and values—forms and norms—of these social movements were not new to the 1970s. As we noted in the previous chapter, the precursors of the extraparliamentary opposition of the 1950s had developed the techniques of protest and demonstration, which were expanded in the 1970s.

The social movements of the 1970s and 1980s are clearly not understood without the concept of the new middle-class intelligentsia. As Claus Offe has argued in an essay on social movements, there are other elements often lumped under the new middle-class concept that need clarification. He does see the radical reforming students—now professionals in the service sector—as a key element of the social movements. However, he also notes: "But it is also true that in most cases, new social movements do not consist exclusively of 'middle class radicals' but are composed, in addition, of elements from other groups and strata with which they tend to form a more or less stable alliance. Most important among these groups are (a) 'peripheral' or 'decommodified' groups and (b) elements from the old middle class."[31]

By peripherals or decommodified groups Offe means people who are not tied to regular jobs, who have a flexible time budget, and who exist in a social category that "rubs up against" authoritarian and bureaucratic organizations. His examples included middle-class housewives, high school and university students, retired people, and unemployed or marginally employed youths.[32] Several of these groups are important elements of the Green party. The old middle class (independent and self-employed farmers, shop owners, and artisan-producers) is often made up of citizens who are directly affected by mammoth technological projects, such as nuclear plants or large-scale urban renewal projects, that mobilize their political activity, but they are not a significant part of the Green electorate. Offe's elaboration of the class structure of the social movements helps us put into perspective the way in which the nuclear issue affected West German politics and the formation of the Greens. Once again, there were student protests in most industrial democracies and there have also been nuclear plants built in many democracies especially after the oil crisis of the early 1970s. But it was in West Germany that the nature of the protest and the consequences of the alliance against nuclear plants and nuclear weapons had a singular impact on the formation of the Greens.

We have a rich store of information about the issue of expanding nuclear power in industrial democracies. In addition to several comparative studies, we have many excellent case studies. West Germany is a key example in much of this research.[33] The politics of nuclear energy encapsulates in a nutshell the issue of modernity. Massive technological projects, often planned by technocratic elites far from the local scene in conjunction with powerful energy companies, are targeted for communities where prior consultation has been pro forma. Modern science and technology offered nuclear energy as an efficient source of power and promised the state the opportunity not to be held hostage by foreign suppliers of oil. But many citizens of West Germany, especially the adversarial intelligentsia of the new middle class, saw these projects as life-threatening. After noting that the rise of the left-libertarian party "would be incomplete without an examination of the major role of social movements," Herbert Kitschelt adds that "the anti-nuclear power movement in particular was a crucial catalyst of the late 1970s and early 1980s" that drew on the broad infrastructure of environmentalist, feminist, peace, student, and neighborhood movements.[34] As Offe has stated, this antinuclear power coalition had a more diverse class coalition than that of the adversarial younger intelligentsia, and our earlier comments on the formation of a local party in Lower Saxony support this interpretation. It is telling that West Germany has been the country where the opposition to nuclear power sites and nuclear weapons has provoked the greatest political mobilization and controversy. It is also significant that West Germans, in contrast to other populations, are peculiarly sensitive to the problems of the "risk society."[35] Nuclear plants were hot issues in a number of ways. They stood for potential destructive power, the danger of radiation, and the feeling of powerlessness. The emotions unleashed by the numerous demonstrations and site occupations generated considerable support for a future ecology party that would speak to this powerlessness.

So there are very particular reasons why West Germany's postindustrial society exhibited a variety and intensity of grass-roots politics that was unlike that of other polities and unlike the previous "politics as usual" of the traditional parties. A subset of the larger middle class, radical reformers practicing surrogate politics on issues of a noneconomic nature—quality-of-life issues—had dared to risk more democracy. The political structures and culture of West Germany were being slowly transformed.

The changing social structure and political actions make it increasingly difficult to explain politics simply in terms of class. A decreasing proportion of the working class votes for the left-of-center parties such as the Social Democrats in West Germany. The salaried middle class votes across the party spectrum, and the New Left draws progressive voters away from the Old Left parties for a clear reason: The Old Left has moved so far to the center promoting economic growth that it has created space to its left by parties such as the Greens who are critical of the paradigm of progress through continual growth and development.[36] Overall, Inglehart sees electorates becoming politicized and "less constrained by established organizations" and suggests that "politics in Western societies is gradually becoming less institutionalized and less predictable."[37]

We have described the changes in postindustrial societies and their implications for political change in West Germany in order to understand the origins of the Green party. Analyzing social structure and occupational changes is necessary to set the context, but the major theories remain to be assessed. One theory, associated mainly with Ronald Inglehart, emphasizes the role of cultural values in shaping postmaterial, New Left, or Green politics. Other scholars stress a combination of cultural values in a matrix of issues, political opportunity structures, and the mobilization of resources and institutional forces in explaining New Left parties. Offe sizes up these various approaches in a useful phrase: "The interest and explanatory approach has in most cases been in the 'push' of new values, demands, and actors that provide 'issueness' to certain questions, rather than in the 'pull' of objective events, developments or systemic imperatives the cognitive perception of which might condition or give rise to issues."[38] Those suggesting that it is the "push" of changed political and cultural values that is the prime cause of New Left or postmaterialist values, which eventually result in new social movements and Green parties, paint on a broad canvas that depicts many parties over a long time period. They see these values as a major causative factor that shapes issues and institutions. The other major interpretation uses both detailed case studies and comparative studies and insists that changing political events—period effects—and the political actors and structures that react to these events provide a more complete explanation. Those focusing on the "pull" of events want to place the competition for political power among electorates, pressure groups, and parties in the middle of their frame: They paint a detailed portrait of the power struggle instead of the broad landscape that the cultural-value approach prefers. And, quite obviously, we have interpretations of the rise of the Green party in West Germany that use these "colors" and "ways of seeing" in an eclectic manner. How well do changed political and culture values explain the rise of the Greens?

Postindustrial Society, Postmaterial Politics, and the Greens

According to Inglehart,

> Advanced industrial societies are undergoing a gradual shift from emphasis on economic and physical security above all, toward greater emphasis on belonging, self-expression, and the quality of life. The rise of the West German Greens, for example, reflects both the emergence of a postmaterial constituency whose outlook is not captured by the existing political parties and the emergence of a growing pool of voters who are politicized but do not feel tied to the established parties.[39]

One of the major interpreters of New Left politics—also called new politics or postmaterialist politics—has been Ronald Inglehart. It would do him an injustice to list him too categorically under the rubric of cultural-value analysis, for he has carried out an accomplished synthesis of political values, skills, and structures in both of his major works, *The Silent Revolution* (1977) and *Culture Shift in Advanced Industrial Society* (1990). In the second work he has sought to integrate his findings with the research by S. M. Lipset (*Political Man*, 1960) and G. Almond and S. Verba (*The Civic Culture*, 1963) on the prerequisites for stable democracy. In short, his research is a major source of generalizations about the political discontent of the economically secure, adversarial, middle-class intelligentsia.

basic hypotheses at the core of the reasons for the rise of
alist politics are:

scarcity hypothesis: Priorities reflect the environment—one
places greater value on things that are in short supply.
2. The socialization hypothesis: One's basic values reflect the conditions that prevailed during one's preadult years.[40]

Quite simply, if you belonged to an age cohort that grew up in a period
of security and prosperity—no wars, plenty of material benefits—you are
later likely to place more emphasis on nonmaterial issues—the quality of
life, a society of more opportunities for participation. Inglehart, especially
in his latest work, *Culture Shift*, does acknowledge that persons' worldviews "are shaped by their entire life experiences" and that later influences—higher education, dramatic events such as the Chernobyl catastrophe or the Vietnam War, and the persistent stimuli of the mass media—
are important to consider, but the effects of those later influences are
superimposed on the original cultural imprint: "The values of a given
generation tend to reflect the conditions prevailing during its pre-adult
years."[41] Furthermore, there is a careful—indeed, exhaustive—analysis of
life cycle or aging effects (with time, radicals become moderates) compared
with period effects (economic recession turns radicals to philistines) before
concluding that cohort or generational effects are the most decisive. Period
effects make some difference, but it is the embeddedness of the formative
socialization experience that anchors this approach.

Most important for politics, postmaterialists do not give high priority
to economic growth or much deference to traditional hierarchies of authority, and Inglehart notes that their sphere of action is shifting: "Initially
manifested mainly through student protest movements, their key impact
is now made through the activities of young elites. . . . It seems to be a
major factor in Western society—a stratum of higher educated and well
paid young technocrats, who take an adversary stance toward their society."[42] We have scarcely captured the sophistication of Inglehart's approach, which applies to eighteen industrial democracies; our focus is how
well this emphasis in postmaterialist values explains the origins and
development of the West German Greens.

Testing Inglehart's Theory in West Germany's Political Reality

The gist of our critique of Inglehart's postmaterialist value cleavage in the
West German case is that too much emphasis is given to the preadult

formative period in shaping basic values without accounting for the particularities of the political culture. We believe that not enough emphasis is directed toward the unusual impact of the university and student movement experiences and the way in which emotionally laden issues shape political values. As we have noted, these political values do not always work in tandem with the values of the earlier preadult period; they often set the tracks in a decisive way.

Early political socialization of the postwar generation in West Germany suggests that a long period of prosperity and a lack of war do not inevitably engender basic values predisposed toward postmaterialist ideals. It is uncertain what exactly these basic values are. Several studies talk about a "skeptical generation" that lacked firmly held political ideals, which caused it to experience considerable anxiety and uncertainty about future directions.[43] This vacuum or absence of a solid value base because of the discontinuities and tragedies in recent German history was aggravated by extremely rapid social and economic change in the period from 1950 to 1970.[44] Finally, the intensity of the generational conflict in West Germany is missed if one overemphasizes the period effects of affluence and security.

In summary, it is the volatility and explosiveness sparked by that generational conflict and the double crisis of authority and identity that explains the configuration of later postmaterialist values rather than the abstractness of moving up the hierarchy from physiological to nonphysiological needs.[45] It is understood that a theory encompassing eighteen democracies cannot cover the particularities of each preadult socialization period, but given West Germany's burden of the past and its extremely rapid growth in the post–World War II period, there is reason to discount the security of the environment in which basic values were formed.

There is additional evidence to note here. If we assume that those from comfortable middle-class homes who later went to the university are potential postmaterialists, how do we explain the variety of political styles—from violent terrorists of the Red Army Faction to dropout hippies and urban Spontis—that came upon the scene in the 1960s and 1970s?

Furthermore, these queries direct us to another hypothesis, which places more explanatory weight on the student movement and the university experience as the forces under which postmaterialist values really took shape. As we noted earlier, the impact of the student movement has been more influential in West German politics than in other countries. Leftist intellectuals also had their influence on a sector of students who, disaffected because of West German rearmament, weak oppositional politics, and authoritarian university structures, decided to "march through the institutions" to democratize the society and polity.[46] Without reaching for a final judgment on the influence that intellectuals exerted on radical students, we can say that many young students were mobilized and radicalized in significantly new ways.

The case need not be overstated, but a valuable short essay by Friedrich Neidhart makes the point simply and clearly. Calling new social movements a "network of networks," he examines the rise of the women's movement, offering close detail on the organizational opportunities in the university milieu. His point can be interpreted as meaning that these opportunities did not merely complement earlier basic values; they also pointed in a very new direction.[47] Rounding out this critique, we should give some attention to comments by Claus Offe and Robyn Eckersley. Offe calls attention to the "recency of the educational experience" and to the fact that activists in new social movements "are relatively secure in their *present* economic positions as opposed to the prosperity enjoyed, as in Inglehart's theory, in their *formative* years."[48] Eckersley sums up his argument in this manner: "In short, Inglehart seems to have overplayed the importance of childhood socialization in accounting for new class radicalism and underplayed the higher-education experience of his post-1945 cohort."[49]

Even when one considers that Eckersley and Offe wrote their criticisms before Inglehart's extension and refinement of his postmaterial thesis in *Culture Shift* (1990), one can still assert—especially in the West German case—that the nature of the historical legacy, the generational tension released in the student movement, and the organizational and normative consequences of that period were crucial for social movements and the Greens and that these circumstances would favor a cohort interpretation strongly modified by period effects.[50]

Wilhelm Bürklin's challenge to Inglehart's explanation of postmaterialist politics is not easy to summarize. In one sense, it has the simplicity of asserting that Green party activists are motivated not by the values they formed in a period of peace and prosperity but because they are blocked from elite positions by an older, closed-governing elite.[51] Bürklin is paradoxically arguing that depressed economic conditions that restrict job opportunities for Green activists and supporters form the underside of their idealism. He is saying that Green partisans are activated not by earlier values but by the present inadequacy of economic and political opportunities. Recent work by Herbert Kitschelt on the percentage of Green unemployed supporters and the rate of elite circulation cast doubt on Bürklin's argument, but it is a useful and imaginative synthesis that reminds us that a mix of materialist and postmaterialist motivations often direct political actions.

Now we turn to a final approach that also finds fault with Inglehart's emphasis on the political culture approach. Inglehart's "camera focus" is wide angle with an extended times series and essentially longitudinal in a broad comparative sense. The school of resource mobilization, which highlights the role of political opportunity structures, is inclined to the close-up taken within a limited time series and narrower longitudinal reach. One scholar notes that "grievances and institutional change are endemic in most societies, but they rarely translated into collective political action. Instead, the actors' skills and resources and the broader opportunity structures determine when individuals are able to engage in collective mobilization. In particular, the choice of a specific vehicle of mobilization, such as a political party, can be explained only in terms of actors' resources and opportunities."[52] This political world is dense with tangible structures where individuals who jockey for tactical advantages wage real dramatic conflicts with ascertainable costs and benefits. Instead of relying on the profile of political values garnered through survey research, it emphasizes organizational competition, political action, and more immediate conflict. Does this approach extend our understanding of the West German Greens?

The "Pull" of Institutions and the Battle for Power

Politics can be defined as the study of power and accountability; the political party is the crucial institution in mass democracy for providing opportunities for holding public elites accountable. Political parties are probably the sine qua non of democracy, and it is these political structures that the resource mobilization scholars often put at the center of their attention. Lipset and Stein Rokkan note that an "understanding of contemporary politics must . . . begin with the genesis of the current party systems and voter alignments."[53] In their influential essay of 1967, "Cleavage Structures, Party Systems and Voter Alignments: An Introduction," they talk about a "freezing of different types of party system and voter alignments." But writing late in 1986, Lipset notes that alignments could have "thawed" and states that economic growth and prosperity had caused the "development of new cleavages clustering around postmaterialist values" that "have changed the divisions between the left and the right and have affected their bases of support. These new issues are linked to an increase in middle-class political radicalism and working-class social conservatism."[54]

After noting how cleavage structures are transformed into party systems, Lipset and Rokkan state that "cleavages do not translate themselves into party opposition as a matter of course." They then proceed to list the preconditions needed for a party (or parties) to emerge. That is our distinct task for the Green party of West Germany. Have there been useful schemes for analyzing the emergence of New Left parties? There have been a number of them, but one that is attractive to a student of politics not looking for a single magic lever to explain all is a carefully constructed synthesis of approaches by Herbert Kitschelt. He combines aspects of the structural approach (the focus of our earlier discussion of postindustrial society) and resource mobilization theory with some critical remarks about the "breakdown" of the relative deprivation approach of Bürklin. He includes the Inglehart value theory within the structural approach with some useful criticism of that guide to understanding. What we will do in this final section is use the "pegs" of his conceptual framework with special attention to how they apply to the West German Greens.

Factors Explaining the Emergence of New Left Parties

Kitschelt's comparative approach, which synthesizes a range of factors, groups them under structural, institutional, and precipitating conditions. The scheme looks like this:

Structural Factors:	1. Modern welfare capitalism.
	2. Economic prosperity.
Institutional Factors:	3. New Social Movements.
	4. Political parties, especially labor corporatism.
	5. Electoral Systems.
Precipitating Conditions:	6. The nuclear issue.[55]

There is little to add about structural factors beyond what we have discussed about the postindustrial society and polity. This research echoes that of Offe and others, indicating that the safety net of the welfare state gives security and that affluence encourages the expansion of educated people with resources poised for mobilization. Kitschelt does point out that the size of the tertiary (service sector) in the eighteen countries for which he has collected data does not correlate with the existence of New Left parties, but the number of activists within the professionalized service sector and specific political culture traditions would help explain individual cases. There is an increasing number of radical reformers in the public service in West Germany, and many of them have voted for the Greens.

New social movements are, we have noted, hybrid organizations with protean institutional shapes that give them flexibility.[56] They appeal to New Left supporters because they offer a type of *Gemeinschaft* solidarity without the accoutrements of elaborate bureaucratization. Kitschelt asserts that the rise of New Left parties "would be incomplete without an examination of the major role of social movements"[57] and that is especially true in West Germany. His analysis does not assign the centrality to the student movement that we have suggested, but his comment that these movements—environmental, feminist, peace, student, and neighborhood—generated a lasting infrastructure of networks of power is certainly correct.

In his comparative research, Kitschelt points out that West Germany has a more mobilized and diversified social movement sector.[58] At this juncture an array of evidence indicates how a critical mass formed a new political party in West Germany. The limitations of the movements and the fear that the issue of violence would undermine the effectiveness of the antinuclear movement "pulled" the founders of Green parties toward the electoral arena.[59] The social movements in West Germany were more active, more diverse, and, as Kitschelt suggests, driven along by an "adversarial political culture" that embodied the outlook of the cutting edge of a generational force determined to create grass-roots democratic tradition apart from the traditional parties.

The step up from a movement to a party is not an easy one, but the main forces were in place. The younger new middle-class actors were on hand with the supporting cast of peripheral and locally affected older middle-class citizens. The issues of the nuclear sites acted as a generational pull for groups suspicious of technology and corporate and state power. And the existence of a strong—and in some ways unhealthy—animus against the traditional parties aided the mobilization process. Kitschelt's comparative findings attributed low influence to the role of electoral systems, but that is not the case for the Greens in West Germany. A low-percentage electoral hurdle in Lower Saxony along with very generous measures for public financing of parties were critical institutional devices that helped generate momentum—and media—in the late 1970s.

Anna Hallensleben concludes in her study of the Green party in Lower Saxony that the relative ease of creating and sustaining a party encouraged confidence in the West German democracy.[60] There is also sufficient evidence to remark that without the 5 percent electoral hurdle on the national level, the strange bedfellows of ecologists, socialists, and New Leftists of diverse persuasions would not have found themselves in the "common bed" at the creation in Karlsruhe in January 1980.[61] But the grass-roots movement and the Green party were sustained by the attitude toward the party system and the feeling that major parties—both government and opposition—were working hand in glove with each other.

As Kitschelt writes, "For this reason, labor corporatism is one key to understanding the emergence of Left libertarian parties. As labor organizations are drawn into corporatist interest intermediation they become preoccupied with tangible short-term material benefits to their constituencies rather than profound institutional change in capitalism."[62] In simple language, this means that the SPD, especially under Schmidt, had cozy relationships not just with their traditional allies, the labor unions, but also with large corporations. These relationships encouraged preservation of the status quo, not reformism, and generated a New Left opposition.

This generalization fits a wide range of countries, but the fit in West Germany is custom-made. When left of center parties, like the Social Democrats, lose their reform capacity, especially when they are in power, political space opens to their left. The extreme low frequency of strikes in West Germany indicates that the party of reform, the SPD (1969–1984), and its trade unions eventually embraced the "cartel of growth" over ecological concerns. Helmut Schmidt's technocratic and managerial style of crisis management, together with his barely veiled disdain of antinuclear plant and antinuclear weapon activists, helped the Greens find their identity. Certainly the political and economic context narrowed Schmidt's options. The oil crisis of 1973 created the push for nuclear plants. The initiatives of the United States and the modernization of nuclear weapons by the Soviets forced the dilemma of more missiles on West German soil. And as Braunthal notes in his detailed study of the Social Democrats in power, 1972–1984, Schmidt turned to the right as an activist sector of the younger generation moved left. Schmidt's personal style and the substance of his policy preoccupation—stability over reform—drove young activists and voters from his party and aided the Greens' entry to the Bundestag in 1983.[63]

The pattern of party competition in West Germany has changed considerably since Otto Kirchheimer wrote about the waning of opposition in 1966. He was correct. A refurbished pragmatic Social Democratic party had unburdened itself of ideological ballast and set out to appeal as a Volksparty to the burgeoning middle class. Very few scholars or politicians in the mid-1960s could foresee the opposition of the New Left to a more establishment-inclined Social Democratic party.[64] As Joachim Raschke has argued persuasively, the major parties in West Germany became overinstitutionalized and that factor contributed to the plethora of semi- and quasi-institutionalized movements that eventually coalesced into the Green party.[65] Kitschelt concludes that "social changes drive the transformation of citizens' wants" but political parties form only when the mix of opportunities and constraints look good to them in balance. "Polarizing conflicts of high symbolic importance"[66] is seen as a precondition for setting the groundwork. In the West German case, the student movement and the nuclear controversy would fulfill this precondition.

Summary: Approaches Explaining Green Politics in West Germany

We said at the outset of this chapter that there is no one major theory of political, cultural, or institutional change that best explains the rise and development of the West German Green party. We suggested in an earlier chapter that the particular nature of the German historical legacy—its discontinuities, its traumas, its want of legitimate democratic revolution from within—has cast its shadow in West German politics. All political systems are affected in some way by their past histories, but we have underscored the Greens' self-identification as a party-movement of ecology and democratic revitalization interested in bringing forth a new political culture with decentralized political structures. This New Left political force is critical of capitalism but does not favor or support the actual institutions of socialism. The ideals of socialism are the subject of much rhetoric, but the "Greenprint" for reaching these ideals hardly moves beyond incantations about a third way beyond a capitalism without an ecological conscience or a socialism without democratic institutions. The events of post-1989 Europe shift the phrasemaking; now we look for capitalism with a human face.

The approaches we have labeled as structural, cultural values, or institutional really attempt to integrate all of the various elements, but there is an undeniable emphasis in Inglehart's approach on the early socialization period as there is an obvious focus in Kitschelt's synthesis to the role of parties as the key players in the political opportunity structure. Our synthesis in this chapter calls attention to the historical legacy and the generational conflict that issue from a dialogue with past events in order to shape present and future events. It is clear that the center of gravity of the Greens has been in the young and educated new middle class. Their future may well depend on whether they can reach beyond just middle-class radical reformers for support and how successfully they coalesce with their eastern German counterparts. It is also clear that postmaterialist values are part of the Green identity, though, we have noted, there is also a mix of materialist values in their policies. Pollution is not just an aesthetic issue. In West Germany, the term *Risikogesellschaft* (risk society) has clear implications for most citizens. Health and safety are material issues of personal security. Inglehart's research shows these postmaterialist values as deeply anchored over time, but we have asserted that a cohort effect will be influenced by period effects that modify political and cultural values inculcated earlier.

By using Kitschelt's synthesis as our way of summing up our eclectic way of explaining the rise of the Greens, we call particular attention to the struggle for power waged by citizens in movements, pressure groups, and parties in a matrix of institutional settings that constrain and encourage a variety of tactics and strategies. Whatever the comparative analysis suggests, the role of the electoral system and the public financing of parties were important for the Greens. In addition, the changing patterns of party competition contributed to the formation of the Greens. The flexibility and adaptability of those competing parties to the issues that the Greens put on the public agenda—peace, women's concerns, ecology—could well limit the future influence of the Greens. With the creation of a unified Germany, the more industrial society in eastern Germany has been joined to an expanding postindustrial one that is certain to bring a new mix of political values. The institutional framework is the same, but for all intents and purposes it's a new game. That is for future analysis. Our next task is to chronicle and analyze the developmental pattern of the Greens in the area of electoral politics.

Notes

1. Helmut Plessner, *Die Verspätete Nation* (Stuttgart, 1959).

2. The electoral results for December 1990 show 5.2 percent support for a New Left/ecology party. Obviously the traditions of this new party will be heavily influenced by the former West German Greens.

3. S. M. Lipset, *Political Man*, expanded edition (Baltimore: Johns Hopkins Press, 1981), pp. 58–63 (methodical appendix to chapter 2, "Economic Development and Democracy").

4. Daniel Bell, *The Coming of Post-Industrial Society* (New York: Basic Books, 1973), p. 20. Other scholars have written on this concept, but Bell's treatment is most cogent.

5. Ibid., p. 15.

6. I have simply compressed the arguments in ibid., pp. 14–32.

7. Ronald Inglehart, *The Silent Revolution* (Princeton: Princeton University Press, 1977), pp. 3–18.

8. Of course, in Aristotle's scheme, women and slaves, who didn't count as citizens, help him envisage his middle-class mixed system, which he termed a polity.

9. Frank Parkin, *Middle Class Radicalism: The Social Bases of the British Campaign for Nuclear Disarmament* (New York: Praeger, 1968), pp. 175–191.

10. Ronald Inglehart, *Culture Shift in Advanced Industrial Society* (Princeton: Princeton University Press, 1990), p. 6.

11. Bell, *The Coming of Post-Industrial Society*, p. 44. For an explanation that ties this tension to the formation of what Herbert Kitschelt calls left-libertarian parties, consider this comment: "Theories of post-industrial society argue that the growing tension between citizens' demands for autonomy and participation on the one hand and the increasingly comprehensive and complex hierarchies of social control on the other, lead to the formation of left-liberation parties." Herbert Kitschelt, *The Logics of Party Formation: Ecological Parties in Belgium and West Germany* (Ithaca: Cornell University Press, 1989), p. 16. Kitschelt calls the Greens left-libertarian.

12. Samuel Huntington, "Post-Industrial Politics: How Benign Will It Be?" *Comparative Politics* 6, no. 2 (January 1974):163–191.

13. Lipset, *Political Man*, p. 230.

14. Arnold Heidenheimer, Hugh Heclo, and Carolyn Adams, *Comparative Public Policy: The Politics of Social Choice in America, Europe, and Japan*, 3d ed. (New York: St. Martins, 1990), Chapter 2, "Education Policy."

15. Inglehart, *The Silent Revolution* and *Culture Shift*.

16. Inglehart, *Culture Shift*, pp. 335–370.

17. Frank Parkin, *Middle Class Radicalism: The Social Bases of the Campaign for Nuclear Disarmament* (New York: Praeger, 1968), p. 171.

18. In ibid., p. 168, Parkin quotes S. M. Lipset, one of our most perceptive scholars on student politics.

19. As we noted earlier, Gerd Langguth in his study of protest movements in West Germany reminds us that this group is a small percent of the university student population.

20. Ernest Barker, *The Politics of Aristotle*, Book 4 (New York: Oxford University Press, 1958), and Lipset, *Political Man*, pp. 127–182.

21. Parkin, *Middle Class Radicalism*, p. 57.

22. Gerd Langguth, *Protestbewegungen: Die Neue Linke Seit 1968* (Köln: Wissenschaft Verlag, 1983), p. 7.

23. Murray Edelmann, *Constructing the Political Spectacle* (Chicago: University of Chicago Press, 1988).

24. Inglehart, *The Silent Revolution*, pp. 289–290.

25. Lewis Edinger, *West German Politics* (New York: Columbia University Press, 1986), pp. 32–70.

26. Erik Andrlik, "The Farmers and the State: Agricultural Interests in West German Politics," *West European Politics* 4, no. 1 (January 1981): 104–119.

27. David Conradt, *The German Polity*, 3d ed. (New York: Longman, 1986), pp. 25–30.

28. Joschka Fischer, "Identität in Gefahr," in *Grüne Politik*, Thomas Kluge, ed. (Fischer: Frankfurt, 1984), pp. 20–35.

29. Inglehart, *Culture Shift*, p. 331.

30. Samuel Barnes and Max Kaase, eds. *Political Action: Mass Participation in Five Western Democracies* (Beverly Hills: Sage Publications, 1979).

31. Claus Offe, "New Social Movements: Challenging the Boundaries of Institutional Politics," *Social Research* 52, no. 4 (Winter 1985):817–866.

32. Ibid., p. 834.

33. Dorothy Nelkin and Michael Pollak, *The Atom Besieged: Extraparliamentary Protest in France and Germany* (Cambridge: MIT Press, 1981).

34. Kitschelt, *The Logics of Party Formation*, p. 25.

35. Ulrich Beck, *Risikogesellschaft: Auf dem Weg in eine andere Moderne* (Frankfurt: Suhrkampf, 1986).

36. Russell Dalton, "The West German Party System Between Two Ages," in *Electoral Change in Advanced Industrial Democracies* (Princeton: Princeton University Press, 1984), pp. 104–133.

37. Inglehart, *Culture Shift*, p. 370.

38. Offe, "New Social Movements," p. 843.

39. Inglehart, *Culture Shift*, pp. 11, 369.

40. Ibid., p. 56.

41. Ibid., p. 82.

42. Ibid., p. 67.

43. Helmut Schelsky, *Die Skeptische Generation: Eine Soziologie der Deutschen Jugend* (Düsseldorf-Köln, 1957).

44. Richard Löwenthal, *Der romantische Rückfall* (Stuttgart: Verlag Kohlhammer, 1970). A gap in the socialization process results because some parents and teachers are uncertain where to anchor values because of the discontinuities of the Nazi experience.

45. Friedrich Tenbruck, "Alltagsnormen und Lebensgefühle in der Bundesrepublik," in *Die zweite Republik: 25 Jahre Bundesrepublik Deutschland—Eine Bilanz*, Richard Löwenthal and Hans-Peter Schwarz, eds. (Stuttgart: Seewald Verlag, 1974), pp. 289–310.

46. Löwenthal, *Der romantische Rückfall*, and Gordon Craig, "Professors and Students," in *The Germans* (New York: Putnam, 1982), pp.170–189.

47. Friedrich Neidhardt, "Einige Ideen zu einer allgemeinen Theorie sozialer Bewegungen," in *Sozial Struktur in Umbruch*, S. Hradil, ed. (Opladen: Leske, 1985), pp. 193–204.

48. Offe, "New Social Movements," pp. 850–851.

49. Robyn Eckersley, "Green Politics and the New Class: Selfishness or Virtue?" *Political Studies* 37, no. 2 (June 1989):218.

50. In writing this, we are also aware of Inglehart's fine effort to call attention to political issues and events that affect postmaterial values. Inglehart, *Culture Shift*, p. 380.

51. Wilhelm Bürklin, *Grüne Politik: Ideologische Zyklen, Wähler und Partein System* (Opladen: West Deuscher Verlag, 1984). Also Jens Alber, "Modernisierung, neü Spannunglinien und die politischen Chancen der Grünen," *Politische Viertelsjahressehrift* 26 (1985). Heft 3, S. 211–226.

52. Herbert Kitschelt, "Left Libertarian Parties: Explaining Innovation in Competitive Party Systems," *World Politics* 40, no. 2 (January 1988):225. The fears of unemployment and the consequences of a radical decree restricting "radicals" from public service should not be completely discounted in understanding the motivations of some Greens. Gerard Braunthal, *Political Loyalty and Public Service in West Germany: The 1972 Decree Against Radicals and Its Consequences* (Amherst: University of Massachusetts Press, 1990).

53. S. M. Lipset, *Consensus and Conflict: Essays in Political Sociology* (New Brunswick, N.J.: Transaction, 1985), p. 115.

54. Ibid.

55. Kitschelt, *The Logics of Party Formation*, pp. 9–40.

56. Joachim Raschke, *Sociale Bewegungen: Ein historisch-systematischer Grundviss* (Frankfurt: Campus, 1985).

57. Kitschelt, *The Logics of Party Formation*, p. 25.

58. Ibid., p. 35.

59. Anna Hallensleben, *GLU zur grünen Partei: 1977–1980 in Niedersachsen* (Göttingen: Musterschmidt, 1984).

60. Ibid.

61. Detlef Murphy and Roland Roth, "Die Grünen-Artifakt der 5% Klausel," in *Neue soziale Bewegungen in der Bundesrepublik Deutschland,* Dieter Rucht and Roland Roth, eds. (Frankfurt: Campus Verlag, 1987), p. 296.

62. Kitschelt, *The Logics of Party Formation.*

63. Gerard Braunthal, *The West German Social Democrats; 1969–1982: Profile of a Party in Power* (Boulder: Westview, 1983), p. 235. Bürklin's analysis of Schmidt and the SPD is similar. Their action cleared a path for the Greens.

64. Charles Hauss and David Rayside, "The Development of New Parties in Western Democracies Since 1945," in *Political Parties: Development and Decay,* Louis Maisel and Joseph Cooper, eds. (Beverly Hills: Sage, 1978), pp. 31–58, especially p. 54.

65. Frank Nullmeier, "Institutionelle Innovationen und neue soziale Bewegungen," *Aus Politik und Zeitgeschichte* B26/89 (June 23, 1989):3–16.

66. Kitschelt, *The Logics of Party Formation,* p. 37.

The Greens
and the Electorate

A s WRITTEN IN *Die Zeit,* "It is one thing to state an idea, another to flesh it out, and yet another to build a coalition for it, either in the electorate or with other parties—and to get a majority for it. The Greens are strong on the first part, weak on the others."[1] Given the fact that competitive political parties are the preeminent institutions of modern mass democracy and the essential prerequisite for the electoral debate that leads to the allocation of political power, one could imagine that having a new party competing for votes would have been welcomed at the end of the 1970s. Yet not everyone who was part of the Green movement was pleased when local and state Green parties filed to run as "The Greens: Another Political Association" (Die Grünen: SPV) in the 1979 European Parliament election and then, after the founding of the Greens in early 1980, to run a campaign in the 1980 national elections.

Some activists in the local citizen initiative groups and other social movements (peaceniks, feminists, environmentalists) felt that their energies and independence of direction would be drained off in the institutional framework of a political party. Jo Leinen, executive director of the national organization of environmental citizen lobby groups, was quite direct in his comments about the new party. In an article for the *Frankfurter Rundschau,* "Effective Lobbying More Important Than a Few Legislators," Leinen argues that a party like the Greens would slow down concrete action on the local level, impede the flexibility and mobility of citizen action groups, and redirect the spontaneity and openness of the ecology and other movements into the hierarchical and bureaucratic organizational form of a political party. For Leinen, the aim of citizen initiatives was to march through *society,* not through *institutions,* to bring about long-range cultural changes. He concludes: "The party garb does not fit a grassroots, extraparliamentary and politically heterogeneous movement."[2]

There were other skeptics and critics besides Leinen. Several political observers in the scholarly and journalistic circles saw the Greens as a sectarian, minor protest party pushing the single issue of ecology. They saw them as a motley crew of leftists of the student movement generation, conservative ecologists, feminists, and antimilitarists who lacked clearly defined goals—especially in the area of economic policy; these critics did not expect much influence from the newcomer. Still others welcomed the new ideas of a predominantly younger generational cohort but were convinced that a movement/party was fated to a difficult passage. It would be a party with schizophrenic organizational identities: One identity would be flexible, plastic, and informal as it preached radical democracy for the polity and society and tried to implement it internally; the other would be disciplined, pragmatic, and structured, the result of inevitably succumbing to the dynamic of professionalization and institutionalization that is dictated by electoral competition.[3]

Theoretical arguments to the contrary, the disaffection with the major parties, the organizational skills and tactics gained from decade-long participation in local politics, and the intensity of feelings generated by the nuclear issue all contributed to form the critical mass that helped create the Green party. The generational cohort felt a sense of adventure in creating a new organizational form that, they hoped, would combine the best features of movement and party. They were as interested in changing the political culture as in garnering votes, and they also understood that access to the media and to the bureaucracy and a measure of attention from the major parties would be a benefit in capturing legislative seats. If these somewhat finger-wagging young Greens were cultural pessimists—as their critics asserted—they were also hopeful and energetic enthusiasts ready to challenge the status quo.

More Than a Decade of Green Campaigns: An Overview of the Record, 1977–1990

Whatever the hopes of the founders or the nagging doubts of the naysayers, the Green electoral record over more than a decade has been remarkable for the first party to break the troika (Christian Democrat/ Christian Social Union, Free Democrats, Social Democrats) monopoly over the electorate. Since 1961 these three major parties had regularly received 94 percent of all of the votes on the national election, garnering over 99.1 percent of the total vote in 1972 and 1976. Challenging these major parties, the Greens broke through on all levels—local, state, national, and European. Their success is even more remarkable given the factional squabbles, the lack of clarity on economic proposals, and most pointedly, as Andreas

TABLE 4.1   Votes for Greens: National Elections, 1980–1990

	Percentage of Vote	Impact	Average Vote
1980	1.5	no seats	1.5
1983	5.6	won 27 seats	5.6
1987	8.3	won 42 seats	8.3
1990	4.8(W)	no seats(W)	
	6.0(E)	won 8 seats(E)	5.1

Source: Unless otherwise stated, all electoral statistics in this chapter are from Clause A. Fischer, ed., *Wahlhandbuch für die Bundesrepublik Deutschland: Daten zu Bundestags-, Landtags- , und Europawahlen in der Bundesrepublik Deutschland, in den Ländern und in den Kreisen 1946–1989*, 2 vols. (Paderborn: Schöningh, 1990).

von Weiss has quipped, the fact that this party of radical reformers adhered to the organizational principle of the New Left with its hostility to organizational hierarchies.[4]

The most obvious successes to students of West German politics have been the votes in national elections (see Table 4.1). After a poor start in 1980 in which the contest between Helmut Schmidt and Franz Joseph Strauss for the chancellorship overshadowed other issues and kept Social Democratic voters in the fold, the Greens polled 5.6 percent of the vote in 1983, which gave them twenty-seven seats in the Bundestag,[5] and 8.3 percent of the national vote in 1987 (over 2 million votes), which increased their legislative delegation to forty-two seats. The epochal events of the rapid unification, the special election law on December 1990, and the Greens' own internal problems left them below the 5 percent hurdle and out of the Bundestag.

Less obvious to outsiders—there is sparse coverage of state or local elections in the U.S. media—but nevertheless of critical importance was a series of electoral battles from the late 1970s through the 1980s on the state (Länder) level in which the Greens obtained representation by jumping the 5 percent hurdle in nine of the eleven states. We will give details on these state campaigns, but the general pattern of success included rapid victories in the earlier 1980s with representation in six state legislatures by the end of 1982 and then slower growth in the late 1980s.

As Table 4.2 indicates, the success of the Greens often meant (1) displacing the Free Democrats as the third strongest party, (2) reducing the political power of the Social Democrats, (3) creating the possibility (and actuality) for coalition government with Green participation, and (4) forcing the necessity of new elections when no acceptable majority coalition could be formed. Quite clearly, the pattern of political party competition in West Germany was significantly changed from earlier decades.

Least noticed of all, but in many ways the cornerstone of Green electoral success in the past thirteen years, were the decisive victories won by the

TABLE 4.2   Votes for Greens: State and City-State Elections, 1978–1992

State	Percentage of Vote	Impact	Average Vote
1978 Hamburg	4.5	(FDP out)	
Lower Saxony	3.9	(FDP out)	
Bavaria	1.8		(3.05)
Hesse	2.0		
1979 Berlin	3.7		
Schleswig-Holstein	2.4	SPD below 50%	(3.73)
Bremen	5.1	won seats	
1980 Baden-Württemberg	5.3	won seats	
Saar	2.9		(3.73)
North Rhine Westphalia	3.0	(FDP out)	
1981 Berlin	7.2	won seats	(7.20)
1982 Lower Saxony	6.5	won seats	
Hamburg (June election)	7.9	won seats	
Hesse	8.0	won seats	(6.76)
Bavaria	4.6		
Hamburg (December election)	6.8	won seats	
1983 Rhineland Palatinate	4.5	(FDP out)	
Schleswig-Holstein	3.6	(FDP out)	
Bremen	7.8	won seats	(5.45)
Hesse	5.9	won seats (coalition later)	
1984 Baden-Württemberg	8.0	won seats	(8.0)
1985 Saar	2.5		
Berlin	10.6	won seats	(5.9)
North Rhine Westphalia	4.6		
1986 Lower Saxony	7.1	won seats	
Bavaria	7.5	won seats	(8.33)
Hamburg	10.4	won seats	

(continues)

grass-roots activists on the local level. In towns, cities, and counties the infrastructure of the Green organization helped create the stability that enabled the party to weather the factional storms and the fogginess of the Greenprint for policy reform that beset state and national party units. In the research on Green party politics, the area of local politics has been neglected, but any full assessment of the party must analyze the critical contribution on that level.[6]

Finally the Greens have consistently improved their national vote for seats in the European Parliament, achieving 8.4 percent of the vote in 1989 after a vote of 3.2 percent in 1979 and a vote of 8.2 percent in 1984. In a comparative sense, there is not a New Left ecology party in any other industrialized democracy that has so changed the pattern of political

Table 4.2 (*continued*)

State	Percentage of Vote	Impact	Average Vote
1987 Hesse	9.4	won seats	
Rhineland Palatinate	5.9	won seats	
Hamburg	7.0	won seats	(8.13)
Bremen	10.2	won seats	
1988 Baden-Württemberg	7.9	won seats	
Schleswig-Holstein	2.9		(5.4)
1989 Berlin	11.8	in coalition; won seats	(11.8)
1990 Saar	2.6		
Lower Saxony	5.5	in coalition; won seats	
North Rhine Westphalia	5.0	won seats	
Bavaria	6.4	won seats	
Mecklenburg-West Pomerania	9.3	no seat; ran separately	
Brandenburg	9.2	in coalition; won seats	(6.48)
Saxony Anhalt	5.3	won seats	
Thuringia	6.5	won seats	
Saxony	5.6	won seats	
United Berlin	9.4	won seats	
1991 Hesse	8.8	in coalition; won seats	
Rhineland Pfalz	6.4	won seats	
Hamburg	6.2	won seats	(8.2)
Bremen	11.4	in coalition; won seats	
1992 Baden-Württemberg	9.5	won seats	(7.78)
Schleswig-Holstein	4.97		

Note: The average votes for the city-states of Berlin, Bremen, and Hamburg are considerably higher than that of any other groups. The Greeens and their counterparts in the East have jumped the 5 percent hurdle to win seats in all states except Saar and Schleswig-Holstein, where the SPD has strong party organizational strength.

Source: Clause A. Fischer, ed., *Wahlhandbuch für die Bundesrepublik Deutschland: Daten zu Bundestags-, Landtags-, und Europawahlen in der Bundesrepublik Deutschland, in den Ländern und in den Kreisen 1946–1989,* 2 vols. (Paderborn: Schöningh, 1990).

power on so many levels of government as the Greens of West Germany. They have tapped a cleavage of political values and raised a range of issues that the traditional parties had neglected. It may well be that the awakened sensitivity of these same parties to the issues of New Politics— environment, feminism, more participation—will eventually undermine a Green party resistant to organizational discipline and professionalization. Then, too, the issue of unified Germany must be carefully considered. If the Greens had resisted the inevitability of this historic change and insisted on their traditional policy of two German states, their demise on the national level would have been certain. As it happened, their confusion on this issue lost them representation in western Germany. Their fate in the new electoral arena of an expanded Germany will be discussed in a later chapter.

First, the problem at hand is to explain the Green electoral success of the past decade. What changed the hyperstable West German party system of the first three decades of the Bonn Republic to one in which four parties competed with a widened spectrum of policy options? What was the setting in the Bonn Republic (1949–1990) that will enable us to understand the political scene in this second, revised and enlarged, "Berlin" republic?

An Electorate in Transition

Observers of political parties agree that voters are influenced both by long-term changes in the class structure and in the political culture and short-term factors such as rates of inflation, environmental disasters like Chernobyl, or the choices of party strategy in a campaign. Choosing the pugnacious Strauss from Bavaria to run against technocrat-manager Schmidt of Hamburg proved to be a poor tactic for the Union parties in 1980. The complex way in which voters balance their assessments of issues, party identification, and candidates with their class position, values, and earlier political loyalties is the subject of much analysis by students of politics. Research in a number of industrialized democracies indicates that party loyalties are waning, independent issue-oriented voting is waxing, and the old cues—religion, class, and urbanization—are gradually losing resonance with the voters, especially the younger, educated members of the new middle class.[7] These trends are referred to as dealignment: when a voter uncouples from one political affiliation without hitching on to another. Dealignment is marked by more calculating assessments of policy outputs and by tactical voting that chooses a political direction by voting for a potential coalition partner with a different agenda or tempo on certain issues.

Ronald Inglehart points out that high levels of education and the general affluence in Western polities have increased the number of politically active and attentive nonpartisans, especially from the new middle class. These well-informed voters are making politics "less institutionalized" and "less predictable" while at the same time subjecting political actors to "increasing close public scrutiny."[8] In general, there are more educated voters with sophisticated political skills who want to try many levers rather than pulling the same old straight party switch.

In our previous chapter on the changing class structure of postindustrial polities and the West German society, we noted those long-term structural changes that are shaping the changing electorate in the Federal Republic.

The working-class electorate continues to decline, as does the self-employed class, while a great expansion has taken place with the new middle class. Ever since Theodor Geiger's study of this class in the 1930s in Germany, it has been clear that members of this class do not neatly choose parties of the Right or Left. Speaking of the fluidity and volatility of the new middle class in 1978, Gerhard Loewenberg noted, "No political party could take their support for granted. None of the old political ideologies attracted their loyalty—they are an electorate . . . newly available for political mobilization."[9] As we will see, the younger new middle class forms the center of gravity of the Green electorate. It is these younger, educated voters with job security—or expected job security, because many are pupils or students—who are the "carriers" of the New Politics. These carriers are but a segment of the new middle class whose generational political experiences were formed in the student movement of the late 1960s and the citizen initiatives and social movements of the 1970s that could not be held and integrated by the party. For them the SPD had become the establishment, just like the other parties. With this as background, we can now turn to the changes in public opinion among the potential Green voters and assess their actual electoral performance in the late 1970s and 1980s.

"Green" Clouds on the Horizon for the Social Democrats

The survey data about political attitudes in Ronald Inglehart's *The Silent Revolution: Changing Values and Political Styles Among Western Publics* have particular significance for West German politics. They show that the growth of postmaterial political values among West German youth was more widespread than in any of the ten other Western democracies and that the generational gap in political values between the older and younger age cohorts was greater in the Federal Republic than in the other political systems.[10]

Those postmaterialist or New Politics attitudes—environmental concerns, demands for a more participatory society, a priority for quality-of-life issues over economic growth goals—had already translated into political actions of which the SPD was well aware. The Social Democrats were in a constant wrangle with the JUSOS, the youth organization whose New Politics agenda included a greater distance from NATO, disarmament, decentralization of power with greater authority to local government, and more openings in the party for women. In addition, declining membership figures in the SPD, especially among the younger generation, indicated that the outstanding gains made by Willy Brandt and his party in 1972 among voters eighteen to twenty-four years of age were slipping away.

Whereas from 1968 to 1972 the SPD party membership had increased, from 1976 to 1982 it decreased; it is obvious from electoral analyses that many of the defecting SPD members and voters moved to the Greens.[11]

The expansion of citizen initiative groups and social movements in the 1970s—which were unattached to political parties—was a further sign that disaffection with the traditional political parties and politicization and mobilization of the younger citizenry were occurring at the same time. Clearly, confidence in the major parties was declining. Eva Kolinsky has summarized these trends: "The detachment among the young from the major political parties has increased during the seventies. . . . The impression that parties remained aloof from society and people had grown not merely among the young. In 1976, 40 percent of the West German population thought that not everybody was represented by the major parties and 16 percent felt they themselves were not represented. The detachment or the cleavage grew faster still among the younger age groups."[12]

In summarizing the causes of the SPD's severe losses to the Greens in the 1983 national election, Manfred Güllner points to the decline in Social Democratic party strength in urban areas—especially university towns—both in membership figures and in local political races during the 1970s. Some workers were disenchanted that local posts were going to new middle-class types; many of these new middle-class types were tied only loosely to the party, and the New Left voters were not tied to any party at all.[13] Events did not help the SPD in the 1970s. Helmut Schmidt's technocratic style, his politics of pushing the nuclear options for domestic energy and, later, for modernized nuclear missiles, and his aloof crisis-manager style certainly drove away many in the growing New Left electorate. As many Greens later noted, Schmidt was one of their best recruiters.

Charting the Green Wave: Electoral Performance, 1978–1991, and the Diversity of Green State Parties

Einheit in der Vielfalt (unity in diversity) is one of the many slogans the Greens have bandied about to convince themselves that their pluralism is not as unstructured as it really is. However, there is more diversity than unity both in factional positions relating to how pragmatic or principled a Green activist may be and also in the different Green parties in the West German states.[14]

In the city-states of Hamburg, Bremen, and West Berlin, New Politics cleavages are strongly represented. These are the urban centers in which the politics of space—land use (expansion of harbors or airports), urban renewal, transportation, nuclear power—contend for attention with the politics of social identity, which involves civil rights, feminist concerns, and expanded participatory opportunities. This is the left faction of the Green party, states where green is mixed with red and multicolored tinges. It is in the city-states where the ecosocialists have had their strength.

In contrast, the more rural large states, Baden-Württemberg and Lower Saxony, have been dominated mainly by pragmatists and ecolibertarians within the Greens who concentrate on the politics of space. The political stance of the party in Parliament is moderate and open to coalition with another party. The Hamburg Greens rejected coalitional opportunities, and the West Berlin coalition with the SPD was a rough-and-tumble affair. In contrast, Lower Saxony has a coalition with the SPD, as the Hessians also do, and the Baden-Württemberg Greens cooperate with the other parties. The color of these two large rural states is a soft, not a bold, green.

Hesse and North Rhine Westphalia have contending factions of realists and fundamentalists that reflect their large urban centers—Frankfurt, Cologne, and Düsseldorf—and their diverse geography. As in the city-states, the politics of space and social identity compete with each other. The green color here covers a wide spectrum; there are fierce arguments about what Green means.

There are two other categories. First, two states, Bavaria and Rhineland-Palatinate, are in areas of strong conservative traditions. The Green parties here are operated by low-key pragmatists who focus mainly on the politics of space. Green organizational activity has been slow to develop and both states barely jumped the 5 percent electoral hurdle in the latter part of the 1980s. A moderate green dominates the landscape here. Second, Saar and Schleswig-Holstein are states where the Greens have never won seats in the state legislature. The predominant fact here is strong SPD leadership that has co-opted many of the Green themes. The states are neither heavily urbanized nor postindustrial, which results in a weak new middle class. There are fewer university towns, and the strong personalities and Green tendencies of the SPD leaders—Oskar LaFontaine in the Saar and Björn Engholm in Schleswig-Holstein—have muted the color and appeal of the state Greens. Keeping in mind the varied strengths of the state Green parties and the wide assortment of differences—in tactics and policy—makes one appreciate why the national Greens "have made a virtue of pluralism from the plight of factionalism."[15]

Background to the Electoral Battles

The Greens began the decade of the 1980s with the wind at their backs. The Social Democrats had an unsteady hand on the rudder of power and their coalition partner, the Free Democrats, were, like the SPD, losing votes to the Greens on the local and state level and preparing again to change coalition partners. Public opinion polls and election results pointed to a trend that prevailed through the 1980s: the Greens' core voting constituency was made up of young, educated, new middle-class citizens in large cities and university towns who worked in personal service jobs—teaching and social service and health professions—and salaried employees in high-tech jobs. They also had—thanks to the progressive Social Democratic law of 1972 that lowered the voting age to eighteen—the largest vote from citizens still studying at the *Gymnasium* or at the university. The Greens were weak in their appeal to workers, the self-employed, and successful businessmen; their core voters held postmaterial political values that were sensitive about the limits to and costs of rapid economic growth. Through the 1980s, the Greens added to this coalition voters in areas affected by massive projects—nuclear plants, airport expansions, highway developments—who were disaffected because they had been taken for granted by parties. The causes of disaffection were many. The parties were heavily financed from the public till, subject to corruption and scandal in corporatist sweetheart agreements, and seemingly oblivious to the Greens' call for more concern for the long-term effects and unintended deleterious consequences of economic growth. The criticism from the Greens—about more integrity in public affairs, more independence in foreign affairs with disentanglement from a military bloc armed to the teeth, and, most telling, more democracy in political and economic affairs via experiments in decentralized authority—had its impact.

Beyond the true believers, the core voters who had the idealistic phrases of the student movement still ringing in their ears, the Greens attracted citizens who were less convinced of the Greens' solutions than they were of the Greens' forthright critique of a political system in need of renewal. These voters, tactical rather than core, were set on sending a clear signal to the traditional parties to clean up their act and to deal specifically with the threat to human and natural resources in the risk society of the postindustrial age.

The "clean Greens"—those with no record of blemishes—had an air of innocence, dynamism, and generational conviction mixed with *Besser-wisserei* (know-it-allness), which gave them a string of electoral victories from 1978 to 1984. Then a second part of the cycle, termed crosscurrents here, kicked in between 1985 and 1987. The Green slogan "Neither left, nor right, but forward" became more of a tired cliché. The freshness was gone and the naïveté and factional backbiting less excusable. The older parties began to adapt by revising their party platforms, and the voters, especially the tactical voters of the new middle class, looked critically and in vain for stable leadership and detailed policy recommendations from the Greens.

The last phase of the electoral competition (still in motion), which we have termed "Ebbing More Than Flowing, 1988–1992," catches the Greens in a legitimate *Identitaetskrise* (crisis of identity) and in a battle for survival. The balance sheet is subject to negative and positive judgments about their long-term project. The Greens continue to do well in local government, have had mixed results in state elections, and had a good result in the European Parliament election of 1989. They have experienced an organization shakeout that caused prominent representatives—fundamentalists and ecosocialists—to leave the party. The unification of Germany caught the Greens flat-footed; they moved indecisively as they abandoned their decade-old policy of the two Germanys. As we have noted, a failure to jump the 5 percent hurdle in the all-German election in December 1990 eliminated the western Greens from the Bundestag, but the shock of that defeat brought on party reform and a string of electoral successes on the state level in 1991. Their major challenge, which we discuss in more detail in the final chapter, is adapting their political style and program to the unified Germany.

With this overview as background, let us look at the details of their electoral performance. We have divided up the electoral cycle in the following phases: (1) The Green Wave Kicks Up, 1978–1980, (2) Incoming Tide, Running Strong, 1981–1984, (3) Crosscurrents, 1985–1987, (4) Ebbing More Than Flowing, 1988–1990, and, described in Chapter 10, (5) Election Results, December 2, 1990. Besides noting the key events of each period, studies of the different types of state Green party will be used to show diverse patterns of tactics and competition.

The Green Wave Kicks Up, 1978–1980

In 1978, the first year in which the Greens participated in state elections, they failed to jump the 5 percent hurdle in four states, achieving a high of 4.5 percent in Hamburg. However, a pattern for the next several years was already clear. The Greens drew votes away from the Social Democrats and the Free Democrats, especially among the younger voters. In Hamburg and Lower Saxony, the Free Democrats failed to jump the 5 percent hurdle for the first time in several elections.

In 1979, the Greens scored two major successes. They achieved 3.2 percent in the vote for the European Parliament. Although the Greens did not gain any seats, the financial support and media attention aided them in their election to the city-state of Bremen with 5.1 percent of the vote. Their vote in Schleswig-Holstein, the Saar, and West Berlin was not great, but it continued to draw from Social Democratic voters. In 1980, the Greens followed the founding in Karlsruhe in January with a series of typical Green party conferences characterized by much wrangling and polemical debate. Nevertheless, a more pragmatic Green party achieved their first victory in a large, southern, geographically diverse state, Baden-Württemberg with 5.3 percent of the vote. This success showed that the city-state victory in Bremen with its left-tinged New Left politics was not an isolated occurrence. It also shows the distinct political settings in which the various Green state parties operate. The Free Democrats failed to make it into the North Rhine–Westphalia Parliament, and the SPD was reduced below the 50 percent mark. Putting together a hastily arranged campaign for the national elections in October 1980, the Greens received only 1.5 percent of the vote, but, once again, extensive media coverage, public financing, and continued participation in local politics showed that a Green organizational infrastructure was developing. The nuclear issue was in the forefront during this year. The NATO decision to station Pershing missiles in West Germany if the Soviets did not pull back their SS-20 rockets had been made in late 1979, and the unrest because of this decision, along with large demonstrations at the proposed nuclear power plants at Brokdorf and Gorleben, kept the political activists and many Green sympathizers highly mobilized. At the end of 1980, political actions and rhetoric in West Germany were changing rapidly from the stable, conventional patterns of the past decades.

Incoming Tide, Running Strong, 1981–1984

At first glance, 1981 appears to have been a quiet year for the Greens. Their party in West Berlin, another city-state with a variety of urban problems, highly politicized university students, and a lively countercultural tradition, achieved 7.2 percent of the vote, cutting sharply into the Social Democratic vote. The Alternative List of the Greens campaigned against the credit scandals, the housing problems, the excesses of party patronage, and the need for long-range planning for urban renewal. Their voters included the usual core of the new middle-class professionals and university students. They even managed to bring out nonvoters in SPD areas. In the country at large the demonstrations against the missiles decision and against nuclear sites reached massive proportions. Over 100,000 individuals demonstrated against the building of a nuclear plant in Brokdorf, and 300,000 supporters of the peace movement attended a rally in Bonn for disarmament. There continued to be violence, charges of police brutality, and countercharges of violence sanctioned by Greens at various sites. A good segment of the population was not convinced of the

Greens' sincerity on their principle on nonviolence, but research has shown that an overwhelming number of Greens adhered to the principle of nonviolent protest behavior.

The election activity of 1982 and 1983 can be summarized together. There were nine state elections and a national election in 1983. The national coalition of the Social Democrats and Free Democrats collapsed in 1982, and the Christian Union and Free Democrats took over the government and ran a successful campaign for national power in 1983. At the end of 1982, the Greens had entered the parliaments of Hamburg, Lower Saxony, and Hesse and barely missed clearing the hurdle in Bavaria. The Free Democrats failed to get above 5 percent in four more state elections, and the Social Democrats continued to lose voters—again from the young educated middle-class-voters—to the Greens, who for the first time brought up coalition possibilities in Hamburg and Hesse. The Hamburg case deserves some attention, for it shows another long-term problem of Green party politics.

The vote in June 1982 put the Greens in a crucial bargaining position in Hamburg. They had won their 7.7 percent with mainly SPD votes and enough FDP votes to barely oust them from the legislature. The vote for the Hamburg Greens came from the area of university students, the art area, the area where house squatters were, the area of young professionals, and the section of Hamburg where the harbor expansion plans were a controversial environmental issue. Over two-thirds of the Green voters were under thirty-five years of age, a phenomenon rarely experienced in other party systems. This clearly defined generational vote had been occurring regularly in the state, local, national, and European elections of the late 1970s and early 1980s. The coalition talks in Hamburg lasted for many hours, and the Social Democrats rejected the demands of the Greens as too far-reaching. The election of December 1982 showed a pattern that was to repeat itself in Hamburg in 1987. The tactical voters, shunting back and forth between the Greens and the SPD, moved enough votes from the Greens to the SPD to give it a majority. The message was clear. The Green party leadership was more fundamentalist than their electorate, which placed value on a constructive opposition.

This mild rebuke for the Greens in Hamburg did not diminish the overall successes of the Greens in 1983. A vote of 5.6 percent in the national election made the Greens the first fourth party since 1953 to break through the three-party dominance in the Bundestag. Votes on the local level in a number of states ran higher than the state and national percentages, and the traditional party elites realized that the pattern of competition had been dramatically rearranged. By the end of 1983 the major parties no longer looked at the Greens as merely a band of "sunshine soldiers" pushing a sometime thing. They were now seen as something more than just a single-issue protest party with a capacity to collect votes despite their heavy baggage, which consisted of extraordinarily decentralized party organizational procedures, sketchily detailed economic policies, and—for the traditional parties—radical proposals such as immediate withdrawal from NATO.

1984 continued the pattern of increased votes for the Greens. The vote for the European Parliament more than doubled the earlier vote in 1975, from 3.2 percent to 8.2 percent, and the party also increased their vote for the moderate constructive opposition in Baden-Württemberg from 5.3 percent in 1980 to 8 percent in 1984. Even more encouraging for supporters was the local-level vote in North Rhine–Westphalia in September 1984 in which the party polled 8.6 percent of the vote. In this state, which contains one-third of all the voters in the Federal Republic, the vote was a stinging rebuke to the Social Democrats, who had built their party successes on strong local political activity. The party scandals, the extremely high mobilization of the citizenry through the social movements promoting peace and combating nuclear sites, the cutbacks in social programs, and high unemployment all had their effect. This year could be seen, in retrospect, as the peak of Green overall political strength. Rolf Zundel, political correspondent for *Die Zeit*, summed up his comments on the Greens: "This is not a short wave of protest and also not just an ecology party. Rather it's a result of a long-simmering eruption of a cultural-critical revolt; much stronger, more enduring, and more unwavering than the earlier extraparliamentary opposition—perhaps it's a groundswell."[16]

In the mid-1980s the environmental issue was near the top of the political agenda. The mass media's coverage on issues of ecology increased. The dire predictions of the Greens about the corrosive effects of acid rain were proven true by knowledgeable experts. International events such as a cloud of poison gas in Bhopal, the near nuclear meltdown of Three Mile Island in Pennsylvania, and the repeated news stories of chemical dumping gave undergirding to the Green critique among the voters. Yet the wind was changing.

Crosscurrents, 1985–1987

On the positive side, the Social Democrats, wobbling along without a majority in Hesse, offered a coalitional opportunity to the Greens that, sweetened with an important ministerial post, the minister of environment, brought the Greens the new role of power wielders. The conditions for accepting power included complex demands about nuclear processing plants, a subject that remained controversial for the two years of the coalition. The Alternative List party in West Berlin became the first state, albeit a city-state, where double-digit percentages were achieved by a Green party (10.4 percent). In 1986, the Green party of Bavaria entered the Parliament for the first time there, and in 1987, the Greens of Rhineland-Palatinate became the ninth Green party to achieve legislative representation. Also in 1986, several months after Chernobyl, the Greens were elected again in Lower Saxony and, to everyone's surprise, received 10.4 percent of the vote in Hamburg, where they ran a historic all-female slate. In 1987, in addition to achieving legislative status in Rhineland-Palatinate, they racked up sizable percentages of 9.4 percent in Hesse and 10.2 percent in Bremen.

The capstone of their electoral efforts came with a 8.3 percent vote in the national election in 1987. The Social Democrats suffered one of their worst defeats of the postwar period, and the West Germans confirmed the coalition of the Christian Union and the Free Democrats. The Greens had come up with programs for restructuring the industrial society with some innovative ideas and more specific cost-benefit analysis, which had been absent from earlier party programs. Their vote in national elections in Schleswig-Holstein was solid even though they did so poorly in local and state votes, and the party organization was slowly fumbling its way from its celebration of the amateur and its disdain of the organizational imperative to small measures of professionalism. Why would one speak of crosscurrents?

The coalition formed in 1985 in Hesse collapsed in 1987 because of disagreements between the Social Democrats and the Greens on a policy toward a nuclear waste facility. The factional fighting within the Hesse Greens set a low tone of polemical bickering. The Greens lost elections in the Saar and North Rhine–Westphalia by failing to get above 5 percent, the first major setbacks in their continual climb to power. The state election in North Rhine–Westphalia showed quite distinctly the volatility of the Green electorate. It also indicated the obvious rational calculations of tactical new middle-class voters who helped reward the local Green candidates in 1984 with almost 9 percent of the vote and then only mustered 4.6 percent for the state party. The election in West Germany's largest state, which has a diverse working force, a high degree of urbanization, and a sizable university population, was instructive for Green party strategists. The fundamentalists controlled the party and dominated the list of candidates, but the Green electorate was considerably more pragmatic. The ongoing internal party conflicts, the weakness in certain policy areas, and the amateurish gaffes on sensitive issues concerning penalties for sexual offenses did not help the party. Meanwhile the Social Democrats had gathered themselves together, pumped up their organizational effort, and captured 52.1 percent of the vote behind the effective personable campaigning of Johnnes Rau. In this election, and in subsequent state elections, the Green vote of the youngest age group (eighteen to twenty-four) declined whereas the twenty-five to thirty-four age group increased slightly. The Greens were taking on more generational markings, and the SPD was reclaiming some of the younger voters.

The inability of the Greens to win legislative representation in the Saar and Schleswig-Holstein also pointed to increasingly defined limitations for the party. In both of these states, the Social Democrats ran young, dynamic leaders—LaFontaine and Engholm—who competed effectively for New Politics voters on the issues of the environment, feminist policies, and controlled growth and followed the electoral strategy of telling their voters that a vote for the Greens was a vote for the CDU. Where the SPD had a chance at a majority, tactical voters, who may have temporarily "parked" with the Greens, moved back to the SPD. Finally, these SPD organizations showed that a balance between the New Left and the Old Left was possible within the party, if only in states with fairly low urbanization and few university students.

Claus Offe, a professor of political sociology, understood the shifting currents.[17] His diagnosis of the Green malady has a startling clarity and a touch of prophecy. The Greens, in his view, were caught in a developmental crisis. The political and organizational forms of the breakthrough period, the late 1970s to the mid-1980s, became difficult obstacles in the following phase. The German folk saying that you cannot jump out of your shadow means that people and organizations are often tied to past traditions, even when circumstances change. The Greens as a protest movement maintained those organizational norms and forms but did not carry through the necessary adaptation to being an effective and competitive party. On a policy level this meant that the early slogans were stale, that the major parties were openly adopting their proposals, and that their critique of industrial problems lacked constructive proposals. In short, the Greens were losing their distinctive profile and failing to develop an appeal to a wider variety of socioeconomic groups. Offe, early in the game, perceived that the generational reservoir and the politics of amateurism had their limitations. Offe's prescription for a more formally structured, professional, constructive party of opposition, with a limit to petty squabbling and romantic posturing in its allergy to state power, came to a terse summary: Spontaneous, revolutionary, organizationally unstructured politics that desires social change is just as bad as bureaucratized mass parties with their uncritical fidelity to the constitutional order and their fixation on growth and security.

Thus, the electoral victories disguised a changed momentum. The activities of the supportive social movements had subsided. The peace movement had fought a good fight and the missiles were in place. The patience of the Green voters, especially the tactical ones, was wearing thin, and the traditional parties were on the rebound. The Social Democrats and the Free Democrats were finding new footholds with updated policies, and the organizational experiment in radical democracy was putting a strain on Green activists and their sympathetic supporters. When the Hamburg Greens squandered a 10.4 percent vote in 1986 to prevent an effective coalition—though an overwhelming percentage of their voters wanted a coalition—they were chastised with a 7 percent vote in 1987 and a coalition that brought the SPD and FDP together again. Purist politics had left them on the sidelines. The balance sheet at the end of 1987 was not simple to decipher. The Greens had their largest delegation in the Bundestag, they had reasonable strength in a wide range of different states, and local Green activism seemed healthy. But new challenges, internally and externally, were appearing as the much-criticized traditional parties showed clear signs of resilience.

Ebbing More Than Flowing, 1988–1990

By the end of the decade, the Greens were becoming a familiar part of the political scene. Once again, in 1988, they failed to capture more than 2.9 percent of the vote on Schleswig-Holstein as the Social Democrats won a sizable majority. Shortly after his dramatic victory, Engholm, the SPD minister-president, appointed four women to his cabinet, two of whom received posts in environmental and women's affairs. The SPD's national strategy for the future—with an eye on the reform-oriented middle class—was being shaped in the peripheral states of Schleswig-Holstein and the Saar. The Baden-Württemberg Greens demonstrated the success of a hard-working effective and moderate opposition party by gaining its usual 7.9 percent of the vote, and in 1989 the West Berlin Alternative List kept its vote in double digits with 11.8 percent of the vote and became a coalition partner with the Social Democrats. Although the coalition did not last long, it was a first in a city-state.

The Greens did creditably well in the 1989 elections to the European Parliament and prepared to celebrate their founding in January 1990. In the Saar election of 1990, the Social Democrats, led by eventual chancellor candidate LaFontaine, duplicated the Schleswig-Holstein success by holding the Greens to 2.6 percent and achieving a sizable majority of 54.4 percent. The Greens were no longer causing a hemorrhage of votes from the Social Democrats. The battle for the floating voters of the new middle class and the younger voters was now begun in earnest. The Greens finally achieved representation in North Rhine–Westphalia with just 5 percent of the vote, and the SPD kept their majority. The FDP had slowly, in the late 1980s, worked its way back into most of the state parliaments. The Greens lost votes from their previous percentage in Lower Saxony to obtain 5.5 percent (6.0 percent in 1985), but that number was enough to form a coalition with the Social Democrats, who increased their vote to 44.2 percent. As in previous elections, the Greens were gradually losing their earlier advantage in gaining first and young voters.

The Wall Is Breached; Honecker Has a Great Fall

The political landscape for all of the parties changed dramatically as the events of late 1989 indicated that the Soviet Union was calling off the Cold War because of circumstances beyond its control. The collapse of the Soviet empire in Eastern Europe, symbolized by the breaching of the Berlin Wall in November 1989 and the East Germans chanting "wir sind ein Volk" (we are one people) meant that German unification was a historical inevitability. These events threw the Greens off balance. They had at one time called for the removal of the clause for reunification from the preamble of the Bonn Constitution, and they had been committed to a policy of two German nation-states, unattached to the major power blocs. Had they adhered to that position, their demise would have been guaranteed. Instead they temporized, agonized, and then finally compromised by accepting events in a backhanded way. The clear mandate for one Germany by the East Germans in their first free election in fifty-seven years (1933–1990) set the tracks for rapid unification. The predictably destabilizing Hamburg Greens split on the issue of unification, and the part of the parliamentary block from the fundamental wing that spoke against unification resigned.

The national party accepted with reluctance the coming together of a greater Germany and worked at creating alliances with the East German Greens, feminists, and related citizen movement groups that managed a small vote in the March 1990 elections. After finding a relatively secure place in the West German party structure, the fate of the Greens would be determined by their ability to bring together a coalition that could gather 5 percent of the vote in an electorate that was now 60 million instead of about 45 million. With an unexpected result, the Greens of the west reached on 4.8 percent and lost all their seats in the Bundestag. Their counterparts in the east achieved 6.1 percent and eight seats. The Green presence in the Parliament was severely diminished. An analysis of the December 2, 1990, all-German election is contained in our final chapter.

At the end of the decade, the Greens had no time to rest. The traditional parties, especially the SPD and the FDP, took the very best punches of the Greens in the early and mid-1980s, reeled around a bit, and then came back to the electoral ring with feet firmly planted and with a new jabbing style that had a Green motif to it. Scholars of West German party politics had repeated through the decade that the fate of the Greens was tied to the actions of the SPD and that the flexibility of the SPD should not be underestimated. The Green challenge was to throw some clear—and obviously not polluted—cold water into the face of a mass catch-all party that had become slugglish, somewhat corrupted, too co-opted by powerful interests, and impervious to citizen demands for demonstration and reform that they themselves (the SPD of 1972) had aroused. The Free Democrats had also rebounded quite nimbly, and they shared with the SPD and the Christian Union the competition for the younger educated new middle class. A closer demographic look at how the electorate voted in the past decade will help us understand how the Green party broke into—and made more lively—the party competition in West Germany.

Core Voters and Tactical Voters

How does one distinguish the party loyalists, who stick with the party through thick and thin, from the consumer shopper voters, who are guided by market rationality and place performance and competence above emotional ties to a single party? It is not easy. The decline in party identification, the rise of a more educated and politically informed electorate, the increase in ticket splitting and issue voting are characteristics of all industrial democracies. We are interested in the West German variation on this general theme. In the West German electoral system, the opportunity to cast two ballots and the relative ideological proximity of several of the parties make it plausible for a citizen—especially a younger one— to have voted for the Free Democrats, the Social Democrats, and the Greens in different elections within a short period of time.

We do have some guidelines for trying to identify the core support of the Greens. We can ask how steady the percentage of the vote in elections of different levels (local, state, national, European) is over a period of time. For example, when the Green vote in Schleswig-Holstein was 8 percent in the 1987 election and 2.9 percent in a state election several months afterward, we can surmise that "all-weather" Greens are not plentiful there. On the national level, one gets an indirect clue about core Green voters by looking at how their two votes are cast. A first vote for a Green candidate when the party has never won a district seat is a sign of solid support. In 1987, the Greens received 8.3 percent of the second party vote and 7 percent for the single-member district vote. In contrast, the FDP second party vote was 9.1 percent and the first vote 4.7 percent.

It is helpful to keep in mind that the vote for the Greens was 1.5 percent in 1980 and 8.3 percent by 1987. A close approximation of core support is found in the nearly 60 percent who voted Green on both the first and second ballots. It is also obvious that the tactical voters for the Greens find their closest second choice with the SPD. Once again these two parties are the direct competitors for the left-of-center new middle-class vote.

The core voters in the city-states give the highest averages with a measure of deviation in the various elections. It is more difficult to talk about the size of a core Green national voter than it is to speculate about the core groups on the local and state levels. The fluctuation of the vote for the Greens depends very much on the pattern of political competition in the electoral district at hand. An SPD supporter will not vote for the Greens with the second vote if the Social Democrats stand a chance of winning a majority. This finding applied in the elections of the Saar and Schleswig-Holstein as well as in the votes in the national elections of 1980 and 1983. Electoral analysis shows that in the 1987 election the Greens won 600,000 votes from the Social Democrats and in 1983 two-thirds of the Green vote came from citizens who voted for the SPD in 1980.[18] Some analysts have seen a Green core group with a generational profile emerging. In the elections of the mid-to-late 1980s, the decrease in the lowest age groups (eighteen to twenty-four) was marked by concomitant increases in the next two groups (twenty-five to thirty-four and thirty-five to forty-four). This change was highly probable given the crucial role the student movement generation has played in Green politics. However, one should be cautious here. David Conradt and Russell Dalton conclude their discussion about the possibility of true realignment—a long-term switch of SPD voters to the Greens—with the caveat that the gains of the FPD and the Greens may have been largely the result of tactical voting rather than the beginning of any fundamental realignment.[19] The 1990 vote confirms that speculation, but that election may turn out to be one of unusual voting patterns.

Inglehart's analysis indicates the lasting effects of postmaterial values over time, but he also recognizes that these postmaterialist voters may well be absorbed back into the major parties.[20] Given the relative shortness of the history of the Green party, the volatility of voting choices, and the changed electoral "playing field" that came with the unification of Germany, it is useful to put the core Green vote in the last decade in West Germany on the national level at 4 percent plus with core voters in city-states and the local levels of some states at a higher number (7 percent). Economic issues are preeminent in the new Germany but have not been a strong card for the Greens. Finally, the major parties are quite adroit at designing customized (and limited) postmaterial packages for the tactical voters who want power with their principles. We can gain another perspective on the long-term developmental pattern of the Greens by looking at the extensive demographic data that have been collected about them.

Who Votes for the Greens?

There is remarkable unanimity in the data that we have about the Green voters. In the late 1970s and early 1980s the Greens were overwhelmingly a party of young voters: Two-thirds to three-quarters of the voters were under thirty-five years of age.[21] The developmental pattern of the age cohorts of Green voters is also remarkably consistent over the past decade. Beginning in the mid-1980s, the center of gravity of the average age moved from the lower groups (eighteen to twenty-four) to the next two groups (twenty-five to thirty-four and thirty-five to forty-four). This change has several implications, as we have noted previously. There is a generational core group that consistently supports the party, but the other parties are now recruiting more successfully for the first and younger voters. There is probably no other party among the Western industrialized democracies that has mobilized such a clearly demarcated cohort of voters from a generational group.

These young and middle-aged voters have substantially more formal education than the rest of the voting population. Only 10 percent of the population have advanced education; 22 percent of the Green voters do.[22] The percentage of Green voters who have an *Abitur*—advanced education equivalent to two years of college, which qualifies a person to attend the university—is close to 45 percent. In contrast, 25 percent of those in the FDP have an *Abitur*, and 10 to 12 percent in the CDU/CSU and SPD do. As can be expected, these factors of youth and education in the Green party result from the fact that a large percentage of the Green electorate are currently studying. Through the 1980s, a good one-third of the Green voters were not employed but engaged in study. When one adds to this figure the relatively high percentage of teachers who are voters, activists, and elected officials, it is clear why they are termed a new middle-class intelligentsia. In actuality, both "academic proletariats" and the university graduates in teaching positions at various levels have been important elements of this party.[23]

The Green party has an underrepresentation of workers, self-employed businessmen, retired persons, and housewives and an overrepresentation of white-collar salaried employees in the public and private sector. These younger professionals, who are employed mainly in health, educational, and social services, could be core or tactical voters. They have consistently represented the large bulk of the Green vote.

At the beginning of the decade, there were more men than women among Green voters, but this imbalance has evened out with a higher percentage of women in the younger age categories. The Green voters are mainly secularists (predominantly urban); the Green party has the highest percentage of those who do not attend church among all the parties. The Green vote increases with the increased population size of the urban area, especially in the case of extremely high votes in university towns and cities. We noted earlier that the Greens receive their strong votes in the new middle-class section of large cities, in universities, towns, and cities, and in areas affected by massive projects that threaten the environment. The percentages of the Green vote in university cities have been overwhelmingly higher than the overall vote of the Greens in the Federal Republic. For example, the Greens polled 8.3 percent overall in the national election of 1987. In Bremen and Frankfurt, two university towns, they polled 14.5 percent and 13.9 percent respectively.

Green voters are highly informed and politically active in social movements. Data from the early 1980s and recent information indicate that a high percentage of Green voters have been or currently are members of the following groups: environmental, peace, civil rights for foreigners, and other New Politics organizations.[24]

Has the Green electorate changed substantially over the past decade? Although the average age of its electorate is slowly increasing, it still has, by far, the youngest electorate of all the parties. The occupational base has widened to include more workers, but the party remains predominantly composed of the new middle-class intelligentsia. There are disputes about the percentage of unemployed voters supporting the Green party, yet it is important to note that a sizable segment of this electorate—pupils and students currently studying—is not anchored into the job market compared with the other parties. Green voters are less rural romantics and more urban secularists who, in Inglehart's phrase, tend "to see the sacred in nature than in churches."[25] The demographic markings of this electorate definitely point to a more defined generational profile, which gives support to a generational rather than a life-cycle interpretation of the New Left postmaterialists. But this indication does not at all guarantee the long life of the Green party. Can it hold its loyalty and continue to recruit new voters coming along? The traditional parties have tested the wind and altered course. As we noted earlier, this makes for increased competition. Do the political attitudes of the Green voters help us understand their competitive changes? This question needs some discussion.

Political Attitudes of the Green Voters: A New Position on the Left

The Greens used the slogan "Neither left, nor right, but forward" to paper over factional splits in the founding years. When the older conservative ecologists—Herbert Gruhl and Baldur von Springmann—quickly resigned from the party, it was clearly situated on the left, but as we have said, the New Left. It favored equality in the sense of widened opportunities for a greater number of people, and it advocated redistributing privileges in order to offer talent a chance to express itself. But it was New Left in its disdain for big government, big bureaucracy, and big concentrations of economic power. It was ambivalent about state power.[26] Most of the Greens did not want to dismantle the welfare state, but one faction, the ecolibertarians, wanted more self-help organizations instead of intrusive governmental agencies. For that group the term left-libertarian is truly apt. Few trust the free market to ensure that air and water would stay unpolluted, and few wanted a planned or command economy long before the collapse of socialist economies in the east.

In the compromise between its factions, the Green party accepted state power in order to enhance human resources and protect natural resources but chose to decentralize that power. New Left politics extended the classical (eighteenth-century) liberal critique of preventing concentration of power to economic as well as state power and was strongly biased toward individualism; thus New Left politics can also be described as left-libertarianism.[27] As a result, radical decentralized democratic procedures—plebiscites, stronger worker councils in industries, grass-roots democracy, intraparty democracy, and the right to challenge bureaucratic regulations—are enlisted in the campaign against arbitrary, distant authority as well as against large-scale conglomerations of organizational power.[28]

The Greens are called radical reformers because the procedural and policy changes they promote are hardly of an incremental nature. A complete halt to all nuclear power is quite different from a gradual phasing out, and immediate withdrawal from NATO, instead of a long-term restructuring, was quite radical as a policy demand in 1980. For all of their polemical disputes, the Green party militants and the Green electorate shared a wide variety of political attitudes and values that are distinct from the political views of the other parties and the electorate.[29]

Speaking of long-term value changes in Germany in the past decade or so, two American political scientists see a shift of priorities that they term postmaterial in New Politics values:

At one level, post-materialism signifies growing public interest in societal problems that were overlooked, or even worsened, by the economic progress of the postwar period. Concerns about environmental quality, the complexities of a technological society, and increased international interdependence entered the agenda of politics. Another element of post-materialism is a heightened emphasis on libertarian norms—freedom of expression, participation in the decisions affecting one's life, and individual self-expression.[30]

The Green electorate sees itself very decidedly on the left and the distance between the Social Democrats and the Greens represents the SPD's acceptance of large bureaucratic organizations: trade unions, the present state, the SPD organization itself. The Social Democrats are reformers; the Greens are radical reformers.

It would take us too far afield to specify the differences, but from our discussion of the different types of Green party organizations in the various German states we know that city-state Greens—in Bremen, Hamburg, and West Berlin—constitute the leftist pole of this New Left party. Although it is a large generalization, there is sufficient evidence to assert that with "the appearance of the Greens the party system in the Federal republic has expanded the spectrum of political-ideological attitudes essentially toward the left."[31]

A final comment is worth noting here. The Greens are termed New Left postmaterialists, but there is a discernible trend in the Green electorate and in the Green party militants toward addressing the concerns of the worker. That means not just Green party support for the worker's right to shape campaign decisions, but support for a thirty-five–hour work week, a very material concern. Then, too, the environmental concern about pollution should not be viewed narrowly as a postmaterialist concern to protect nature. The health risks from pollution assume very material consequences, and the evidence of ecological despoilation in the east will only underscore the problem.[32] All this is to emphasize that although the Green party and their electorate moved political attitudes leftward in the 1980s, the Green party activists were also nudged toward the center. This shifting took place while another sensitive set of political attitudes were taking hold: support of the political institutions.[33]

Support for Political Institutions: Toward a More Democratic Republic

To consider a political force a distinct political subculture within a polity, you would have to show support for significant changes on the key questions of political culture: who should have authority and how it should be exercised. For all the rhetoric—usually shrill during election campaigns—from certain right-of-center politicians in the early 1980s that the Greens were anarchic radicals out to undermine the Republic, the evidence consistently shows support from the Greens for constitutional democracy. The Greens, however critical they have been of the present political institutions, have not called for a substitute to constitutional democracy; they have called for a different type of democracy. In the process they have confused—and rendered suspicious—traditional voters

TABLE 4.3 Support of the Political System of the Federal Republic by Party Preference, 1982 and 1989 (percent who "strongly agree/agree")

	Protects Citizens' Basic Liberties		Is Just and Fair	
	1982	1989	1982	1989
CDU/CSU	93	93	93	87
FDP	88	94	88	88
SPD	85	81	81	71
Greens	64	80	63	67

Source: Data for 1982: Forschungsgruppe Wahlen. Data for 1989: EMNID Institut, Bielefeld. Cited in David Conradt, "German Unification and the Remade Political Culture," p. 10. Paper presented at the American Political Science Convention, San Francisco, 1990.

when some Green party militants have spoken in romantic macho fashion about challenging the state's use of force. Those "shoot-from-the-lip" examples of verbal radicalism have disconcerted Green moderates and realists—the majority of the party—because the comments from fundamentalists about the necessity of civil disobedience or the right to resist immoral state power simply provided campaign ammunition for the traditional parties. Once again, the Greens issue out of the student movement. A major topic of debate in the 1960s—quite understandable in what leftists considered a postfascist society—was to resist "illegitimate" power. Those residues, not of any great moment, were part of the rhetoric of a minority of Green militants in the early 1980s. The Green supporters were ill at ease with the Federal Republic and its institutions. In the early 1980s, Green voters regularly showed less confidence in major public institutions. One could read these additional clues of dissatisfaction as the profile of a soreheaded bunch of cultural pessimists, but the evidence of the past decade shows Green political activity on all political levels working within the system to change it. The data as shown in Table 4.3 show the positive changes in the Green attitudes toward the system. Romantic utopianism did surface in those antinuclear demonstrations that got out of hand, but they were not orchestrated by the Green party. Individual Greens, especially fundamentalists from the city-state tradition, looked the other way when "limited violation of the rules" or the right to civil disobedience escalated to violent acts, but, then too, the 1980s do not lack examples of a misuse of police power.[34] In combating a historical legacy in which state power was used in a most perverse way, some Green militants dispensed with fine distinctions.

One singular accomplishment of the Greens and the citizen initiatives and social movements of the 1970s and 1980s is that they expanded the repertoire of dissent and oppositional tactics and thereby added a measure of flexibility to their political institutions.[35] Certainly those new tactics will help in shaping the political culture of the new Germany.

The Green Electorate's Policy Positions

The other major parties in West Germany have moved toward the center on major issues in the past several decades, demonstrating a sure instinct for the issues that the expanding new middle class finds appealing, whereas the Green voters show a very distinct profile on the issues they consider vital.

There is a wide consensus by all party supporters, including the Greens who supposedly play down bread-and-butter economic issues, that unemployment is a critical concern. Given the high rate of unemployment in general and especially in service-sector jobs, these figures are not surprising. Beyond this issue, the gaps between the most important issues for the Green electorate, the other parties, and the general voting population begin to widen. Green voters are most concerned with effective environmental protection, disarmament, and more citizen participation. All other issues pale in significance. The voters of the major parties have the most concern for very different policies: secure pensions, stable prices, deficits, and law and order. David Conradt has worked out a useful statistical comparison that shows the relative proximity of a party's issue priorities to that of the general electorate.

Commenting on this unusual relationship, Conradt emphasizes that "the Greens, of course, had the most distinctive issue ranking of any party."[36] That means simply that the policy positions of the CDU/CSU are very close to those of the general electorate whereas the priorities of the Greens show the greatest distance from the center. Finally, we find further support for an earlier argument that we put forth. We can see a movement from 1980 to 1987 of the electorate and the major parties toward New Politics issues such as environmental concerns and disarmament. The events of Chernobyl, the nuclear issue of plants and missiles, and the increased media attention to chemical dumping of course played a part, but the Greens' role in competitive party politics and their amplification of these issues suggest a move of the electorate to a mix of materialist and postmaterialist issues. For an increasing number of citizens, the Greens were not crying wolf. The problem for them is that the specific policies to handle the "wolf" were not explicit enough for the electorate.

Mobilizing the Green Vote

The generational ideals of the student movement aimed at a more democratic society with restructured political institutions. The successes of the citizen initiatives and social movements of the 1970s convinced Green activists that a party "unlike the others" would serve as a model for the democratic renewal for which they hoped. The organizational experiment of the Greens—as much pluralism, decentralization, and intraparty democracy as possible—began the decade with high hopes and ended it chastened by the imperatives of leadership, organizational coherence, competitive electoral battle, and the limits of grass-roots democracy.

A look at how the Greens' role as organizational innovator affected their nominations process and campaign style and how their electioneering techniques influenced party development shows the party caught in a catch-22 situation. Herbert Kitschelt sees ecology parties as caught between the logic of constituency representation ("faced with a trade-off between breadth of popular appeal and ideological purity of policy and strategic stances, they prefer the latter") and the logic of electoral competition ("adjustment of internal organization, program, and strategy to the condition of the political marketplace to maximize electoral support"[37]). This is a tension that the Greens have faced from the outset. Their uniqueness stems from how they have tried to fight the dominant trend for most parties: trimming the sails to the exigencies of electoral battle.

The broadest generalization that can be advanced in the area of nominations is that the Greens began with a pattern of recruitment that called for prior participation in the structures of New Left politics: the student movement, extraparliamentary organizations, citizen initiatives, and social movements (environmental, feminist, civil rights, urban planning). But under pressure from the demands of effective campaigning, they have moved to more professional criteria: Now they ask what the persons have done for the party and what their political positions are.[38] The party has "upped the ante" for party experience and has a greater concern for more defined policy positions. The Greens also slowly recognized that their negative view on media personalities needed adjustment. From the outset the Greens have been wary of and have reined in charismatic media types who cut their own swath (Petra Kelly, for example), but there is an awareness that the politics of personal campaign is not a negative factor per se. Kitschelt quotes a Hamburg militant who recognizes that an "outstanding political personality" can focus attention on the party's values and also hold loyal supporters.[39]

Other major generalizations about Green nominations are that they are contested more in dense urban settings on state and national levels and that the demographic characteristics of the nominees fall within the general contours of the Green electorate.

The candidates are young, educated, and in the occupational categories of the new middle class. The Greens have paved the way for a higher percentage of women in party politics, and their initiatives have undoubtedly put pressure on the other parties to change their ways. One-third of their delegation to the Bundestag was female in the 1983–1987 session and almost three-fifths (59 percent) in 1987–1990. Most state Green parties follow the party rule of running at least one-half female candidates, and, as we noted earlier, the GAL (Green Alternative List) in Hamburg ran an all-female slate in the 1986 state elections and was quite successful.

A problem peculiar to the Greens concerns its membership size in relation to candidates for office. With only 40,000 members, the Greens had the lowest ratio of members to voters of all the parties in West Germany and a relatively high turnover of that membership. This situation indicates several problems: It shows the antiorganizational bias of many Green voters, it means that the party doesn't do enough recruitment or have adequate incentive to retain a larger membership, and it points to the unusual situation of having such a large percentage of members as active office holders that "minding the store" for the party organization is neglected. When you realize that only 10,000 of the 40,000 members are the real party activists, and that, in some states, on the local level 20 percent of all members were elected to municipal councils, then you understand the comment made by one of Kitschelt's interviewees, an activist in Baden-Württemberg, who noted that "after the last local election, the local party organization essentially collapsed in her district because all committed activists had been elected to municipal councils and the county diet."[40]

The Greens and the Free Democrats have stretched the limits of the framework party, which relies on a small membership to accomplish its party tasks. Compared with the FDP, the Greens have less of a tradition in West German politics, are further from the center, where the majority of the electorate is, and face the problem of how far they can stretch stylized amateurism and still keep a viable party. In the latter part of the 1980s, Green party organizations were coming to grips in a more realistic way with the techniques of modern campaigning, including effective use of the media, and by moving toward recruiting candidates who can help them win votes. Their campaign style seems to be slowly evolving.

It was all too obvious how the organizational problems of the Greens and the inability to define their position on unification hurt the party in the 1990 election. The epochal event of having unification for the taking because of the Soviet collapse was seized as *the* issue by the major parties, but the difficulties that we have discussed in this chapter—increased competition from the other parties, loss of support because of leadership instability, the reliance on too many independent-minded tactical voters, and indecisiveness on the major issue of unification—cost the Greens their representation in the Bundestag from the west and resulted in the election of only a small delegation of eight Greens from the east. The Green wave did not know how to deal with a fallen Wall, and consequently the future of the party was cast in doubt. We noted at the outset that critics felt that the Greens would not do well with a hybrid movement/party and that the "logic of electoral competition" would change their style. Now, after a decade, we can say that though the Greens surprised many in the electoral arena on several levels of competition, their organizational apparatus did not hold up well. As Antje Vollmer, one of the leaders of the Green Bundestag delegation, noted, "we had the right ideas and the wrong vehicle." The stage has been set for a possible new beginning for the Greens in 1991 by their redesigning the vehicle, sharpening and expanding their ideas with specific proposals regarding important economic issues, and finding a new center of gravity, as dogmatic and polemical leftists quit the party in 1989 and 1990. In our final chapter we look at the all-German election of December 1990 and the six subsequent state elections of 1991 and 1992 in more detail, but we now need to look in more detail at the Green experiment in party organization.

Notes

1. Horst Bieber, M. Schwelien, and G. Spörl, "Deutschland soll ergrünen," *Die Zeit*, September 10, 1982.

2. Jo Leinen, "Effektive Lobbyarbeit wichtiger als einige Abgeordnete," *Frankfurter Rundschau*, November 5, 1980.

3. Eva Kolinsky, "The Green Party: A New Factor in the West German Political Landscape," in *Parties, Opposition and Society in West Germany*, Eva Kolinsky, ed. (New York: St. Martin's, 1984), pp. 297–300.

4. Andreas von Weiss, *Die neue Linke* (Boppard, 1969).

5. The West German electoral system is complex in that each citizen has two votes. The first is for a candidate in a single-member district; the second is a party vote. A party cannot obtain any legislative representation without getting at least 5 percent of the second party vote, and it must win at least three district votes to gain any representation. The Greens—and the Free Democrats, for that matter—obtain representation through the second party vote. Generally the percentage gained on the second vote nationally equals the proportion of seats that were received in the Bundestag. As is readily apparent, this system encourages tactical voting and split-ticket voting. Depending on the constellation of contending political forces, a person could vote for the candidate of one party in his or her district and cast the second vote for another party.

6. There is a growing literature in this field. An early work with valuable case study information is Elim Papadakis, *The Green Movement in West Germany* (New York: Croom Helm, 1984).

7. David Conradt and Russell Dalton, "The West German Electorate and the Party System: Continuity and Change in the 1980s," *Review of Politics* 50, no. 1 (Winter 1988):3–29.

8. Ronald Inglehart, *Culture Shift in Advanced Industrial Societies* (Princeton: Princeton University Press, 1990), p. 370.

9. Gerhard Loewenberg, "The Development of the German Party System," in *Germany at the Polls: The Bundestag Election of 1976*, K. Cerny, ed. (Washington, D.C.: American Enterprise Institute, 1978), p. 20.

10. Ronald Inglehart, *The Silent Revolution: Changing Values and Political Styles Among Western Publics* (Princeton: Princeton University Press, 1977), p. 364.

11. William Paterson, "West Germany: Between Party Apparatus and Basic Democracy," in *Political Parties: Electoral Change and Structural Response*, A. Ware, ed. (New York: Blackwell, 1987), p. 162.

12. Kolinsky, "The Green Party," p. 56.

13. Manfred Güllner, "Zwischen Stabilität und Wandel: Das politische System nach dem 6. März 1983," *Aus Politik und Zeitgeschichte* B 14/83, April 9, 1983, p. 28.

14. The categories both lean on and depart from a categorization of the Green state parties in Herbert Kitschelt, *The Logics of Party Formation: Ecological Politics in Belgium and West Germany* (Ithaca, N.Y.: Cornell University Press, 1989), p. 86.

15. Detlef Murphy and Roland Roth, "Die Grünen-Artifakt der 5% Klausel," in *Neue soziale Bewegungen in der Bundesrepublik Deutschland*, Dieter Rucht and Roland Roth, eds. (Frankfurt: Campus Verlag, 1987), p. 304.

16. Rolf Zundel, *Die Zeit*, March 30, 1984.

17. Claus Offe, "Zwischen Protest und Parteipolitik," *Die Zeit*, October 17, 1986.

18. David Conradt, "The Electorate, 1980–1983," in *Germany at the Polls: The Bundestag Elections of the 1980s*, Karl Cerny, ed. (Durham, N.C.: American Enterprise Institute and Duke University, 1990), p. 46.

19. Conradt and Dalton, "The West German Electorate and the Party System," p. 24.

20. Inglehart, *Culture Shift*. Speaking of the Greens, he notes that postmaterialists are twenty-three times as apt to vote for them as materialists (p. 384), but in speaking of New Left parties in general he states: "They have not yet developed stronger voter loyalties or party organizations. Whether they ever will is an open question. If they do not, in the long run, their electorates will probably be absorbed by larger parties that modify their ideological stance" (p. 263).

21. The demographic data referred to in this section are derived mainly from the articles in the *Zeitschrift für Parlamentsfragen* on state and national elections from 1978 to 1990.

22. Russell Dalton, *Politics in West Germany* (Glenview, Ill.: Scott, Foresman/Little, Brown, 1989), p. 288.

23. Helmut Fogt and Pavel Uttiz, "Die Wähler der Grünen, 1980–1983: Systemkritiker neuer Mittelstand," *Zeitschrift für Parlamentsfragen* 15, no. 2, (June 1984). They write, "It is clear without a doubt that *Gymnasium* pupils, students at the universities and recent graduates form the core group of the green electorate" (p. 219).

24. Franz Urban Pappi, "Die Anhänger der neuen sozialen Bewegungen im Parteiensystem der Bundesrepublik," in *Aus Politik und Zeitgeschichte* (Bonn: Bundeszentrale für politische Bildung, 1989).

25. Inglehart, *Culture Shift*, p. 433.

26. Ibid., p. 304. Inglehart notes that the postmaterialist New Left regarded the state as a potential instrument of oppression and exploitation yet favored equality and the regulation of market forces to prevent pollution.

27. The term is Kitschelt's, from Kitschelt, *The Logics of Party Formation.*

28. Peter Gatter, *Die Aufsteiger: Ein politisches Porträt der Grünen* (Hamburg: Hoffman and Campe, 1989), p. 17. Gatter speaks of the Greens' aim to dismantle the authoritarian state and to challenge the hierarchies in the authoritarian society.

29. Hans-Joachim Veen, "The Greens as a Milieu Party," in *The Greens of West Germany,* Eva Kolinsky, ed. (Oxford: Berg, 1989), p. 45.

30. Conradt and Dalton, "The West German Electorate and the Party System," pp. 10–11.

31. Hans-Joachim Veen and Peter Gluchowski, "Wandlungen und Konstanten in den Wählerstrukturen," *Zeitschrift für Parlamentsfragen* 15, no. 2, (June 1984), p. 248. This conclusion is reached after assessment of extensive survey research data, 1980–1987.

32. For an elaboration of the concept of the risk society, see Ulrich Beck, *Risikogesellschaft* (Frankfurt, 1986).

33. Fogt and Uttiz, "Systemkritiker neuer Mittelstand," p. 224.

34. Gerard Braunthal, "Civil Liberties in the Federal Republic," in *Political Loyalty and Public Service in West Germany* (Amherst: University of Massachusetts Press, 1990). pp. 152–176.

35. Samuel Barnes and Mat Kaase, *Political Action: Mass Participation in Five Western Democracies* (Beverly Hills, Calif.: Sage, 1979).

36. Conradt, "The Electorate, 1980–83," p. 51.

37. Herbert Kitschelt, *The Logics of Party Formation,* p. 41.

38. Ibid., p. 203.

39. Ibid., p. 218.

40. Ibid., p. 156.

5

Party Organization and Grass-roots Democracy

Political parties are more than manifestations of social cleavages. They are organizations that interact with their environments in both adaptative and transformative ways. Political scientists have attributed various systemic functions to parties as organizations, for example, integration, leadership recruitment, and policymaking functions.[1] Furthermore, parties are not unitary actors; they are miniature political systems with their own power structures and cultures.

From one viewpoint, the way in which parties democratically organize themselves bears directly upon how democratically a polity functions. From another viewpoint, democracy is a systemic property resulting from the competition of parties (and groups) irrespective of their internal organization. E. E. Schattschneider, in his study of American political parties, declares, "The political parties created democracy and . . . modern democracy is unthinkable save in terms of the parties." But he also contends, "Democracy is not found *in* the parties but *between* the parties."[2] In contrast, European socialists have traditionally maintained that "the party plays the major role in democratizing the political system and needs therefore to practice internal democracy in order to serve as an exemplary model for other institutions."[3]

Upon closer inspection, varying conceptions of the procedural prerequisites of democracy emerge. From the "realistic" perspective, democracy involves the accountability of government via the free choice of the voters among rival teams of leaders. From the "idealistic" perspective, democracy requires more, that is, the participation of citizens in decisionmaking not only within party organizations but also other societal institutions affecting their vital interests. The realists assume that the citizen is preoccupied with private concerns, lacks the expertise to grasp policy complexities, and should defer to political elites. The idealists assume that the citizen is motivated and competent to participate in policy matters directly affecting him or her and that the gaps between rulers and ruled should be drastically narrowed. At the outset, the Greens as a new party organization embraced the idealistic conception both in their rhetoric and their practices. The established parties have presented themselves as democratic organizations; the Greens have viewed them as such only in the formalistic sense. Many of the first generation of Green activists had experienced as party members, mostly in the SPD, the frustrations of intraparty "democracy" in West Germany. However, soon they encountered new frustrations within the Green party. In this chapter we consider the organizational aspirations and experiences of the Greens as a "party of the new type" from 1980 to 1991. First, we shall briefly review the scholarly lineage of the question of party organization and democracy.

Party Development and Democracy

The first political parties originated when parliamentary groups, responding to the enlarging electorates, set up committees to mobilize voters. Soon the approach of universal suffrage set the stage for mass parties created by extraparliamentary forces. Maurice Duverger emphasizes the enduring significance of historical origins for party organization: Parties that originated externally tend to be more centralized, more disciplined and coherent, and occupied with more than electoral activities. He views socialist parties as the best example of this extraparliamentary category and, furthermore, maintains that their mass membership-branch structure is the modern trend.[4] Leon Epstein disputes this contagion from the Left thesis, finding evidence of counterorganizational techniques spreading from the Right during the postwar period.[5]

In contrast to the early parliamentary (caucus) party, the mass party sought to bring societal demands to bear upon government. According to Giovanni Sartori, the essence of a democratic party is this shift of emphasis from "responsible" to "responsive" government.[6] Robert Michels's classic study of mass parties maintains that intraparty democracy soon becomes impossible because of technical and psychological factors that concentrate power in the hands of party leaders; "historical evolution mocks all prophylactic measures that have been adopted for the prevention of oligarchy."[7] Through the years, Michels's study has encountered numerous criticisms, for example, that he overlooked factionalism as an inhibitor of oligarchy. Robert McKenzie, in his monumental study, challenges Michels's presumption that to be democratic a party has to be under the control of its membership. McKenzie argues that major British parties are effectively controlled by the few; however, because they provide a meaningful popular choice of alternative governments in parliamentary elections, they are democratic parties.[8]

Duverger maintains that "the leadership of parties tends naturally to assume oligarchic forms." These may be personal (informal) or bureaucratic (formal). But how far the general tendency goes depends on many factors: the social origins and democratic values of party members, the party's doctrine (and resulting structure), and the age of the party.[9] The power question was simple for the middle-class caucus parties: Parliamentarians dominated the party. The development of mass parties with their ideological activists, formal constitutions, and party bureaucracies posed a challenge to the authority of parliamentary members. Duverger views the mass party as characterized by a state of tension between its internal leaders and its parliamentary representatives. Despite the tendency for power to accumulate in the hands of leaders (party and/or parliamentary), he declares that "the members are the very substance of the [mass] party, the stuff of its activity."[10] The mass party depends on its membership for its democratic legitimacy and its political and financial support; one can argue that ultimately its leaders must be broadly responsive to the needs of the rank and file.

Nearly a century ago, Max Weber predicted the inexorable growth of party bureaucracy.[11] The modern party had no choice but to rationalize its apparatus in order to mobilize ever greater political support. Nevertheless, the mass party can be seen as a party of integration that still remained for its members comprehensible and accessible: "part channel of protest, part source of protection, part purveyor of visions of the future."[12] Otto Kirchheimer argued in 1966 that the era of the mass integration party had passed. Social structural changes, such as growing affluence, and technological changes, such as television, paved the way for the predominance of the "catch-all" party in West European politics.[13] The catch-all party combines structural features of the mass party (large membership) and the cadre party (elites). Its success depends upon voters, not party members. The party leaders, once elected by the members, are left free to determine and to market party programs for "prospective customers."[14] Stephen Wolinetz concludes that catch-all parties succeeded only during the postwar period in West European countries that had experienced crises that loosened traditional partisan attachments.[15]

Although agreeing that the party transformation varied from country to country, Angelo Panebianco sees a general historical trend from cadre parties to mass parties to catch-all parties. Instead of "catch-all," Panebianco prefers the term "electoral-professional" parties to emphasize the central role of professionals (for example, media experts) rather than political-administrative bureaucrats in a party focused on the electorate.[16] Its preeminent leaders are its public-office holders, not party officials. Its stress is on issues and personalized leadership, not on ideology. Finally, by its "very structure" and the "looseness" of its clientele, this type of party does *not* threaten the "functional powerholders" of society: "Via its electoral role it produces that limited amount of popular participation and integration required from the popular masses for the functioning of official political institutions."[17]

Parteienstaat und Basisdemokratie

The Federal Republic, in contrast to the Weimar Republic, has been a stable party state (*Parteienstaat*). The Basic Law's authors sought to facilitate this outcome by explicitly constitutionalizing political parties in Article 21. The Federal Constitutional Court has twice used its power to outlaw antidemocratic parties. The constitutional anchoring of parties paved the way in 1959 for the regular distribution of public funds to the parties for their "political educational" activities. A comprehensive Party Law, first enacted in 1967, sets forth the legal requirements for democratic organization of a party. For example, parties must have a written constitution, a membership or delegate assembly at least every other year to elect an executive board, and internal arbitration courts. In short, the Party Law requires parties to be configured as representative democracies.

Eleven parties from far left to far right won Bundestag seats in 1949, only four fewer than could be counted after the last "normal" Reichstag election in 1928. However, socioeconomic changes *and* electoral law manipulations steadily reduced the number of parties. Then in 1961 only the SPD, CDU/CSU, and FDP were represented in the Bundestag. As Kurt Sontheimer explains, "All three parties are *'staatstragend'*. . .there exists between them agreement based on the Constitution on the principles of democratic order."[18] But all-party consensus can also be seen as all-party cartel. Since 1959, the Bonn parties have voted themselves increasing levels of public funding for campaign expenses, parliamentary salaries, and "educational" foundations. They have monopolized political leadership recruitment and have influenced top appointments in the broadcast media, universities, judiciary, bureaucracy, and even the military. All three have attracted increasing numbers of civil servants as party members. By the 1970s the SPD, CDU/CSU, and FDP had become in many senses *Staatsparteien* (state parties).

The major parties have claimed to be *Volksparteien*, which speak for the people irrespective of their class or religion. The CDU has been the prototype of the people's party. Its thrust has been pragmatic rather than ideological: appealing to diverse social groups and retaining governmental power. The CDU's electoral successes in the 1950s prompted the SPD to drop its working-class label, to pronounce itself also a *Volkspartei*, and to accommodate many CDU policy orientations. The small centrist FDP managed to survive as the third actor in Bonn by appealing to tactical voters as a brake on the leftward or rightward momentum of the major coalitional partner. As *Staatsparteien*, the SPD and CDU are "not merely bland, vote-winning engines," as implied by the catch-all concept; they are vitally connected to the state and accept responsibility for it.[19]

During the 1970s, the "omnipotent" image of the CDU/CSU and the SPD was undercut. Joachim Raschke argued that the *Volksparteien*, as the embodiment of "statist, materialist, and quietist politics" and premised on continuous economic growth, had lost touch with the times. He attributed the party crisis to four tendencies of the *Volksparteien*: overaccommodation to established interests, overgeneralization of appeal (more growth, more welfare, more weaponry), overinstitutionalization (more oligarchy and bureaucracy), and "overload" (declining resources to meet the rising expectations of the people).[20]

Political scientists found declining public satisfaction with all the Bonn parties during the 1970s. Opinion polls indicated that more West Germans were actively involved in nonpartisan citizen action groups (*Bürgerinitiativen*) focused on specific problems than were members of the three major parties. Party elites responded ambivalently to the surging citizen action movement: Grass-roots activism could provide an early warning device, alerting the party leaders to new problems, but grass-roots activism could also undermine the legitimacy of the institutions of representative democracy.

In the early 1980s, the term "new social movements" came into vogue for the citizen action groups, environmental groups, women's groups, peace groups, and alternative life-style groups. Despite the great diversities among and within these movements, they shared protest orientations not only toward the established parties and interest groups' priorities but also toward their centralized bureaucratic structures. In principle, the new social movements rejected charismatic leaders, hierarchical organizations, and representative models in favor of grass-roots democracy (*Basisdemokratie*). In practice, one could find a wide range of organizational patterns from central/formal to decentral/informal within the movements. At one extreme, the citizen action/environmental movement had its national "roof" association, the BBU (Bundesverband Bürgerinitiativen Umweltschutz), which claimed to represent 1,000 local groups. At the other extreme was the alternative movement, which favored no persisting structures above the local level. Nevertheless, the concept of *Basisdemokratie* provided the "counterlegitimacy" of the new social movements; even former Communist activists paid lip service to it.[21]

During the early euphoric phase of movement politics, informal, discontinuous modes of action are compatible with egalitarian values. This phase is characterized by no formal separation between leaders and followers, between members and nonmembers, and between individuals with diverging policy preferences.[22] Yet grass-roots activists soon learned that as movement groups grow and persist, informal hierarchical structures are likely to develop. Many saw decentralization as one antidote for this natural tendency. The new social movements, in contrast to earlier movements, also emphasized the value of internal diversity, which works against the hegemony of any particular current. Differences of opinion emerged in the late 1970s within the movements over the formation of a Green party. Some activists flatly rejected the idea because they equated party organization with hierarchy, careerism, and corruption. However, others argued that parliamentary election campaigns by a Green party would increase the visibility of new politics issues and, if successful, would augment the resources of movement groups.

The early Green parties preferred the name "Liste" (slate) to distance themselves from traditional party organizations. The Lower Saxony GLU (Grüne Liste Umweltschutz), the first state-level Green party, presented itself as the arm of the citizen action groups and as a short-term protest party that would force the major parties to respond to environmental problems. Carl Beddermann, the GLU's prime mover, clearly never conceived of the GLU as a radical democratic party.[23] After his resignation, the GLU restructured itself along *basisdemokratische* lines, which the leftist Bunte (multicolored) and Alternative Lists were popularizing.

The Hamburg Bunte Liste (BL) was an alliance of diverse protest groups dominated by the activists of the KB (Communist League). The idea of an Alternative Liste (AL) was raised in West Berlin by the "Maoist" KPD (Kommunistische Partei Deutschlands). However, given the Hamburg experience, several citizen action groups balked at entering an alliance that might be dominated by Communist activists. The AL was founded in October 1978 only after many compromises; for example, its charter forbids simultaneous membership in other parties and ideological groups.[24] The founders of the AL viewed themselves as an electoral alliance (*not* as a party), rejected sectarianism, and enthusiastically embraced *Basisdemokratie*. This enthusiasm was not shared by the conservative wing of the environmental movement. In July 1978, Herbert Gruhl, after resigning from the CDU *Bundestagsfraktion*, launched a new party, Grüne Aktion Zukunft (GAZ), along more conventional lines to serve as the catalyst for the national integration of local and state Green lists. Gruhl did not find fault with the representative institutions of the Federal Republic but rather with the materialistic values that dominated its politics. He was sharply critical of those who advocated direct democracy.[25]

The Aktionsgemeinschaft Unabhnägigen Deutscher (AUD) was a minor national party of populist conservatism, which sought during the 1970s to become "the" party of environmentalism. The AUD saw environmental degradation as evidence of the crisis of monopoly capitalism and the failure of the Bonn party system. The AUD sought to establish linkages with citizen action groups. After it became apparent that they were not rallying to the AUD, its leader August Haussleiter shifted to the tactics of coalition building. The small AUD served as a midwife during the birth of the Greens by mediating between the leftist Bunte and Alternative lists and the conservatives in the GAZ (and some Green lists). In this formative time period, *Basisdemokratie* appealed to the AUD because it allowed for a clear distinction between the established parties and the emerging Greens, who began to describe themselves as an "antiparty" party.

The Greens as "Antiparty" Party

Despite their organization according to the Party Law, both supporters and opponents in the early 1980s denied that the Greens were really a party. Petra Kelly, who popularized the antiparty term, described the Greens as a movement and not a party.[26] An early critic, after describing the Greens as a "protest or nuisance party," concluded that they were not a real party because they were not prepared to govern.[27] Yet the Greens are clearly a party according to Epstein's minimal definition: "any group, however loosely organized, seeking to elect governmental office-holders under a given label."[28] A decade after their birth, Rudolf van Hüllen portrayed the Greens as "legally a party, structurally an alliance, and, at least according to their self-understanding, a movement."[29] Although the CDU/CSU, SPD, and FDP are legal entities and are alliances that are more tightly coupled than the Greens, they don't see themselves as movements. It would probably make more sense to refer to the Greens as the *Anti-Volkspartei*.

Panebianco maintains that the characteristics of a party's origin "more than any other factor" define its organizational structure even decades later. His three questions are (1) Did the party develop through diffusion (local organizations first) or penetration (national organization first)? (2) Did the party have an external "sponsoring" institution? and (3) Did the party initially have a charismatic leadership? Parties that developed through diffusion, according to Panebianco, are likely "to give rise to decentralized and semi-autonomous structures, and consequently, to a dominant coalition divided by a constant struggle for party control." In parties with an external "sponsor" institution, the party's organizational loyalties will be indirect and the leadership's source of legitimation will be external. Parties formed by "pure" charismatic leaders will have difficulties institutional-izing.[30]

An alliance of activists from citizen action groups, Bunte and Alterna-tive lists, the GLU and local Green lists, the AUD, the GAZ, and alternative life-style groups launched the Greens as a national party in January 1980. It is hard to imagine more diffuse organizational origins and its conse-quences have generally been those predicted by Panebianco. Although the BBU as a national organization never officially sponsored the Greens, one can say that at the regional and local levels the new party had many external sponsors and that the Greens defined themselves as the arm of the extraparliamentary movements. Thus the Greens look like an exter-nally legitimated party that has indeed experienced some of the organi-zational problems that Panebianco anticipated. Finally, the Greens rejected the "situational" charisma of Gruhl soon after their formation but they also endeavored to keep the party organization from becoming more than semi-institutionalized. Panebianco does not really address this possibility but other scholars have hypothesized that parties rejecting strong leaders and strong organizations inevitably confront the problem of informal oligarchies.

In a formal sense, the Greens' organization has the characteristics of modern parties, for example, formal dues-paying membership, ties with like-minded social groups, local and regional branches, large national party congresses to vote policies, and smaller steering committees and executive boards to administer party affairs (see Figure 5.1). During the 1980s, the highest organ of the Greens was the federal delegate assembly. Between its meetings, the federal steering committee was the highest organ and could bind the federal executive board, whose eleven members and three coequal speakers provided collective leadership in daily affairs. The cospeakers were not in command; their role was to represent the views of the party and to coordinate its federal activities. The basic units of the federal party were the local or district associations (*Kreisverbände*), 10 percent of whom could call special party congresses. According to the federal party charter, the local and state associations have the "greatest possible autonomy" regarding programs, finances, and personnel.

The federal model was largely followed by each of the Green state parties, though some had membership assemblies (for example, Hamburg) rather than delegate assemblies (for example, Baden-Württemberg) and some operated without a state-level steering committee (for example, Lower Saxony). The Berlin Alternative List has been unique in terms of intraparty representation because its charter treats local parties and special policy groups (*Bereichsgruppen*) equally.[31] Clearly Green party politics has been quite stratarchical in its configuration.

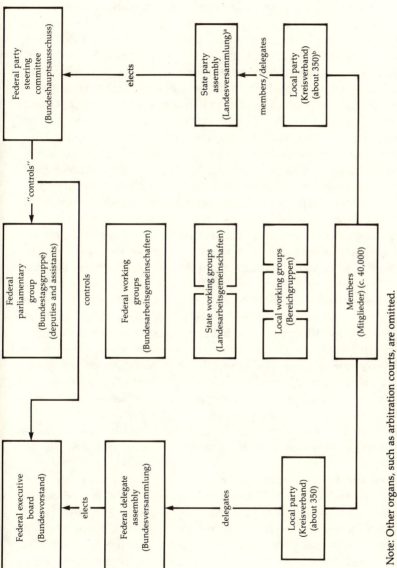

Note: Other organs, such as arbitration courts, are omitted.

[a]Also elects state executive boards (Landesvorstände).

[b]Also sends delegates to state steering committees (Landesausschüsse) (where they exist), who are supposed to supervise the state parliamentary group (Landtagsgruppe).

FIGURE 5.1 The National Organizational Chart of the Greens. *Source:* Adapted from Sara Parkin, *Green Parties: An International Guide* (London: Heretic Books, 1989), p. 145.

Although the formal organization of the Greens has paralleled that of the established parties, *basisdemokratische* procedures have set them apart. The Greens' founders sought to counter inevitable trends toward oligarchization, bureaucratization, and professionalization found in modern parties. With rare exceptions, party meetings at all levels have been open to members. Minorities have had the right to be heard. The optimal decisionmaking was to be by consensus, after the venting of the issues at all levels. Movement groups have had the right to be heard at party assemblies. Nonparty members have been nominated and elected as Green parliamentary candidates. The Greens have embraced the concept of *imperatives Mandat*, which requires the resignation of any deputy who deviates from policy resolutions of the party assembly. Specialized working groups at the local, state, and federal levels have provided technical information for programmatic development from outside experts and interested activists. During the 1980s, the Greens reflexively accorded democracy a higher procedural priority than efficiency.

The founders erected numerous barriers to the development of a professionalized party elite that could use its expertise and resources to entrench itself. The party charter has prohibited the simultaneous holding of party offices and parliamentary seats (*Ämterhäufung*). Party officers were to receive no salaries, though they could be reimbursed for some expenses by party assemblies. The Greens placed short time limits on how long leadership offices could be held consecutively. Members of the federal executive could be elected twice to two-year terms. There were state variations; for example, in Lower Saxony, members of the party executive (Landesvorstand) could be elected by the delegate assembly to two one-year terms. Except for the early period in Baden-Württemberg, the Greens have adhered to the principle of collective leadership at the state as well as federal levels. Each of the established parties elects a party chairman, who is often a parliamentary deputy, is well paid, and has no term limitation.

Basisdemokratie for feminists has meant struggling against not only hierarchical structures, which they see as suppressing the socioeconomic and political rights of women, but also "the aggressive, manipulative 'masculine' political style."[32] Thus women cannot be virtually represented by men. The Greens' party charter calls for their equal representation on party committees, boards, and commissions. More recent rules have required special efforts to assure equal representation of women on parliamentary candidate lists (which has not precluded all-female lists), on speaker lists at party assemblies, and on party employee payrolls. Policy questions deemed by women of particular interest to women may be voted on by only female assembly delegates.

To prevent the development of a class of professional parliamentarians who would concentrate power in the *Fraktion* (parliamentary group) and become autonomous from the *Basis*, the Greens established the procedure of midterm rotation of Bundestag seats by the resignation of deputies in favor of their colleagues lower on the party list. Except for Baden-Württemberg Greens, who left the decision up to district parties, Green state parties in the early and mid-1980s also embraced midterm rotation. Furthermore, Green Bundestag deputies were required to give up most of their generous salaries to *öko-Fonds,* which are set up at the state level to assist alternative projects, and to live on the salary equivalent of a skilled laborer. The salaries of Landtag deputies have generally not been seen as so enriching by extraparliamentary Greens.

Under the notion of *Basisanbindung* (grass-roots linkage), the Greens' deputies were not only to maintain continuous contacts with their local parties and movement groups but also to engage in extraparliamentary activism. The latter, according to the Green orthodoxy of the early 1980s, constituted the more important "standing leg" of the movement-party. Most activists at that time maintained that the Greens' deputies should stick to their principles and refuse to participate in any parliamentary power games.

The membership orientation of the Green party has also differed significantly from that of the established parties. During the 1980s, the Greens grew from about 18,000 to over 40,000 members, whereas the memberships of the SPD and FDP declined. However, Green party officials have never aggressively sought to maximize membership size. Some founders were sensitive to the trade-off between size and internal democracy, that is, the larger the party grows, the greater the difficulty in keeping it participatory and "transparent" for members. Furthermore, an active recruitment campaign might make the Greens look like the other parties. Gerd Langguth argued that the Greens are a "cadre" party because they had the highest ratio of voters to members—87:1, compared to 16:1 for the SPD in 1983.[33] But unlike the other parties, the Greens have treated activists of new social movements as de facto members in many circumstances.

Membership contributions have represented a significantly smaller percentage of the Greens' total income than has been the case with other Bundestag parties. The annual portion of the Greens' total income derived from membership (and officeholder) contributions averaged about 15 percent during the period from 1980 to 1986, compared to 50 percent for the SPD, 43 percent for the CDU, 29 percent for the CSU, and 26 percent for the FDP. In the early 1980s, the Greens relied more heavily on campaign expense reimbursements from the state (as high as 69.5 percent of total income in 1983) than did the other parties. But this portion declined in in the period from 1985 to 1986 to under 40 percent (and in 1986 the CSU was more dependent on state funds).[34] It is ironic that during its formative years the antiestablishment party was so financially dependent on the state.

In a qualitative sense, the Greens' membership also has contrasted with the established parties' because "one of the unwritten rules of this party is to reject 'individualist' charismatic leaders."[35] According to Robert Harmel, the Greens are a "new type" of party (unanticipated by Michels) not because of their decentralized power structure or radical program but because of their elite-challenging, highly educated, participation-valuing membership.[36] But what happens to the new party as it wins a significant number of local, state, and federal parliamentary seats?

The Greens as "Eine Stinknormale Partei"?

Beginning in the mid-1980s, as the Greens struggled with intraparty controversies about their development, one encountered the lament that they had become or were becoming "a stinking normal party."[37] In a series of interviews in 1985 and 1987, the overwhelming majority of Green politicians interviewed said that the antiparty phase of the Greens' development was over; some regretted its passing, some favored it, but most accepted it as natural. However, few felt like the Greens were on the verge of becoming just another normal political party.

Throughout the decade, *Basisdemokratie* provided the "counterlegitimacy" of the Greens. Reference to the *Basis* was necessary to legitimize policy proposals, but the meaning of grass-roots tended to be somewhat open. Only a small minority of Green politicians interviewed in 1985 and 1987 defined the Greens' electorate as the *Basis*. The general tendency was to express the view that the *Basis* was larger than the party—that it encompassed the movement—though the latter was seen as the receding component by many. Jo Müller of the Realos (realist) wing of the Bonn *Fraktion* observed that the meaning of *Basis* depends upon the context and that *Basisdemokratie*, in practice, means that leaders must show a large backing for their ideas, that they cannot say "I" want this or that.[38]

The policy formulation process of the Greens required repeated referral of matters back to the local party and local movement activists for deliberations. Roland Schäffer observed in Hesse that the local parties were almost completely overloaded in dealing with just local matters. He charged that the federal and state steering committees often spoke for the *Basis* whether or not grass-roots linkages had been made.[39] Furthermore, most sources have estimated that typically about 10 to 20 percent of party members have shown up at the local and state membership assemblies, which raises the question of "accidental" majorities. Prominent Greens expressed concerns about the cumbersome, slow-moving process of policy formulation at the state and federal levels. Speakers at federal assemblies have been selected by lot so that, in contrast to the situation in the major parties, leading figures won't monopolize floor debates. However, observers have maintained that informal leaders cut the key deals outside the framework of the open sessions.[40] Nevertheless, compared with the major parties, the Greens' federal and state party assemblies have been generally characterized by vigorous participation in deciding—or delaying—policy decisions rather than formal ratification of the proposals of party leaders.

During the 1980s, the Greens were the most decentralized of the parties represented in the Bundestag. The federal party had at best "moral" control over the diverse state parties. Exceptions to the rule are rare. In face of neo-Nazi infiltration of the West Berlin Greens during 1984 and 1985, the federal party disbanded the state Greens and recognized the Alternative List as its association in West Berlin. The federal party leadership refused to recognize the Green Forum, the *Realos* splinter party in Hamburg formed in 1990. Differing federal-state factional balances were responsible for a number of attempts by the federal party executive to influence state party decisionmaking about strategy toward the SPD. In these cases, the state parties successfully defended their autonomy against Bonn. When factional infighting at the federal level escalated in spring 1988, the "crisis council" that convened (outside the party charter) included several members of state party executives.

A decade of experience raised questions about *basisdemokratische* procedures adopted to hinder the emergence of an SPD-style professional party elite. For example, only unrepresentative types of members have been motivated to hold nonsalaried, burdensome party offices. Per diem reimbursements for expenses allowed part-time pay for what amounted to a full-time job for federal party speakers. Finally, in March 1989 the federal party assembly approved salaries for leading members of the federal executive board. Partial professionalization also has occurred in some of the state parties. Party charters, however, still limited the tenure of federal and state party leaders. In most cases, the tenure of nonelected party functionaries has not been formally restricted. Above the local level, the prohibition of the simultaneous holding of multiple party offices or a party office and a parliamentary mandate remained in place, as did the provision for collective party leadership. However, trade-offs were increasingly recognized within the party. Intraparty communication tends to suffer as a result of the separation of party office and parliamentary seat. Collective party leadership tends to produce a divided leadership fighting for factional interests rather than attempting to integrate the party around the common interest.

Although the candidate lists of the Greens have remained open to nonparty members, except for women, the opportunities for breathtaking upward mobility of newcomers and outsiders via the Green party structure had lessened by the late 1980s.[41] As reflected in the historic proportions of Green party leaders, parliamentary candidates and deputies, and parliamentary leaders who were women, the Greens delivered on their promise to provide an alternative model for West German society in regard to representation of women. This representation has occurred even though males during the 1980s tended to outnumber women as Green voters, members, and activists. The federal working group specializing in women's issues has played a significant role in policy development.

Midterm rotation proved to be the most contentious *basisdemokratische* procedure among Bundestag Greens. The majority of both deputies and successors (*Nachrücker*) admitted that though midterm rotation of seats had theoretical advantages, there were just too many practical disadvantages.[42] (We shall discuss the specific problems in Chapter 7.) Although only two of the Green deputies elected in 1983 refused to rotate, the *Fraktion*'s assessment underlined the immense amount of organizational stress in delivering on the promised midterm rotation.[43] By the late 1980s, the federal party and nearly all state parties had moved toward allowing deputies to be eligible to serve one or two full terms.

The original idea behind rotation (and tenure limits) was to prevent the development of a class of Green professional politicians. This had been subverted by "diagonal" rotation: the practice of moving between party bodies and parliamentary groups or across federal and state levels or both. The founders had envisaged amateur politicians who would return after a few years to the *Basis*, enriching it with their experiences while reacquainting themselves with everyday realities. Ironically, rotation worked against the accountability of parliamentary deputies to the party. Individuals barred from reelection (or from even serving a full term) have less incentive to comply with party resolutions with which they disagree. Although the party's parliamentary group could expel a maverick deputy, it could not constitutionally force him or her to resign from Parliament. During the period from 1983 to 1990, irreconcilable differences produced a small number of ex-Green independent (*fraktionlos*) deputies. In 1990, conflict between the party and the parliamentary group in Hamburg resulted in the defection of most of the GAL deputies, who reorganized themselves as a new *Frauenfraktion*. Also, in more routine circumstances, the formal leaders of the deliberately "weak" party organization simply lacked the resources to match those of Green parliamentary groups. This is hardly surprising given Duverger's observations about the historical ineffectiveness of mass parties (characterized by strong organizations) in regulating their deputies' access to power resources.[44]

Fundamental opposition, the orientation favored by most Green activists in the early 1980s, soon became difficult to maintain as opportunities arose for the Greens' deputies to hold the balance of power. By the mid-1980s, the original "Red-Green" (left) versus "Green-Green" (right) cleavage had been supplanted by the *Realo* (realist) versus *Fundi* (fundamentalist) cleavage. The latter camp included both those who called themselves radical ecologists and those who called themselves ecosocialists. The *Realos* favored cooperation, including formal coalitions, with the SPD. The *Fundis* rejected cooperating with the SPD on anything other than an issue-by-issue basis. The *Realos* emphasized parliamentary politics, whereas the *Fundis* emphasized extraparliamentary politics. However, distinctive groups existed within each wing, and, furthermore, there were noteworthy nonaligned groups, such as autonomous feminists and ecolibertarians, and numerous issue specialists. Whereas the rivalry between *Realos* and *Fundis* absorbed much energy among the Greens at the federal level, the factional situations of the state parties varied significantly. During the 1980s, Baden-Württemberg Greens and Lower Saxony Greens were not so polarized along the fundamentalist-realist axis. In the Hamburg GAL, the fundamentalist ecosocialists dominated until 1990 while *Realos* triumphed in the mid-1980s factional struggle among Hesse Greens.

Ambitious Green politicians, by capitalizing on the mass media's hunger for interesting personalities, sought to become de facto party leaders. Parliamentary "stars," such as Petra Kelly, Otto Schily, Joschka Fischer, and Wolf-Dieter Hasenclever (in Baden-Württemberg), became the early foci of intense distrust from activists. According to a member of the Hesse Greens' party executive, "Petra Kelly says *Basisdemokratie* but does her own thing."[45] Schily and Fischer were distrusted because of their eagerness to play power politics within the system. Baden-Württemberg ecosocialists reacted against Hasenclever's leadership as too parliament-oriented. In the mid-1980s, the *Fundis* also generated their own national *Promis* (celebrities), most notably the strident Frankfurt radical ecologist Jutta Ditfurth. The open and bitter factionalism that characterized the Greens' intraparty politics throughout the decade vividly contrasted with that of the established parties.

The Crisis of Party Development ·

In the late 1980s, the Greens found themselves immobilized not just because of factional infighting between *Promis* at the federal level. Media headlines had obscured chronic problems at the *Basis* level, which threatened the Greens' development as much as schism between rival factions. Party activism, as measured by attendance at party meetings, had sunk to new lows, hardly compatible with the Greens' identity as a participatory party. In some states, the active membership pool was so shallow that, for practical purposes, the Greens' local councillors had become the local parties. Even in the boom years in the early 1980s, there had been local reports of difficulty in filling candidate lists, which obviously made midterm rotation an impossibility. The Greens' entry into state and federal parliaments tended to siphon off active party members essential for outside scrutiny of the activities of parliamentary groups. The irony is that Green party leaders did not aggressively recruit members because of their preference for remaining a movement-party. Issue specialists, advancing their causes via the Greens, tended not to be interested in the maintenance and development of the party organization. *Basisdemokratie* presumes an activist rank and file. If this should be lacking, then the Greens would be on their way, despite their rhetoric, to becoming an "electoral-professional" party.

A moderate group of Greens (Grüner Aufbruch '88) organized to reawaken the *Basis* through the direct democratic device of membership balloting on rival manifestos. The Aufbruch group's reform agenda included parliamentary rotation after one or two terms, liberalization of the *imperatives Mandat* doctrine to allow minority dissent, professionalization of the party executive, and cumulative time limitations on party and parliamentary officeholding to stop diagonal rotation. However, the Aufbruch group in the late 1980s rejected ending the separation of party office and parliamentary mandate. The *Realos* in their draft manifesto advocated restructuring the Green party for a *Reformpolitik* that could be supported by a wider social base. They were eager to bargain with coalitional partners to accomplish concrete changes. They favored abandoning the separation of party office and parliamentary mandate so that power could be more democratically concentrated in the hands of elected Green leaders.[46] In short, prominent *Realos* sought a more fully parliamentarized Green party whereas the Aufbruch group favored a "rationalized" alternative party.

Seeing no need for party reform, the prominent *Fundis* declined to develop their own manifesto. They favored the existing *basisdemokratische* framework, which had allowed their supporters to have a disproportionate influence in the development of Green party programs and strategies. Following a series of financial scandals, the fundamentalist-dominated federal executive was voted out by a majority of assembly delegates in December 1988. *Fundis* failed to regain their predominant role in the federal party leadership, which became somewhat more representative of party factions and tendencies in 1989 and 1990. While Thomas Ebermann and Rainer Trampert, who were prominent in the GAL, resigned from the Greens in early 1990 to launch a new radical leftist formation, fundamentalist Ditfurth chose to continue the struggle within the Green party (until 1991).

Also noteworthy in the late 1980s was the organization of the nondogmatic Left (Linken-Forum), which opposed the Aufbruch group's membership balloting proposal and rejected the *Realos'* pursuit of coalitions with the SPD. They favored the toleration of minority SPD governments. The formation of a Red-Green coalition in West Berlin in 1989 by the leftist Alternative List shifted the intraparty debate about strategy to the disadvantage of the nondogmatic Left. However, the SPD's opportunistic approach to reunification caused the Greens' federal party assembly to back off from a coalitional strategy during the 1990 all-German election campaign. The attempt of the Aufbruch and the *Realo* leaders to push aside the nondogmatic and the fundamentalist Lefts so that the party structure could be reformed and the party program's "obsolete" rhetoric could be jettisoned met with little success. The majority of party delegates favored a pluralistic federal leadership that included prominent leftists to counterbalance the realists and moderates who have tended to predominate in the parliamentary groups.

Questions of structural reform were quickly overshadowed after spring 1990 by the need to close ranks and to work out alliances with East German Greens and citizens' movements in order to survive the all-German elections. During the campaign, the federal party leadership distanced the Greens from any alliance with the PDS (the reform Communist party in East Germany). Subsequently some disgruntled Green leftists resigned and aligned themselves with the PDS/Left List campaign in West Germany. In areas such as the Saarland where the Green party had not been strong, active members were lost to the PDS on the left and to the SPD on the right. Some *Realos* sought to seize the opportunity to encourage the wholesale departure of the fundamentalist Left; however, most who were prominent in the party shunned intraparty brinkmanship in face of the uncertainties of the all-German election campaign.

The electoral debacle of the West German Greens in the December 2, 1990, elections shook the party from top to bottom. Ironically, the Federal Constitutional Court's positive response to the complaints from the Greens as well as the small parties of the GDR about the unfairness of early all-German elections with a national 5 percent threshold for representation worked against the West German Greens' success. With separate East-West 5 percent thresholds mandated, the pressure to link the West German Greens and the East German citizens' movements dissipated and the merger of West Greens and East Greens was delayed until after election day. Together with the East Greens and their allies, the West Greens would have cleared a national 5 percent threshold and qualified for Bundestag seats. (The eight Bündnis 90/Grüne deputies elected from the former

Deutsche Demokratische Republik [DDR; GDR]) included two East German Greens.)

During 1990, negotiations had revealed that the diverse East German citizens' movements were reluctant to submerge their separate identities. As a gesture of solidarity, some West German Green state parties nominated prominent East German citizen activists to promising list positions. Although the West German Greens and the East German citizens' movements have shared many policy views, the latter's leaders have included many who were uncomfortable with socialist sympathies evident within the former's membership. For their part, prominent East German Greens have tended to respond pragmatically to issues. Therefore, the successful merger of East and West Green parties would seem likely to augment moderate and realist groups.

The formation of the East German Green party in November 1989 was not without dispute. Many environmentalists favored developing as a decentralized movement, not as a political party; proponents of a Green party in the GDR argued that the rush of events ruled out such an organic evolution. As a small party, claiming 3,000 to 5,000 members, with sparse resources, the East Greens had no reason for being obsessed with *basis-demokratische* controls on their leaders. The December 3, 1990, formal merger with the West German Greens brought two Easterners on to the federal executive board. Inevitably, the defeat of the West German Greens generated second thoughts among some Eastern leaders about the wisdom of the predetermined merger. And in the case of Saxony Greens, the immediate course of action was to seek ties with their state's citizens' movements while remaining autonomous from the federal Green party.

In the aftermath of electoral defeat, Joschka Fischer and Antje Vollmer, *Realos* and Aufbruch leaders respectively, seized the initiative by proposing major structural reforms to remedy the lack of forceful leadership in the party. Among their proposals were abolishing rotation, making party office and parliamentary mandates compatible, electing two party chairs who would propose a party manager to be elected by the party assembly, replacing the federal steering committee with an expanded committee that includes state party and parliamentary leaders, and phasing out or trimming back the unaccountable federal working groups (Bundesarbeitsgemeinschaften [BAGs]). Vollmer reiterated (unsuccessfully) her long-standing proposal for a membership ballot on the future course of the party, which she has visualized as becoming an ecology and civil rights party of the all-German center.

Although dissenting from Vollmer's vision, spokespersons of the Linken-Forum also urged rationalizing the party organization and providing for a more responsible leadership. Yet they favored retaining the separation of party office and parliamentary mandate. Fundamentalist Ditfurth, speaking for a fading minority, argued that the Greens' future lies not in restructuring the party organization so that it is more like the old parties but in reviving *Basisdemokratie* through extraparliamentary opposition. However, even the left-leaning federal executive board advocated reforms of party structure. The reforms accepted at the Neumünster party conference in April 1991 did eliminate rotation, reduce the size of the federal executive board, increase the role of the elected state party leaders and parliamentary deputies by replacing the federal steering committee with a new Länderrat (council of state party leaders), and set up dual chairs with a Green from the East and a Green from the West. However, the proposal to change the rule forbidding the simultaneous holding of a party office and a parliamentary mandate failed narrowly in attaining the necessary two-thirds majority. But it is very likely that individual state parties will soon accomplish that change with their own reforms. A decade of experimentation with alternative party forms was being brought to a close by the new realities of party politics in a united Germany.

Conclusion

The historic transformation of German politics during the period from 1989 to 1990 found the West German Greens largely immobilized. The major parties, just a few years ago discounted as overaccommodated, overgeneralized, overinstitutionalized, and overloaded, quickly responded to the new circumstances (in the case of the Christian Democrats, boldly!). The Greens' formal leadership sought to draw warring factions together in a federal campaign that emphasized the survival of the global ecosystem at a time when old-fashioned materialist concerns of economic growth and security had been reinvigorated by German reunification. Although sharing the West German Greens' reservations about Kohl's fast-track approach to reunification and many of their other policy views, the East German citizens' movements showed little enthusiasm for any early fusion with Europe's most well-known *basisdemokratische* party.

In 1980 the Greens proclaimed themselves to be a new type of party that not only advocates grass-roots democracy in West German society but also practices it within its own organization. Early critics dismissed *Basisdemokratie* as little more than a facade for domination by left-wing activists. Although it is true that a sizeable number of Green activists began their political careers in leftist groups, a conspiratorial explanation overlooks the fact that most were determined to learn from the sectarian mistakes of the 1960s and 1970s. Green activists favored political alliances with diverse groups and advocated open, nonhierarchical party structures. The organizational contrast with the established parties, in both formal and informal senses, was sharp enough that one can conclude that the Greens constituted an alternative model.

However, a large body of political science literature maintains that new parties, if they survive, tend to change organizationally over time toward resembling old parties. For example, Panebianco observes that as parties institutionalize they evolve from a system of solidarity with a movement type of participation to a system of interests with a professional type of participation.[47] The founders of the Green party were particularly sensitive to Michels' "iron law," according to which even prodemocracy parties inevitably become oligarchical as they grow. There were also concerns about the impact of quick electoral success on the new party's development, that is, that it would accommodate itself, like the SPD had historically, to the established norms of parliamentary politics.

The idealist objective of Green party innovators was to preserve the open, participatory character of social movements within the legal framework of a party organization competing with others in electoral and parliamentary politics. The realistic outcome of the Greens' antielitist procedures has been a weakly institutionalized party, which in a period of surging movement mobilization can be functional. However, movement politics is cyclical and party politics is continual. Because the Greens denied their elected party leadership conventional resources, power dissipated within a "stratarchical, disjointed framework party" that was not particularly responsive to movement activists nor accountable to party members. According to Kitschelt, the power vacuum was filled by "political entrepreneurs" (informal elites) and parliamentarians.[48] Who has power in the party? Without hesitation a veteran GAL party official responded in 1987, "The *Promis* and the issue-specialists."[49]

The Greens thus developed during the 1980s as a new complex party phenomenon. They valued participation more than efficiency, but they were not a participatory movement-party. They evolved a generation of party careerists, but they were not an electoral-professional party. As a national party the Greens combined both qualities in an unstable, convoluted hybrid organization with dysfunctional consequences not anticipated by their founders. During the late 1980s, the political environment of the Greens was changing and the party was not adapting. Sympathetic voters were no longer overlooking the organizational chaos of the party; they were looking for evidence of the organizational competence to tackle policy problems, not simply to dramatize them. The Greens' electoral debacle on December 2, 1990, provided the acute crisis to catapult overdue structural reform to the top of the party's agenda. In the following chapter, we turn to the related question of the Greens' programmatic integration.

Notes

1. Angelo Panebianco, *Political Parties: Organization and Power* (Cambridge: Cambridge University Press, 1988), p. 268.

2. E. E. Schattschneider, *Party Government* (New York: Rinehart, 1942), p. 1.

3. William E. Wright, "Comparative Party Models: Rational-Efficient and Party Democracy," in *A Comparative Study of Party Organization*, William E. Wright, ed. (Columbus: Merrill, 1971), p. 30.

4. Maurice Duverger, *Political Parties* (New York: Wiley, 1963), pp. xxiii–xxxv.

5. Leon D. Epstein, *Political Parties in Western Democracies* (New York: Praeger, 1967), pp. 126–129, 257–260.

6. Giovanni Sartori, *Parties and Party Systems: A Framework for Analysis* (Cambridge: Cambridge University Press), pp. 21–22.

7. Robert Michels, *Political Parties: A Sociological Study of the Oligarchical Tendencies of Modern Democracy* (New York: Free Press, 1962), p. 368.

8. Robert T. McKenzie, *British Political Parties*, 2d ed. (New York: Praeger, 1963), pp. 644–645.

9. Duverger, *Political Parties*, pp. 135, 151.

10. Ibid., p. 63.

11. Karl Loewenstein, *Max Weber's Political Ideas in the Perspective of Our Time* (Amherst: University of Massachusetts Press, 1966), pp. 56–57.

12. Otto Kirchheimer, "The Transformation of the Western European Party Systems," in *Politics in Western European Democracies: Patterns and Problems*, Gary C. Byrne and Kenneth S. Pederson, eds. (New York: Wiley, 1971), p. 164.

13. Ibid., pp. 157–158.

14. Kay Lawson, *The Comparative Study of Political Parties* (New York: St. Martin's Press, 1976), p. 17.

15. Steven B. Wolinetz, "The Transformation of Western European Party Systems Revisited," *West European Politics* 2, no.1 (January 1979):24–25.

16. Panebianco, *Political Parties: Organization and Power*, pp. 220–235, 262–267.

17. Kirchheimer, "The Transformation of the Western European Party Systems," p. 165.

18. Kurt Sontheimer, *The Government and Politics of West Germany* (New York: Praeger, 1972), p. 83.

19. Gordon Smith, "The German Volkspartei and the Career of the Catch-All Concept," in *Party Government and Political Culture in West Germany*, Herbert Döring and Gordon Smith, eds. (New York: St. Martin's Press, 1982), p. 69.

20. Joachim Raschke, "Jenseits der Volkspartei," *Das Argument* 25, no. 1 (January 1983):55.

21. Karl-Werner Brand, Detlef Büsser, and Dieter Rucht, *Aufbruch in eine andere Gesellschaft: Neue Soziale Bewegungen in der Bundesrepublik*, 2d ed. (Frankfurt: Campus Verlag, 1984), pp. 246–247.

22. Claus Offe, "Reflections on the Institutional Self-Transformation of Movement Politics: A Tentative Stage Model," in *Challenging the Political Order*, Russell

Dalton and Manfred Küchler, eds. (New York: Oxford University Press), pp. 236–237.

23. Anna Hallensleben, *Von der Grünen Liste zur Grünen Partei?* (Göttingen: Muster-Schmidt Verlag, 1984), p. 258.

24. Burkhard Schaper, "Die Entstehungsgeschichte der AL," in *AL: Die Alternative Liste Entstehung, Entwicklung, Positionen*, Michael Bühnemann, Michael Wendt, and Jürgen Wituschek, eds. (Berlin: LitPol, 1984), pp. 55–59.

25. Herbert Gruhl, "Die grüne Notwenigkeit," in *Die grüne Protest*, Rudolf Brun, ed. (Frankfurt: Fischer, 1978), pp. 117–121.

26. Petra K. Kelly, "Die vierte Partei—Eine wählbare Ökologische, gewaltfreie, soziale und basisdemokratische Anti-Partei," in *Die Grünen: Personen, Projekte, Programme*, Hans-Werner Lüdke and Olaf Dinne, eds. (Stuttgart: Seewald, 1980), p. 80.

27. Sebastian Hoffner, *Überlegungen eine Wechselwählers*, 2d ed. (Munich: Kindler, 1980), pp. 119–126.

28. Epstein, *Political Parties in Western Democracies*, p. 9.

29. Rudolf van Hüllen, *Ideologie und Machtkampf bei den Grünen* (Bonn: Bouvier, 1990), p. 6.

30. Panebianco, *Political Parties: Organization and Power*, p. 50.

31. Bühnemann et al., *AL: Die Alternative Liste*, pp. 91–92.

32. Isaac Balbus, "Das Dreieck der neuen sozialen Bewegungen: Feminismus, Ökologie und Basisdemokratie," in *Neue soziale Bewegungen: Konservativer Aufbruch im bunten Gewand?* Wolf Schäfer, ed. (Frankfurt: Fischer, 1983), p. 59.

33. Gerd Langguth, *The Green Factor in German Politics* (Boulder: Westview Press, 1984), p. 48.

34. *Datenhandbuch zur Geschichte des Deutschen Bundestages 1980 bis 1987* (Baden-Baden: Nomos Verlagsgesellschaft, 1988), p. 101.

35. Elim Papadakis, "The Green Party in Contemporary West German Politics," *Political Quarterly* 54, no. 3 (July 1983):304.

36. Robert Harmel, "Michels + 75: The Iron Law of Oligarchy Revisited." Paper presented at the 1987 Annual Meeting of the American Political Science Association, Chicago, Ill., August-September 1987, pp. 19–21.

37. See Wolf-Dieter Hasenclever, "Die Grünen sind eine stinknormale Partei geworden," in *Die Grünen: 10 bewegte Jahre*, Michael Schroeren, ed. (Vienna: Überreuter, 1990), pp. 135–145.

38. Interview: Bonn-Haus Tulpenfeld, May 13, 1985.

39. Roland Schäffer, "Basisdemokratie. Oder: wenn der Löwenzahn nicht waschen will, Müssen wir eben Kopfsalat essen," *Kursbuch*, no. 74 (December 1983):77–93.

40. See Marie-Luise Weinberger, *Aufbruch zu neuen Ufern? Grün-Alternative zwischen Anspruch und Wirklichkeit* (Bonn, 1984), pp. 117–124.

41. Herbert Kitschelt, *The Logics of Party Formation* (Ithaca: Cornell University Press, 1989), pp. 215–218.

42. Interviews: Bonn-Haus Tulpenfeld, May 13–15, 1985.

43. Die Grünen im Bundestag, *Rechenschaftsbericht* (Bonn: Die Grünen im Bundestag, 1985), p. 9.

44. Duverger, *Political Parties*, pp. 190–195.

45. Interview: Landesgesellschaftsstelle, Frankfurt, April 29, 1985.

46. *Die Grünen* [Wochenzeitung], no. 27 (July 9, 1988), pp. 4, 9–11, and no. 28 (July 16, 1988), pp. 4–5.

47. Panebianco, *Political Parties: Organization and Power*, p. 18.

48. Kitschelt, *The Logics of Party Formation*, p. 295.

49. Interview with Hamburg GAL party manager, June 12, 1987.

6

The Programmatic Development
of the Greens

P ARTIES ARE SUPPOSED TO STAND for something, to have a cause, however broad or specific, grand or mundane. Edmund Burke's early definition of a party as a "body of men united, for promoting by their joint endeavors the national interest, upon some particular principle in which they are all agreed"[1] emphasizes that parties should stand for some collective good. Modern political parties, though they are quite different phenomena from those in Burke's era, generally do endeavor to mobilize popular support behind some common cause, program, or ideology. Political scientists have attributed numerous systemic functions to modern parties. High on most lists is the function of interest aggregation. Parties combine diverse specific demands and restructure them as a more manageable set of policy proposals. Parties may be single-issue parties, though "rarely are such parties 'significant' in a party system."[2] The common expectation is for "real" parties to address a multiplicity of policy issues.

And to make sense out of all the sound and fury, it is most helpful to have some sort of overall perspective. Klaus von Beyme attributes to modern parties the function of goal identification; accordingly, he highlights the role of ideology and programs.[3] As a concept, ideology has proven both indispensable and troublesome in political science; it is weighted down with a lot of historical baggage. The age of *Weltanschauungen* (worldviews), "secular religions," and absolute utopias may be fast fading. But ideology is still around, for good reason, as Willard Mullins conceives it: It is "a logically coherent system of beliefs which, within a . . . conception of history, links cognitive and evaluative perception of one's social conditions—especially for the future—to a program of collective action for the maintenance, alternation, or transformation of society."[4] This conception allows for ideologies that are relatively open or closed, more or less comprehensive, and strongly or weakly articulated. Parties do not necessarily have to have an ideology (or program), but "only parties based on ideology have succeeded in establishing themselves in Europe."[5]

Since 1980, the Green party has hardly been a one-issue party. It has aggregated the demands of not only environmentalists but also of diverse protest movements. From the outset, Green activists have shared a negative consensus that radical changes must be made in Germany and the world. Moving toward a positive consensus on the goals and means of change has been difficult because the Green party has no unified ideology (as defined previously). What one found throughout the 1980s was contentious ideological pluralism. Joachim Raschke's recent study maintains that the Greens' intense factionalism reflects no less than four ideological models, which provide rival interpretations of the causes and cures of societal crises.[6] As a rule, Green parties at local, state, and federal levels have labored to develop alternatives to the policies of the established parties. However, the absence of a positive consensus has hampered the integration (and communication) of the Greens' programmatic efforts.

In this chapter we consider the efforts of the Green party to formulate an alternative perspective of radical reformism toward the policy dilemmas of advanced industrial societies. But first we shall briefly look at some assessments of ideology and programmatic development of modern parties in general.

Parties and Programs

In contrast to political philosophies, ideologies are action oriented. Mostafa Rejai asserts, "Not only do they posit a set of values, they also seek to relate specific patterns of action to the realization of these values . . . [these patterns] may be either reformist or radical in nature."[7] Yet translating party principle into reality has hardly been an easy task for the major parties in Western Europe. Jean Blondel observes that "in most cases programmes are drafted quickly in the context of elections . . . are unclear, often limited in scope, and not closely connected to the goals which the party proclaims . . . [and] do not follow a consistent line over any length of time." Furthermore, he concludes, "On balance parties do not really have programmes . . . a critique of other parties' programmes does not constitute a substitute for the formulation of their own positive policies."[8] Blondel's underlying concern seems to be that when modern democratic parties fail to set policy priorities, the job is left to executive and administrative elites.

In his survey of Western political parties, Leon Epstein agrees that parties lack the time and the tools to formulate policies on complex problems but sees the critique as misconceived: The primary function of parties is vote-getting and to do this their candidates must respond flexibily to changing circumstances. One must "look beyond programmatic ideologies with their simplified remedial suggestions."[9] Epstein opts for pragmatic parties unfettered by party doctrine (and a mass membership) with the task of policy development lodged elsewhere.

In her comparative study of parties, Kay Lawson differentiates among parties that are issue-less (which is rare), pragmatic, programmatic, and ideological. Pragmatic parties are reactive and focused on immediate problems; programmatic parties are concerned with developing "an integrated long-range plan of action . . . [linking] present needs and future goals"; and ideological parties address "issues only in an abstract, future-oriented way in strict accordance with a known doctrine of thought."[10] Her scheme allows for the occurrence of parties with an ideology but without a credible program and also illustrates how political scientists associate the word ideological with a rigid style of behavior of party activists. Although the policy controversies within Green parties above the local level often featured an ideological style of behavior, we will argue that their decade-long development was toward being a programmatic party, as defined by Lawson.

The scholars of the "end of ideology" school of the 1950s and 1960s welcomed the decline of total ideologies and the resulting moderation and even convergence of major parties within Western party systems during the postwar period. For some it seemed self-evident that politics would become managerial and that problem solving in politics would become technical. However, by the end of the 1960s, Western political systems had experienced a resurgence of "radical" ideologies and extraparliamentary opposition against established norms and values. Von Beyme observes a cross-national trend toward "re-ideologization" within major Western parties rooted in the same time period.[11] By this he does not mean that total ideologies were coming back in vogue but that goal formulation was being taken more seriously by party activists. One manifestation of the trend was the reinvigoration of ideological factionalism. A prime example during the 1970s was the Young Socialists (JUSOS), who wanted the SPD to stand for more than crisis management.

Party programs have both internal and external roles. From the pragmatic view, programs should above all broaden the party's electoral base by winning new voters and holding old voters. The "good" program should signal credibility to potential coalition partners, opinion leaders in the media, and the attentive public. Internally, the party program should help recruit new members and mobilize old members and should provide policy guidance to members and leaders alike. Votes on the provisions of the program reflect the relative strengths of intraparty groups. But the final draft is likely to include compromised wording and specific provisions with contradictory implications. Although major German parties have been more programmatically constrained than major U.S. parties, the CDU and, since the late 1950s, the SPD leaderships have underlined in word and deed the external role of programs.

In contrast, Green programs have been primarily inner-directed, Rudolf van Hüllen argues in his study of the Greens.[12] The formulation of common programs should help to integrate the demands and identities of heterogeneous activists. But van Hüllen maintains that because there is no Green party consensus on even the role of programs, their provisions reflect the evolving balance of power among ideological subgroups more than the outcome of creative efforts to grapple with real world problems. From his perspective, those outsiders who criticize the irreality or inconsistency of Green programs are missing the point because their primary significance relates to inner representation rather than external representation of views. However, the dynamics of program formulation may be even more complex. Herbert Kitschelt's study discerns three categories of Green party activists: ideologues, lobbyists (issue specialists), and pragmatists. The latter emphasize "external practical policy achievements."[13] Wherever pragmatists and lobbyists form a majority coalition, programs are more responsive to the needs of electoral appeal.

Many political scientists contend that minor parties play an important role in the programmatic development of major parties by raising new issues. The major parties selectively absorb popular provisions of the minor party's program. Robert Rohrschneider's study of the environmental policies of major parties in Western Europe suggests that however inner-directed the Greens' programs may have been, their proposals have contributed to policy changes by the major West German parties, especially the SPD.[14] Hence we maintain that the substance as well as the process of Green program formulation warrants attention.

Early Programs: The Late 1970s

The first Green parties were little more than small protest parties seizing the opportunity of low-cost local elections to send a message to the major parties. In Lower Saxony, the Umweltschutzpartei (USP) outlined its environmental concerns in a one-page program. In 1978 the USP merged with other voter initiatives to become the Grüne Liste Umweltschutz (GLU), whose seven-page program identified the central problem of our times as "the maintenance and improvement of the basis of life." Except for brief attention to education, research, and democratic reforms, the GLU program was preoccupied with ecology, which for its authors stood above left-right controversies. Green lists with similar inclinations were soon emerging beyond Lower Saxony, as were rival Bunte (multicolored) and Alternative Lists.

In the latter's vanguard was the leftist-dominated Bunte Liste (BL) in Hamburg. Although the BL subtitled its fourteen-page program "Initiatives for Democracy and Environment," it devoted only 10 percent of the contents to environmental policies, compared with 50 percent for social policies.[15] For example, the BL advocated equal rights for women, homosexuals, and foreigners. It addressed the concerns of workers, such as the right to strike and the demand for a shorter workweek. It cataloged reform demands about schools, housing, health care, and prisons. In other words, environmental problems were just one symptom of the crisis of late capitalism. The BL program of 1978 reflected no prioritization of policies; it, as did the Berlin Alternative List's program of 1979, simply added the demands of affected groups in order to mobilize a grass-roots alliance of leftists, from anarchists to Marxist-Leninists (K-Gruppen). Van Hüllen maintains that the hidden agenda of the K-Gruppen was to undermine the legitimacy of West German political institutions by exposing their inability to cope with surging demands for reforms.[16] In contrast, the GLU never had overturning the political order as its goal.

Neither did the Grüne Aktion Zukunft (GAZ), the national environmental party that Herbert Gruhl launched in July 1978. Gruhl's program consisted of a list of thirty points. His prime target was the "growth ideology" of the modern industrial economy, which he believed was destroying the "ecological foundations of all life." The GAZ advocated a simpler, less materialistic life-style. It stood up for the protection and recognition of the role of mothers (which feminists viewed as regressive). There was no attention paid to the socioeconomic demands of workers or minorities. In contrast to the GLU's and BL's programs, the GAZ's included foreign and defense policy goals: peaceful relations with the East bloc, national self-determination, Third World assistance, and nuclear disarmament. According to Gruhl, political institutions should be reformed in line with traditional values, *not* replaced by new radical democratic or socialist institutions.

Whereas the GAZ sought to establish lines of demarcation with leftist groups, the Aktionsgemeinschaft Unabhängiger Deutscher (AUD) sought a broad alliance spanning right and left. The AUD began as an antiestablishment party of populist conservatism, which during the 1960s attempted to build bridges to the leftist Extra-parliamentary Opposition (APO). During the 1970s, it moved environmental protection to the top of its program. The AUD rejected "back-to-nature" romanticism as well as the racist and biological notions of the far right. Its program embraced neutralist nationalism, a vague "new" socialism, grass-roots democracy, and equal rights for women. The AUD's leader, August Haussleiter, carried the stigma of a political origin on the far right, but many of the AUD's policies resembled the themes of the new left.

The Grüne Liste Hesse (GLH) platform for the 1978 state elections combined socialist, radical democratic, and ecological themes. However, the GLU and the GAZ disassociated themselves from the GLH and ran separate campaigns; the result was a three-way split of 2 percent of the Hesse votes. Although the Green votes were also meager in the 1978 Bavarian election, these votes are noteworthy because the AUD opened its candidate list to members of citizen groups and nature protection associations under the label AUD/Die Grünen and agreed to a joint program with the GAZ. Leftist alternative groups sat out the Bavarian campaign.

The leaders of the GLU, AUD, GAZ, and GLSH (Grüne Liste Schleswig-Holstein) pushed ahead without the Bunte and Alternative Lists to draw up a common program for a nationwide electoral alliance (SPV-Die Grünen) to contest the 1979 European parliamentary elections. What were to become in 1980 the four pillars of the Green party—ecology, social responsibility, grass-roots democracy, and nonviolence—appear at the outset of the 1979 Euro-program. Yet the core concern of this fourteen-page program was clearly the environment. The Euro-electoral alliance called for a "dynamic equilibrium" society whose goals would be environmental protection, stable currency, and jobs with human dignity. Contemporary society's preoccupation with quantitative growth and materialistic living standards was criticized. The Euro-program's authors posed intellectual and spiritual self-development as their alternative. They attacked the consequences of rampant industrialization but not capitalism per se. Though preoccupied with environmental protection, the Euro-program included positions on other policy issues as well: social (for example, rights of minorities), economic (for example, worker participation), and foreign (for example, "Europe of the Regions").

After winning 3.2 percent of the Euro-votes in West Germany, SPV-Die Grünen leaders moved to organize a national Green party to contest the 1980 Bundestag elections. In October 1979 the Bremen Green List, a loose grouping of populist reformers, won the first Green seats in a state parliament despite competition with a leftist Alternative List. However, the leaders of the Euro-electoral alliance felt that to have any chance of clearing the 5 percent threshold in the 1980 federal election they had to broaden their electoral base. Therefore, they allowed leftists who had not participated in the Euro-campaign into their membership and onto their program commission. The formulation of a federal program (Bundesprogramm) to glue together such a heterogeneous alliance as a party was to prove troublesome.

Das Bundesprogramm

Left-right ideological conflict at the founding conference of the Green party in January 1980 focused on whether those who were also members of other parties (primarily leftist) should be allowed into the new party. The resulting compromise left the decision to the state parties, which enabled the conference to launch the Greens with their ecological, social, grass-roots democratic, and nonviolent "pillars." The approval of a federal program was postponed to the March 1980 party conference in Saarbrücken.

On the program commission, the more professional politicos of the ideological Left soon outmaneuvered the more amateurish conservatives. Simply put, conservatives wanted to maintain a programmatic focus on environmental issues and leftists wanted—and got—a broad program with radical stands on a full range of domestic and foreign issues. Although the new wave of members that had surged into the party since late 1979 were more to the left, they still did not constitute a majority. According to van Hüllen's estimate, about 36 percent of the delegates in Saarbrücken were on the left (a small minority of whom were Marxists), compared with 28 percent for Gruhl's allies on the right.[17] Leftist activists proved to be more skillful in manipulating conference procedures and benefited from their more established network.

Yet the key to the Left's success was the Mittelgruppe (middle group, or moderates), which formed a majority with the Left on key issues. These moderates differed with the conservatives by orienting ecology to society and differed from the Left by favoring an evolutionary strategy not shaped by such notions as the class struggle. The middle group, including the AUD, favored a "third way" between capitalism and socialism. Despite the blurring of ideological perspectives in programmatic compromises, their vision is often reflected in the Bundesprogramm.

Although the final version of the program also included the ideas of conservatives, Gruhl and his allies believed that they were overshadowed and distorted by the antisystem agenda of the Left. Quantitatively, the environmental protection section constituted only 14 percent of the text of the forty-six page program compared to 44 percent for its social issues section.[18] Qualitatively, Gruhl attacked a Green party program whose social policies would necessitate more economic growth and whose foreign policies echoed anti-Western propaganda. At the Dortmund conference in June 1980, the moderate-left majority attempted to mollify the conservative minority by passing a Wahlprogramm (election program) that removed or watered down several provisions hotly contested at and after the Saarbrücken conference. Nevertheless, over the summer, a couple of state parties disassociated themselves from the federal election campaign and about 1,000 conservatives resigned from the party of around 15,000 members. In 1981 Gruhl launched a rival Ecological Democratic party (ÖDP), which has failed to develop any real appeal on the center-right of German politics.

The thesis of the Greens' federal program is that West Germans are in the midst of an ecological and economic crisis threatening the future of industrial societies. The symptoms of this crisis are environmental destruction and human exploitation; its roots are in profit-seeking competition and quantitative economic growth. The federal program maintains that "economic goals should only be realized within a framework of ecological necessities." It opposes "an economic system in which the economically powerful control the work process, the end products, and the living conditions of a vast majority of the population," and it asserts that affected people should decide "what, how, and where products will be produced."[19] The Greens call for the just distribution of goods and services to the socially disadvantaged, a guaranteed income for all, the gradual shortening of the workweek (with full pay), an end to sexual discrimination, and a host of other policy changes.

To accomplish the fundamental realignment of industrial society, the federal program espouses decentralization and self-administration. For example, large corporations should be dismantled into self-managing units and small alternative companies should be promoted. Yet the state would not wither away because many proposed changes would necessitate enhanced enforcement powers. For example, a federal environmental ministry is proposed to protect nature; sexual discrimination would have to be countered by enforcing agencies; and an open planning process would still require the authority of the state to prevent negative land use. The federal program provides a segmented vision of the alternative society by enumerating—not integrating—the domestic policy demands of the diversity of special interests within the Green movement. It neglects the questions of costs, trade-offs, and priorities, which is hardly surprising for a new small party.

The Greens' federal program also offers a radical alternative to the foreign policies of the major parties. The newcomers maintain that "an ecologically-conscious foreign policy is based on nonviolence." They oppose the insanity of the arms race and the folly of the strategy of nuclear deterrence. They demand the removal of all medium-range nuclear missiles from Europe. Further, the Greens call for the dissolution of both military blocs and the withdrawal of all foreign troops from Germany. They advocate nuclear-free zones in Central Europe and the unilateral reduction of the West German army; in the long run they favor the replacement of conventional armed defense with nonviolent social defense.

"In this way, the groundwork would be laid for a solution to the division of Europe and Germany."[20] (That is the federal program's sole reference to German unification.) Beyond the European arena, the Greens favor peaceful support of national liberation movements struggling against repressive regimes. They advocate the end of the world arms trade, a worldwide moratorium on debt repayments, and increasing assistance for Third World countries.

The federal program portrays the Greens as the champions of underdogs abroad and at home. The Greens advocate full equality for women. They promote the rights of foreign workers, homosexuals, gypsies, the handicapped, prisoners, and the aged. For all citizens they stress the right of free speech and assembly, the right of conscientious objection to military service, and the right to be free of surveillance.

Although the federal program aspired to a comprehensive scope, some key policies—tax, currency, and finances and children and youth—were disputed and left out for future development. Appended to the federal program is the statement that the development of policies will continue with "new findings and perceptions gathered from practical experience."

Changing Policy Circumstances

All parties must adapt in some way, sooner or later, to their changing political environment if they are to be viable forces. Despite their weak showing in the October 1980 federal elections, the Greens were well positioned during the early 1980s to respond quickly to the surging peace movement, ignited by NATO's decision to deploy hundreds of Pershing II and cruise missiles in West Germany. Although Greens constituted a small minority of the peace movement, they were able by conspicuous involvement in protest demonstrations to present themselves as the "eco-peace" party. Not until the SPD was able to reverse its stand on the missile deployments could its peace appeal be competitive.

At the October 1981 Offenbach federal party conference, the Greens' major item of business was the approval of the Friedensmanifest (peace manifesto). The peace manifesto largely reflects the "equidistant" reasoning of the peace movement: The threat to peace stems from superpower rivalry. The draft of the Hamburg GAL would have placed the blame squarely on Western imperialism, to which the USSR had defensively (and dangerously) reacted. The manifesto sees the arms rivalry as growing out of the growth dynamics of industrialism to expand worldwide one's sphere of resource domination. The Greens demand a bloc-free, demilitarized Europe and a Third World free of superpower rivalry. A necessary first step would be the loosening of West Germany's ties with the Western

Alliance. The Greens' policy resolutions became progressively more anti-NATO through the mid-1980s.[21]

As the West German economy stagnated in the early 1980s, the Green party came under increased pressure to delineate its economic alternatives more specifically. At the November 1982 Hagen party conference, factional struggles occurred over a draft economic program. Although the Greens have long included a small ecolibertarian group (which has no qualms about the marketplace), both sides of the grand debate in Hagen opposed the capitalist system. The basic difference was between the radical ecologists, who favored decentralization, self-administration, and nature protection even at the cost of more unemployment, and the ecosocialists, who favored a more democratic, more ecologically sensitive social state with full employment.

At the January 1983 Sindelfingen conference, the Greens approved the economic action program entitled Sofortprogramm gegen Arbeitslosigkeit und Sozialabbau (Immediate Program Against Unemployment and Declining Social Expenditures), which proclaims, "The ecological and social belong inseparably together."[22] The cautious wording of many provisions reflects tentative compromises among contending factions. In contrast to the federal program's enumerative approach, the Sindelfingen economic program is organized as fundamental perspectives, concrete proposals, and political strategies. However, its theme is the same: the disastrous costs of "not too little production, but too much." The Sindelfingen program brackets capitalist and existent socialist systems as variants of the same industrialism, which is destroying the environment and repressing the citizenry. Although it admits that private property is necessary for individual freedom, the program declares that holders of private *and* state property should no longer be allowed to exploit nature or humanity. The Greens reject the traditional form of nationalization in favor of new forms of social property allowing for self-administration and democratic controls. The steering functions of the market are cautiously admitted, though certain resources, for example, land, are to be removed from the market.

To counter the worst effects of the crises of industrialism, the Greens advocate the creation of jobs by shortening the workweek and restricting overtime; ecological investments in energy, transportation, housing, and agriculture; conversion of industries away from destructive products; support for alternative projects and self-help organizations; full maintenance of social programs; and special training for unemployed youth. The Greens briefly indicate the budget reallocations, tax changes, and state borrowing that could cover the costs of their economic program.

The final section of the Sindelfingen program recognizes the massive resistance that even short-term measures would encounter from established interests. Its answer is mobilization of the new social movements *and* the progressive forces in the trade union movement. The compromises at Sindelfingen hardly resolved the programmatic debates within the party, which became entangled with the troublesome question of political strategy toward the SPD.

Greens Between Reformism and Radicalism

During the 1980s, the Greens' federal and state conferences were, compared to German party norms, characterized by active participation of members in deciding or delaying policy decisions. The movement-party was supposed to develop the policies and its parliamentary deputies were supposed to implement them (or resign). But the election of Greens as full-time paid politicians in Bonn with the resources of staff, budget, and media access transformed intraparty relationships. Soon the Bundestag Greens were eclipsing the federal party leadership. During the mid-1980s, the split personality of the Greens crystallized: The majority of deputies tended to be reformist and the majorities of the federal party executive and steering committees tended to be radical.

After the 1983 federal election, the SPD accelerated its programmatic renewal. During the campaign, SPD chancellor candidate Hans-Jochen Vogel had credited the Greens with asking the right questions—but giving the wrong answers. The SPD's dilemma was how to co-opt the policy appeal of the postmaterialist Greens without alienating its traditional materialist working-class supporters. The March 1985 Dortmund special congress, Arbeit und Umwelt, indicated that there was growing trade union support for new SPD formulas that combined the issues of employment and environment. Party leaders argued that the development of environmentally benign technologies would promote long-term growth of West German industry. SPD spokesperson Volker Hauff dismissed the Greens as being incapable of ecological reform politics because of their anti-industrialism.[23]

The Bundestag Greens were determined to compete with the SPD across the full range of issues. An early discovery by Green deputies was the programmatic deficits of their party, particularly in regard to economic policy. By rejecting fundamental opposition, Green deputies were obliged to work out concrete proposals as credible steps toward the Green utopia. However, media coverage, such as of the *Kindersex* episode during the 1985 North Rhine–Westphalia campaign (in which a proposal for decriminalization of sexual relations between children and adults turned up in the Greens' state election program), nicely reinforced the SPD's argument that the Greens were irresponsible.

The national push for a more programmatic party came from within the Greens' parliamentary group, not from the party leadership. A cluster of deputies and staff assistants felt that the Greens had to move beyond the negativism of protests to present positive alternatives in order to expose the shortfalls of the major parties' policies. They saw the Greens' early programs as catalogs of demands lacking in the policy integration necessary to cope with their changing political environment. The party could no longer avoid the tough questions of costs, trade-offs, and time-tables if it was going to project the image of a responsible political force. The concept of *Umbau* (reconstruction) appealed to many as the way to differentiate the Greens' radical reformism from the merely reparative ideas of the established parties and to counter the criticism that the Greens were reckless utopians who favored the collapse of industrial society.

Das Umbauprogramm

Throughout the Umbauprogramm's formulation, the initiative remained with the Bundestag Greens' working group on economic issues. At its core were four deputies—two prominent *Realos*, one self-declared *Neutralo*, and an ecosocialist (though not of the Hamburg GAL variety). The Greens' left wing reacted suspiciously to the Umbauprogramm as some sort of *Realo* plot to reconstruct the party, not society. Party cospeaker Rainer Trampert attempted unsuccessfully to derail the special congress to discuss the draft program. It reached the agenda of the May 1986 Hanover party conference but because of complaints about the lack of time for local activists to discuss its provisions and because of the conference's over-loaded agenda consideration was delayed until the September 1986 Nu-remberg party conference. There the amended Umbauprogramm was passed by an overwhelming majority. The Umbauprogramm is an action program focused upon concrete steps within a four- to five-year time frame. It carries over various concepts from earlier Green programs but differs by striving to demonstrate the technical and financial feasibility of proposals in the near future. It culminates in an inventory of state measures and an accounting of financial resources.

The authors of the Umbauprogramm saw Kohl's government as subor-dinating all policy problems, including mass unemployment and environ-mental destruction, to the growth and competitiveness of the corporate sector. However, their main target was the SPD, whose reparative policies addressing unemployment and environment were indicative of its unwill-ingness to consider radical change. According to the Umbauprogramm, the economic system of industrial capitalism must be replaced—step by step—with one that is "ecological, social, and grassroots democratic" and whose overriding goal would *not* be economic growth.[24] Work would be shortened, redefined, and redirected. The consumptive life-style would be transcended. New forms of social ownership and democratic planning would be developed. Its basic theme is that steps can be taken toward the alternative economy now.

The program focuses on twenty-five domestic problem areas. Most of these ideas are hardly new for the Greens, but their more structured treatment contrasts with earlier programs. In some areas, such as industrial conversion, state subsidization of private enterprises would be employed. In other areas, such as toxic waste, state interventionism would be greatly extended. Yet a guaranteed minimum income would represent a less interventionist state. Democratic planning and social ownership are advocated for coping with particular problems and a series of new taxes are envisaged elsewhere to steer the behavior of private enterprises. A cornerstone for the reconstruction of industrial society, referred to in virtually all areas, is the extension of the participatory rights of the citizenry.

The Umbauprogramm is sensitive to the likely effects of proposed changes, particularly upon employment. The Greens support the restructuring of the steel industry as autonomous decentralized public enterprises responsive to economic *and* ecological efficiency. The chemical industry would remain in private hands though within a tough framework of state regulation. The Greens take a distinctly conservative approach to the new communication technologies, automation, and computerization. They carry over numerous proposals from earlier programs: decentralization of energy, extension of public transportation, humanization of health care, and promotion of alternative enterprises. What stands out is the nonideological eagerness to make skillful use of an entire range of state instruments, from public ownership to pollution taxes.

During the formulation of the Umbauprogramm, Christian Schmidt of the Hamburg GAL was its most vocal critic. He saw it as a first step toward a common government program with the SPD. Schmidt argued that the Umbauprogramm too readily accepts the private economic structure in many areas and that the Greens' programs must be fundamentally different from those of the SPD, not merely outpromise them. From the viewpoint of the leftist Alternative List, the Umbauprogramm was too cautious, too preoccupied with redistribution rather than with the control of production and less important than the more radical program for the 1987 Bundestag election.[25]

Das Wahlprogramm 1987

The May 1986 Hanover party conference, where ecosocialists and fundamentalists constituted the absolute majority, passed the 1987 election program. Compared with the Umbauprogramm, its rhetoric is sharper and its scope is wider, covering foreign policies, but its provisions are less detailed. The authors of the Wahlprogramm placed ecological and economic policy as the *last* of five policy sections, which is striking because polls have indicated that environmental protection is where the Greens have been seen as the most competent. This sixteen-page section incorporated ideas from the Sindelfingen 1983 program and the draft Umbauprogramm. The motion of Baden-Württemberg moderates to incorporate even more concrete proposals from the latter was narrowly defeated in Hanover. Nevertheless, this section concludes that both capitalist and real socialist systems are unsuitable models for economic reconstruction.

The media's coverage concentrated on the radicalism of the 1987 Wahlprogramm, particularly its foreign and defense policies. The Greens make the case for West Germany's disarming unilaterally, getting out of NATO, recognizing fully the existence of two German states, and mobilizing all forms of civil disobedience in the pursuit of peace. The authors of the 1987 program see the danger of war as rooted in the U.S. pursuit of military superiority over the USSR. The program stresses that NATO is "not reformable"[26] and is incompatible with peacemaking; it notes (but does not dwell on) Soviet intervention in Afghanistan and the struggle of democratic oppositions in East Europe. Its fourteen-point plan advocates the immediate and unconditional removal of Pershing II and cruise missiles, the end of West German involvement in "star wars" missile defense research, the withdrawal of atomic and chemical weapons, the removal of NATO strike forces from the Federal Republic, and so forth.

The 1987 Wahlprogramm also calls for the immediate shutdown of all West German nuclear power plants. Party cospeaker Trampert declared at the conference that all the atomic parties—also the SPD—are the Greens' opponents. The *Realo*-dominated Hesse Greens at this time were the coalition partners of the SPD. The Hanover party conference resolved that the Hesse Greens must end the coalition unless concrete steps toward nuclear shutdowns by the end of the legislative period were agreed to by the SPD. The Hesse coalition was to break up in early 1987 over nuclear policy differences.

The Wahlprogramm upgrades women's issues. An entire section is devoted to *Frauenpolitik* (women's issues), which is subtitled, "We want everything!" Women's issues received nearly twice as much attention in the 1987 federal program as they did in the 1980 program.[27] At the Hanover conference the leftist and feminist viewpoints of the federal working group (BAG) on women's policy prevailed over more moderate viewpoints of the Hesse autonomous women's group. The Greens' program declared, "We are making women's policy not family policy. Women as human beings stand at the center of our political work, not women in their function as wives or mothers." The goal is a new society without the repression, domination, force, and role definition directed against women that have characterized West Germany's patriarchal society.

The Greens demand the abolition of section 218 of the West German legal code, which restricts abortion. Although it acknowledges the conflict between the life of the fetus and the life of the mother, the program comes down squarely on the side of the woman's right of self-determination without the legal pressures of the state. This feminist stand contrasts with the ambivalence of the Greens' initial position on abortion in the 1980 federal program. The Greens advance proposals to maximize the opportunities of women outside of traditional housework and child-care roles. They demand a minimal 50 percent quota of all training and work positions in employment areas where women are underrepresented. They demand equal pay for equal work. They advocate women commissioners at local, Land, and federal levels to make sure that antidiscrimination law is enforced. They favor the neutrality of tax codes for married and single people. They believe that the state should, however, support various self-help projects, such as autonomous women's houses. Laws regarding rape should be rewritten to include punishment of marital rape. Homosexuality and heterosexuality are declared to be "equivalent forms of sexual orientation."

Though the preamble of the 1987 election program reiterates the four pillars of 1980, feminist principles had in effect become the fifth pillar of the Greens. In September 1986, the Greens' Nuremberg conference changed the party charter to require a 50 percent quota of women on the candidate lists of the party and left open the possibility of all-female lists, as in Hamburg 1986–1987. Furthermore, women should hold at least half of all party leadership and staff positions, and women delegates were given veto rights over policy resolutions particularly pertinent to their interests. Eva Kolinsky concludes that on closer inspection such policies were actually halfhearted concessions to the feminist faction within the party.[28]

The Greens went to the electorate on January 25, 1987, on the basis of a program that reminded supporters that there was *no* alternative to the Greens. The overall goal of the Greens, in contrast to the old parties, remained the democratization of society. This would require the direct participation of citizens from below, as in initiatives and referenda, to deepen the parliamentary-representative democracy of the Federal Republic. To counter the power-oriented old parties, beholden to vested interests, the Greens reassert their eagerness to utilize parliamentary and extraparliamentary means to advance toward a new society.

Policy Debates and Factional Manifestos

After the weak electoral gains of the Lower Saxony Greens in June 1986, which *Realos* blamed on the radical rhetoric at the Hanover conference, the balance of power tipped to the side of the parliament-oriented members at the Nuremberg conference. Not only was the Umbauprogramm finally passed, but the door was also left open for SPD-Green cooperation, if together they could form a majority after the federal election. However, the SPD followed a centrist strategy, distancing itself from the Greens. This allowed the latter's contending factions to close ranks during the campaign. The Greens, despite the decline of the new social movements since the early 1980s, scored significant gains in the 1987 election. Yet, as Werner Hülsberg observed, "the Green Party lacks an inner equilibrium. The excitement of an unexpected electoral success is followed by inner-party strife and fierce factional battles."[29] Even the party consensus about defense policy had begun to erode. Although the *Realos'* origins are on the left of West German politics, second thoughts about the "get-out-of NATO" policy had developed among them during the mid-1980s. They saw the verbal radicalism of the ecosocialist and fundamentalist majority as no substitute for responsible policy formulation. *Realos* envisaged a more gradual process of bloc dissolution and sought common ground with the SPD left wing. After the 1987 election, prominent *Realos* began speaking out against immediate withdrawal from NATO. Joschka Fischer warned that "a unilaterally-declared West German withdrawal from NATO would only heighten tensions, lead to the revival of the ill-fated German *Sonderweg*" (special way).[30] A bloc-free West Germany would mean instability, facilitating the revival of German nationalism.

The Umbauprogramm makes the case for realistic short- and medium-term steps toward an alternative society. Its implication is that the Greens cannot simply wait for the imminent collapse of industrial society, which would galvanize the masses behind the radical demands of the party. However, fundamentalists fear that Green reforms could help industrial capitalism save itself without eliminating socioeconomic inequity. Therefore they have shunned technical details and have advanced absolutist demands—to shut off nuclear power right now—to counter the "Socialdemocratization" of the Green party. The proposals of the Umbauprogramm would reallocate one-third of the federal budget, hardly an incremental change, yet budget figures lend themselves to bargaining. Successful engagement with the complexities of economic policies also implies a more professional leadership, which directly clashes with the movement-oriented ethos of the *Fundis*.

The Greens' programmatic emphasis on the representation of women as candidates soon resulted in historic high percentages of women within their parliamentary groups and party leaderships. However, at the Dortmund conference in 1987 policy disagreements among Green women sharpened. In general terms, there have long been frictions between those interpreting feminism as pursuit of equality within the current system and others interpreting it as pursuit of an alternative system. The latter viewpoint has been taken by the federal working group (BAG) on women's issues. In 1987 its leaders were challenged by the Mothers' Manifesto group, which had "rediscovered" woman's traditional role of mother. In the words of the "Mothers," "It is high time that other women or men stopped instructing mothers in how to plan their lives. . . . To demand scope and room for mothers does not mean weakening the women's movement. It does also not mean excluding men."[31] The authors of the manifesto targeted what they consider know-it-alls—childless feminists and single career women—as obstacles. On the other side, the supporters of the women's BAG attacked the conservative implications of the Mothers' Manifesto.

A number of prominent Green women parliamentarians who had formerly backed the women's BAG signed the Mothers' Manifesto. Although the issues are complex, one can find some correspondence in the two sides of the disputes over women's policy with the realists and fundamentalists in the strategy debate. The "Mothers'" campaign sought to broaden the Green constituency by appealing to nonfeminists with such concrete demands as neighborhood mothers' centers. In contrast, as Michael Hoexter observes, "the Women's Working Group and the 'Fundis' maintain their distance from this 'common sense' and hope that by confronting conventional wisdom they will change it."[32] In 1988, radical feminists together with fundamentalists and ecosocialists (of the Hamburg GAL) constituted the majority in the federal executive committee.

In the late 1980s, Green factionalism, driven by the conflicting power and protest imperatives, overshadowed programmatic development. It was no media exaggeration to speak of a crisis of party identity. The Aufbruch (Awakening) '88 moderates favored a Green party that was pluralistic and stood above left-right ideological lines. They saw no future for the Greens as a small party to the left of the SPD. Although largely preoccupied with structural reform, the authors of the Aufbruch manifesto put human rights and ecology at the core of Green politics.

The 1988 manifesto of the *Realos* emphasized restructuring of the party to make it a more effective organization for carrying out reforms via parliamentary politics. The *Realos* rejected the "warehouse catalog" of demands approach to programmatic development; political priorities must be set and "conscious compromise" must be a foundation for Green politics.[33] The leading *Realos* had in mind a professionalized party that appealed to the new middle classes and worked as the junior partner of the SPD. Some *Realos* even spoke out as converts to ecocapitalism.

The small but articulate group of Green ecolibertarians has long argued that ecology, grass-roots democracy, and the free market go together. They hold a misalliance of state power and private capital responsible for the superindustrialization that threatens both humanity and nature. Their manifesto portrayed both *Realos* and *Fundis* as sharing leftist predispositions toward state interventionism.[34] According to the ecolibertarians, the Greens must become an ecological reform party that would appeal to the voters of the SPD *and* the CDU. They advocate an ecological humanism that is based on the decentralization of the economy and of the state.

The June 1988 Perspectives Congress marked the emergence of the nondogmatic Left (later Linken-Forum) as a distinctive faction within the Greens. Although sharing the anticapitalist viewpoint of the GAL ecosocialists, the nondogmatic Left differed by advocating positive steps (including tactical compromises) toward changing the extraparliamentary balance of societal forces to support radical reformism. In contrast to the *Realos*, the nondogmatic Left portrayed themselves as looking beyond parliamentary politics and not being fixated on governmental participation per se. From their viewpoint, the *Realos* and *Fundis* shared equal blame for the Greens' inability after the mid-1980s to regain the political initiative on major policy issues.[35]

Although the Greens' ideological pluralism could be seen as a creative plus in the early 1980s, it became an obstacle in responding to the rapidly changing political environment of the late 1980s. No party consensus about strategy was to emerge from the Second Perspectives Congress of November 1989, which was attended by representatives from East German citizen movements. Green activism seemed to them largely misspent in intraparty competition. For East Germans, the West German Greens were both a positive and negative model.

East German Green Programs

The Green party of the GDR was founded on November 26, 1989, by about 150 environmentalists. Hardly could they claim to be the parliamentary arm of the citizen movements, which at their peak mobilized hundreds of thousands supporters. These diverse movements incorporated in their programs many of the environmental, peace, human rights, and grass-roots democratic themes that are found in the West German Greens' programs of the 1980s. But, in contrast to many of the West Germans, East German activists harbored no ideological illusions about the performance of socialism. The founders of the East German Green party placed themselves alongside all forces seeking democracy and freedom through radical reforms. Their preliminary declaration of November 6, 1989, described the Green party of the GDR as "ecological, feminist, and nonviolent."[36] Shortly after their founding, the East German Greens declared their support for a confederation of two sovereign German states committed to nonaggression, ecological priorities, sexual equality, and antifascism. Thereafter the pace of East German political change was so rapid and the resources of the new Green party so sparse that it could formulate only a framework program for the March 1990 East German parliamentary election. The program's basic theme is that ecological catastrophe looms unless there are fundamental changes in the pattern of production and consumption. Although equal space is allocated to ecological and social policies, the program deals first with the threats to the foundations of life from the shortsighted power and profit motives of industrial society. Its specific environmental proposals could have easily been lifted from those of the Baden-Württemberg Greens. Much of the social section also echoes the programmatic themes of the West German Greens.

There are provisions shaped by experiences under the SED party-state. The program views neither democratic centralism nor parliamentarism based on parties as sufficient for democracy. Social policy should include rent controls and social subsidies. The program favors maintenance of agricultural cooperatives. In short, there is a general suspiciousness about market mechanisms without restrictions. The East German Greens advocate "a solidarity, grassroots democratic, multicultural, and nonviolent society."[37] In foreign policy, they declare that the GDR must not become a direct or indirect member of NATO. They view German unification as interlinked with European unification, which is premised on bloc dissolution and total disarmament.

After their weak showing in the March 1990 elections, the East German Greens joined forces with the citizen movements of Bündnis 90 in the Volkskammer (East German Parliament) as a parliamentary group and later as an alliance for the all-German elections. Some West German Greens preferred to work with the broader citizen movements rather than with the small Green party in East Germany. But many East German citizen activists found troublesome the West German Greens' more ideological approach to politics. Bowing (some reluctantly) to electoral realities, five citizen movements along with the East German Greens agreed to a common electoral platform with the West German Greens in autumn 1990.

The electoral platform does not supercede the programs of the six allies, whose separate identities are to be respected. In its enumerative style, the platform emphasizes the alliance's goal of a society characterized by solidarity, ecology, radical democracy, emancipation, feminism, nonviolence, and cultural diversity. Its eight pages provide scant opportunity for details on implementation. The authors steer clear of ideologically loaded terms that might disrupt formal consensus; for example, "capitalism" is not explicitly attacked. Although the old GDR is in no way defended, the platform dwells only on the dark side of German reunification, suggesting that its net outcome will be negative in all policy areas. The economic oppression of the command economy has been replaced by that of the profit economy. The SED party-state has been replaced by a de facto Grand Coalition. The East German democratic revolution of 1989 and 1990 has been betrayed by power-hungry party elites determined to carry out the annexation of the GDR, whatever the costs. The alliance presents its common platform as the only alternative to the major parties. To halt the destruction of nature, there must be a fundamental change in the ruling economic system. Germany must be totally demilitarized (though this can be accomplished in stages). There must be massive financial support for the socioeconomic transformation of the former East Germany by taxing the rich and cutting the military budget. Furthermore, the platform declares, "The structure of representative democracy and the emanicipation of citizens have proven to be contradictory."[38] There must be a new all-German constitution to be ratified by popular referendum. The platform endorses the full agenda of the women's movement, including child support, abortion rights, and quotas. It takes a stand for the human rights of German social minorities, such as homosexuals and foreign workers, and for the exploited nations of East Central Europe and especially of the Third World.

Das Wahlprogramm 1990

The West German Greens declare, "Green is essential—Green is doable!" in the preamble to their own 1990 electoral program.[39] They once again present themselves as the real alternative. But self-righteousness is shunned: "We are not better human beings and we don't have ready answers for all questions." However, the crisis of industrial society has worsened and necessitates nothing short of radical rethinking. From the Greens' viewpoint, the collapse of real socialism hardly legitimates capitalism as the best of all possible worlds. And the Greens reject all forms of power and hegemonic politics at home and abroad in favor of the democratization and pacification of social life.

In contrast to the 1987 program, the 1990 electoral program's first and largest section deals with environmental policies. The threat to world climate is given top priority in this section. Other environmental proposals have been largely replayed from earlier programs. The 1990 program embraces diverse mechanisms to implement its objectives. It does not get into price tags, except for indicating that 1 percent of the GNP should go into an international climate fund to compensate Third World countries for not exploiting their rain forests.

The Greens' foreign and defense policies emphasize long-standing demands for unilateral disarmament, conversion of military production, and "social defense" as a replacement for the German armed forces. They reject both NATO and a military role for the European Community. Special concern is expressed about the danger of Eastern Europe becoming an economic colony of the West. The Greens favor the development of a new social structure in the former Communist states as well as a more just world economic system.

In contrast to the common platform, the Greens' electoral program is more explicitly anticapitalist. For example, in their lengthy women's policy section, the Greens declare themselves in favor of "a noncapitalist and nonpatriarchal society." The Greens favor new social and economic councils to democratize decisionmaking at all levels. Their social policies include demands for a six-hour workday and a guaranteed minimum income for all.

The 1990 electoral program takes a clear stand for "multicultural democracy," which grows out of an appreciation of the positive learning experience of cultural diversity. Foreign residents should have the right to vote in all elections. Asylum seekers, whether they come for political or economic reasons, should have the right to stay. The Greens reiterate their stand for equal rights for the aged, the handicapped, and homosexuals. Overall, though relative emphases may vary, there is a basic continuity of policy concerns with those of Green programs of the 1980s.

In a campaign overshadowed by materialist concerns about German unification, the Greens sought to dodge this main national issue by emphasizing the global issue of looming climatic catastrophe. Late in the campaign, an apprehensive Green party leadership advanced a Ten Point Emergency Program to mobilize members and supporters. It included calls for massive transfers of funds from the defense budget to create jobs in depressed areas (the new Länder), taxes to protect the atmosphere, rent controls, and the abolition of section 218 of the criminal code, which restricts abortions.[40] Although such programmatic appeals had rallied Green voters in 1983 and 1987, this time they failed to deter last-minute defections to the SPD, whose chancellor candidate had waged a reformist campaign incorporating many Green themes.

Conclusion

From the outset the West German Greens have aggregated the demands of diverse groups disillusioned with the responsiveness of established elites to the crises of advanced industrial society. Although critics tried to discount the Greens as a one-issue party, this charge was inaccurate even during the formative period of 1979 to 1980. Furthermore, the Greens were launched without a unifying ideological model. Some ideological heterogeneity within parties is the rule. But in the case of the Greens, their heterogeneity was so great that the party's identity was defined negatively by shared protest against the major parties' policies, structures, and styles.

Nonetheless, the small Green party provided a radical alternative to the postwar policy consensus of West German party elites that could hardly be ignored. In contrast to all other parties, the Greens, without reservation, assigned higher priority to environmental protection than to economic growth. Furthermore, the Greens strongly supported unilateral disarmament, withdrawal from NATO, and recognition of two sovereign Germanies. In words *and* deeds, the Greens embraced the cause of women's rights as well as those of various societal underdogs. Although their specific proposals were often attacked from all angles, the major West German parties were by the mid-1980s selectively borrowing Green themes, as the East German citizen movements were to do in 1989 and 1990. In this chapter we have been preoccupied with the programs adopted at the federal level. Yet in most state and local parties, activists also took programmatic development seriously.

An overview turns up more continuity than change in the policy orientation of Green federal programs. Yet there have been changes in the priority of ecology in the Greens' agenda: The Greens of the late 1970s placed ecology at the top of the agenda, then during the 1980s other issues became coequals in treatment, and then in 1990 ecology resumed its top position. Although the level of emphasis on foreign and defense policies was more steady, the programmatic emphasis on women's equality steadily grew during the 1980s. The Greens began the decade with mixed views on the role of the market and the state in the economy and ended the decade that way, despite the collapse of East European socialist systems.

The Umbauprogramm of 1986 is noteworthy because it represents a step beyond simply enumerating demands. Its authors attempted to outline an integrated plan of action linking short-term needs and long-term goals. In doing so, they did not shy away from budgetary considerations, and they ended up being nonideological about means of policy implementation. Yet the Umbauprogramm's mixed reception bears witness to the factional divisions over the party's political strategy in the late 1980s. Why emphasize the practicalities of one's proposals unless one is prepared to work for their implementation through parliamentary politics? Strong voices among the Greens still preferred verbal radicalism and the strategy of extraparliamentary protest and fundamental opposition.

Because of the lack of party consensus (and the weakness of the party organization), factional leaders and special interest groups had the leeway to contest the public meaning of the Greens' program. In the words of one critical observer, "With factions and media personalities firmly in charge of the issues . . . the Green party . . . seems little more than a convenient label for a disjointed and divided assortment of policies."[41] An aspiring programmatic party must not only develop its policy alternatives but also communicate to the electorate an image of political credibility. In December 1990 a sizeable number of Green supporters found this lacking and abstained or voted for the SPD. Yet the tumultuous departure of the vocal minority of fundamentalists in spring 1991 has simplified the Greens' internal process of consensus-building on political strategy. Their greater challenge will probably be the external one of working out a common understanding of programmatic means and ends with the Eastern German citizen movements.

Notes

1. Cited by C. F. Padfield and A. Byrne, *British Constitution: Made Simple*, 7th ed. (London: Heineman, 1987), pp. 34–35.

2. Geoffrey K. Roberts, *An Introduction to Comparative Politics* (London: Edward Arnold, 1986), p. 72.

3. Klaus von Beyme, *Political Parties in Western Democracies* (New York: St. Martin's Press, 1985), p. 13.

4. Willard A. Mullins, "On the Concept of Ideology in Political Science," *American Political Science Review* 66, no. 2 (June 1972):510.

5. von Beyme, *Political Parties in Western Democracies*, p. 29.

6. Joachim Raschke, *Krise der Grünen: Bilanz und Neubeginn* (Marburg: Schüren, 1991), pp. 22–25.

7. Mostafa Rejai, *Political Ideologies: A Comparative Approach* (Armonk, N.Y.: Sharpe, 1991), p. 9.

8. Jean Blondel, *Political Parties: A Genuine Case for Discontent?* (London: Wildwood House, 1978), pp. 121–126.

9. Leon D. Epstein, *Political Parties in Western Democracies* (New York: Praeger, 1967), pp. 262–267, 287.

10. Kay Lawson, *The Comparative Study of Political Parties* (New York: St. Martin's Press, 1967), pp. 15, 137.

11. von Beyme, *Political Parties in Western Democracies*, pp. 364–365.

12. Rudolf van Hüllen, *Ideologie und Machtkampf bei den Grünen* (Bonn: Bouvier, 1990), pp. 19–20.

13. Herbert Kitschelt, *The Logics of Party Formation: Ecological Politics in Belgium and West Germany* (Ithaca: Cornell University Press, 1989), p. 51.

14. Robert Rohrschneider, "New Politics in Old Parties: Environmental Issues in Four West European Party Systems." Paper presented at 1990 Annual Meeting of the American Political Science Association, San Francisco.

15. van Hüllen, *Ideologie und Machtkampf*, p. 115.

16. Ibid., p. 116.

17. Ibid., p. 224.

18. Ibid., p. 277.

19. Die Grünen, *Bundesprogramm* [English translation] (Bonn: Die Grünen, n.d.), p. 22.

20. Ibid., p. 19.

21. Hans-Georg Betz, "Strange Love? How the Greens Began to Love NATO," *German Studies Review* 12, no. 3 (October 1989):487–505.

22. Die Grünen, *Sinvoll arbeiten—solidarischen leben: Gegen Arbeitslosigkeit und Sozialabbau* (Bonn: Die Grünen, 1983), p. 3.

23. SPD, "Für eine ökologische Modernisierung der Volkswirtschaft," *Politik*, no. 7 (July 1985):2–3.

24. Die Grünen, *Umbau der Industriegesellschaft: Schritte zur Überwindung von Erwerblosigkeit, Armut und Umweltzerstörung* (Bonn: Die Bundesgeschaftsstelle, 1986), p. 9.

25. Interview with members of the Berlin Alternative List in Rathaus Schöneberg, Berlin, June 29–30, 1987.

26. *Bundestagswahl Programm 1987: Farben bekennen* (Bonn: Die Grünen, 1986), p. 31.

27. van Hüllen, *Ideologie und Machtkampf*, p. 445.

28. Eva Kolinsky, "Women in the Green Party," in *The Greens in West Germany: Organisation and Policy Making*, Eva Kolinsky, ed. (Oxford: Berg, 1989), p. 217.

29. Werner Hülsberg, *The German Greens: A Social and Political Profile* (London: Verso, 1988), p. 212.

30. Quoted in Betz, "Strange Love? How the Greens Began to Love NATO," p. 497.

31. *Müttermanifest 1987*, p. 2, quoted in Kolinsky, "Women in the Green Party," p. 210.

32. Michael Hoexter, "It's Not Easy Being Green," *New Politics* 2, no. 1 (Summer 1988):110–112.

33. "Sein oder Nichtsein: Manifestentwurf der 'Realo,'" *Die Grünen* [Wochenzeitung], no. 28 (July 16, 1988):4–5.

34. "Von der Grösse des Kleinen: Das Manifest der ökolibertären," *Die Grünen* [Wochenzeitung], no. 30/31 (July 30, 1988):4–5.

35. "Illusionslose Bestandsaufnahme: Thesenpapier von 'undogmatischen' Linken," *Die Grünen* [Wochenzeitung], no. 29 (July 23, 1988):4–5. Radical feminists, fundamentalists (Frankfurt variety), and ecosocialists (Hamburg variety) declined to develop their own manifestos.

36. "Erklärung der Gründungsinitiative für eine Grüne Partei in der DDR," in *Die Opposition in der DDR*, Gerhard Rein, ed. (Berlin: Wichern Verlag, 1989), p. 120.

37. Hallenser Rahmenprogramm der Grünen Partei DDR (February 10, 1990), p. 9.

38. Die Grünen/Bündnis 90 Wahlprogramm (September 1990), p. vii.

39. Die Grünen, *Das Programm zur 1. gesamtdeutschen Wahl 1990* (Bonn: Die Grünen, 1990), pp. 4–8.

40. "Greens Adopt 10-Point-Plan for December Elections," *The Week in Germany* (German Information Center), November 9, 1990, pp. 1–2.

41. Eva Kolinsky, "Introduction," in Kolinsky, *The Greens in West Germany*, p. 8.

7

Parliamentary Politics
and the Alternative Party

FROM AN AMERICAN TEXTBOOK PERSPECTIVE, political parties are "tripartite systems of interactions" encompassing the party organization, the party-in-government, and the party-in-the electorate.[1] Ordinarily the ideological and programmatic orientations of U.S. party activists end up being subordinated to the pragmatic quest for a broad electoral coalition. And party candidates as incumbent public-office holders typically enjoy wide autonomy from the party organization—inside and outside of government—in deciding how to vote on policy issues. Political scientists have listed policymaking as one of the functions of political parties, but traditionally the U.S. majority party has not operated as a responsible party-in-government committed to implementing its electoral platform. In West European parliamentary systems, the norms (and sanctions) of party discipline have been generally stronger. In some countries, they have been so strong that critics bemoan the decline of parliamentary democracy and the rise of "party-ocracy." In Western Europe, the party-in-the-electorate has hardly been the factor that it has been in U.S. politics; symptomatically, there are no primaries in these systems.

Particularly on the left side of the European party spectrum, the party organization has sought to control the party-in-government (in-parliament) so that the programmatic views of party activists will be translated into actions. Yet early mass movement-parties, such as the German SPD, after their electoral breakthroughs soon encountered the normalizing forces of parliamentary institutions. A couple of generations later, the Greens sought to develop as the model of decentralized participatory democracy both inside and outside of Parliament. However, by the mid-1980s, the Greens found themselves divided on how to respond as a movement-party to the "parliamentary embrace."

As a party becomes "parliamentarized," one would expect its parliamentary group to grow more independent of party activists, to be more willing to bargain and compromise, to play a larger role in developing party programs, and to be more preoccupied with maximizing votes in parliamentary elections.[2] Radical parties that win parliamentary seats do not inevitably become "parliamentarized." For example, the French Communist party after decades in Parliament exhibits few of these characteristics. A multitude of factors obviously shape the outcome of the process. Furthermore, because parties are not unitary actors, a party can become "semiparliamentarized," as the Greens became during the 1980s despite their founders' intentions.

In terms of the U.S. tripartite scheme, the Greens at the outset attributed the highest place to their grass-roots sector, the party-in-the-movement (rather than party-in-the-electorate), followed at some distance by the party organization and lastly by the party-in-government. This chapter begins with an overview of the German parliamentary system, reviews the Greens' early perspectives on parliamentary democracy, describes the organization and activities of Green state and federal parliamentary groups, and assesses the impacts of the alternative party on the parliamentary system and vice versa.

German Parliamentarism

The parliamentary system of the Federal Republic has become well institutionalized since 1949. In contrast to earlier federal parliaments, the Bundestag has not only endured but also has enjoyed strong popular support compared to some other Western parliaments.[3] Loewenberg's landmark study of the Bundestag detected both a rising class of professional politicians among the membership and a bureaucratization of the legislative process stemming from institutional norms that emphasize specialization.[4] Bernhard Badura and Jürgen Reese's longitudinal study found that new deputies tend to internalize prevailing norms during their first term.[5] The Bundestag and the Landtag are working parliaments with well-established specialized standing committees and subcommittees, which the parties' own specialized working groups (Arbeitskreise) parallel. Winfried Steffani concludes, "The work of the specialized committees . . . is in final analysis controlled by the parties represented in the Bundestag."[6] However, William Paterson and David Southern maintain that because of a high degree of membership continuity the standing committees develop a "sense of identity" and "a spirit of cooperation" that moderates partisanship.[7] Although the federal government typically gets its bills passed, most bills are subject to amendment during the legislative process. Nelson Polsby labels the Bundestag a "modified arena" legislature because of trends toward more legislative independence and classifies the British House of Commons as an "arena" legislature, which is merely the formal setting for the confrontations of electoral parties.[8] Because the German deputies rarely initiate legislation, in contrast to members of the U.S. Congress, the Bundestag can be labeled reactive, but it is not powerless. Its deputies utilize well-established devices, such as plenary debates, parliamentary questions, interpellations, and investigative committees, to represent constituents and to constrain the executive. Compared to British members of Parliament (MPs), German deputies have been generously paid and endowed with staff assistants.

The organizing forces of West German federal and state parliaments have been the *Fraktionen* (parliamentary groups). Only with *Fraktion* status do a party's parliamentary deputies receive seats on committees and on the Council of Elders, participate fully in parliamentary proceedings, and obtain significant financial resources. SPD, CDU/CSU, and FDP party leaders have tended to hold parliamentary seats concurrently, which has worked to smooth relationships between the party organization and the parliamentary group. The hierarchical power structure of the major parties' parliamentary groups has limited the role of their backbenchers.

Within the West German parliamentary system, the deputies of the majority party or coalition elect the chancellor (minister-president at the state level) and support the proposals of the chancellor's government in committee and plenary sessions; opposition deputies monitor policy implementation and present policy alternatives. Studies have found two patterns of opposition within Western parliamentary systems: "Competitive" opposition seeks to turn out the government, shuns cooperation, wages an electoral campaign in parliament, focuses on plenary activities, and provides a comprehensive critique of the government "Cooperative" opposition seeks opportunities for coalitions with the governing party, offers case-by-case cooperation, focuses on committee work, and provides no comprehensive critique.[9] Manfred Friedrich's study of opposition behavior in the Bundestag from 1949 to 1974 found that cooperative opposition has generally been the rule and competitive opposition the exception.[10] A recent study reports that the majority of all acts proposed between 1972 and 1983 passed unanimously at the third reading.[11]

The federal dimension of the German parliamentary system reinforces the inclination toward cooperative opposition because an opposition party in the Bundestag is likely to be in power in some states and perhaps even control the majority of the votes within the Bundesrat, the indirectly elected upper chamber. The federal government cannot ignore the *Land* governments because of the possibility of the Bundesrat's veto in vital areas and because of the pervasive role of the Länder in implementing federal laws. Within the Landtage there has been even stronger emphasis on cooperative opposition than in the Bundestag.

Parliamentary Democracy and the Greens

The Greens' criticism of prevailing political forms and practices in the early and mid-1980s caused their foes to label them as antidemocratic and/or antiparliamentary. Survey data do indicate that Green supporters have tended to trust parliamentary institutions much less than have the supporters of the established parties. However, the new party was not simply replaying the antiparliamentary themes of the old Extra-Parliamentary Opposition (APO). Rather, the intervening decade of local initiatives and new social movements had resulted in a new composite of views. As described in the Greens' federal program, *basisdemokratische* politics entails decentralization, direct democracy, self-administration, and involvement of those citizens directly affected by public policies. The program of the Hesse Greens cites the failure of representative democracy to defend citizens against the abusive powers of bureaucracy and interest groups. The program of the Baden-Württemberg Greens warns about the "incrustation" of the parliamentary system through bureaucratization, corruption, lack of separation between the executive and legislative branches, and the impenetrable planning process. Hamburg's more leftist Green Alternative List (GAL) declared its opposition to the "bourgeois-democratic state" and proclaimed its lack of illusions about the parliamentary route to emancipatory societal change.

Upon closer inspection, the Greens' early party documents and public pronouncements reveal two different viewpoints on the future of parliamentary democracy. One viewpoint envisages its total replacement by a radical democracy (through nonviolent means); the other, the maintenance of parliamentary institutions that are revitalized by direct democratic features. In other words, these Greens see themselves as the true defenders of democratic parliamentarism. Yet the overall gist of the Greens' programs has been to de-emphasize parliament in favor of new democratic forms.

The founders of the Greens embraced a double strategy of direct actions outside parliament and representative actions within parliament. In the late 1970s, they advanced numerous reasons for seeking parliamentary seats: to draw media attention, to set issues on the parliamentary agenda, to improve the resources of extraparliamentary groups, and to provide the opportunity of protest voting. Leftist critics warned that parliamentary involvement above the local level would absorb the energies of the movement. In 1982, the GAL recognized two future dangers: (1) the loss of contact between its parliamentary deputies and the movement and (2) the assimilation of established values by its deputies. Nevertheless, GAL leaders expressed confidence in grass-roots democratic controls over their elected parliamentary members.

According to the Greens' 1980 federal program, the core idea of their party, which differentiates it from the oligarchical power structures of the major parties, is the control of all party and public officeholders by the *Basis*. The 1984 program of the Baden-Württemberg Greens defines the *Basis* as the extraparliamentary movement. The Hesse Greens equate the *Basis* with the party's state assembly and steering committee (where movement groups would presumably be heard). The principle of *imperatives Mandat*, which compels Green deputies to follow the directives of the *Basis*, clashes with Article 38 of the Basic Law, which guarantees the independence of elected representatives from outside control. A German deputy may be expelled by the *Fraktion* for disobedience of policy resolutions but the deputy cannot be deprived of his or her seat in Parliament. An additional complication is that during intraparty disputes there have been various tactical interpretations of the meaning of the *Basis*, for example, the extraparliamentary movement(s), the party membership, the party activists, the party working groups, and the party electorate; in practice, Green deputies have referred to "the" *Basis*, which is most supportive of their views.

During the early 1980s, the orthodox model of the Greens as a new movement-party reflected the "two-leg" theory: The party is the free maneuvering leg of the movement in parliamentary activities and the other leg, the extraparliamentary *Basis*, is the more important and supporting leg of the Greens. In other words, the Greens must not become parliamentarized, as the older movement-party, the SPD, had become. Most Green activists maintained that the party should adhere to the role of fundamental opposition, that is, refusing both to compromise basic principles and to share overall governmental responsibility with other parties. In particular circumstances, fundamental opposition might involve disrupting parliamentary activities, boycotting parliamentary sessions, utilizing parliament as a forum, or participating in the details of parliamentary work.

The role of fundamental opposition becomes more difficult for a new party to maintain as its opportunity for holding the balance of parliamentary power grows and the expectations of its supporters for achieving concrete results increase. The interim position of toleration of a minority government in exchange for policy concessions becomes attractive. However, toleration at what price becomes the crucial question. By the mid-1980s, the Greens' *Realos* were eager to experiment with modes of cooperating with the SPD, including formal coalitions. Yet, when a party achieves full "coalition capability," its claim of being a new type of party loses credibility; it gets caught by the undertow of the representative system with all its incrementalism, logrolling, and accommodation.[12]

Landtag Greens

West German federalism provides opportunities for a new party (which receives at least 5 percent of the votes) to build up its resources by winning Landtag seats. The Greens (and the Alternative List) held parliamentary seats in six states before they won Bundestag seats in March 1983.[13] This section focuses on the pioneering experiences of Green parliamentary groups in five of these states. We exclude the Bremen Green List, which, as a loose alliance, elected four candidates to the city-state parliament in 1979 but distanced itself from the Greens in the early 1980s. The Greens have been the most regionally diverse of West Germany's political parties. Outsiders have commonly perceived Baden-Württemberg Greens as being relatively more ecological (green), less socialist, and more reformist than other Greens. In 1985, Baden-Württemburg Greens saw themselves as very heterogeneous, nonpolarized, and more balanced than Greens elsewhere.[14] Observers have located the Alternative List (AL) of Berlin on the left end of the spectrum of Green parties. In 1978, the Maoist KPD (Kommunistische Partei Deutschlands) was the prime mover behind the AL, but as the AL developed, it successfully incorporated diverse left-of-center activists. The Lower Saxony Greens have had a more heterogeneous social base than the urban AL. Also, their pragmatic leaders managed to retain moderates and conservatives from the GLU, which dissolved itself in 1980. The Hamburg Green Alternative List (GAL) can trace most of its activists back to the leftist-dominated Bunte Liste of the late 1970s. The Hesse Greens have been more heterogeneous than the GAL but less heterogeneous than the Baden-Württemberg Greens, some of whom have been prominent ecolibertarians. After the disastrous 1979 Hesse elections, which three competing Green lists contested, activists from citizen action groups, Frankfurt's alternative scene, and nondogmatic leftist groups joined together to launch the Greens as a state party.

The successful candidates of these diverse Green state parties entered somewhat different parliamentary institutions. For example, Green deputies in the more professional Hesse Landtag received significantly higher salaries and greater *Fraktion* resources than did Hamburg GAL deputies, who served in a city-state parliament that until 1991 maintained its part-time tradition (and pay). More important, in the early 1980s Green deputies entered state parliaments in which the political opportunity structure differed. In Baden-Württemberg and Lower Saxony, where solid governmental majorities existed, the Greens could not have much leverage in parliamentary politics. After the 1981 Berlin elections, the AL declined to tolerate a minority SPD government, but the question was already moot because FDP deputies had decided to support a CDU government. The GAL held the parliamentary balance of power after the June 1982 elections in Hamburg. Toleration negotiations with the SPD failed and early elections restored the SPD's majority. GAL activists admit that, realizing that the SPD would never submit to their demands, they used the negotiations to solidify the GAL's public image to the left of the SPD.[15] Although well primed for the role of fundamental opposition, the Hesse Greens' nine deputies in September 1982 found themselves in a Landtag where the SPD had lost its majority. Most were quickly "resocialized" by the opportunity to influence governmental policies. Between 1982 and 1985, their relationship with the SPD shifted from opposition to coalition and stimulated bitter intraparty factionalism.

Since 1980, Green parliamentary groups have ranged in size from five to seventeen deputies, which compares with the forty to sixty deputies of the typical CDU or SPD *Fraktion* at the state level. Green deputies have organized themselves nonhierarchically. The role of their annually (or biannually) elected chairperson has been internally to coordinate and externally to represent the *Fraktion*. Some parliamentary groups have had no qualms about electing (and reelecting) strong personalities as leaders. Other parliamentary groups have passed the job around their membership. Because of the small size of the *Fraktion*, the chairperson must also work as a policy specialist.

Green parliamentary groups have struggled to cover the details of committee work. Their deputies have usually found themselves as sole Green members on their assigned committees. Some deputies emphasized in interviews the importance of information from outside policy working groups (Landesarbeitgemeinschaften), but others pointed out that in certain areas there have been no policy working groups to draw upon so they have had to take the initiative.[16] Green parliamentary groups have employed small professional staffs (averaging about ten positions) to cover managerial as well as specialized policy work. The number of full-time paid staff positions of state party organizations has been even smaller.

Rotation of parliamentary deputies became one of the compulsory features of the Greens' "alternative parliamentarism" after the Baden-Württemberg Greens' parliamentary group had organized. Following sharp disputes between the Greens' parliamentary leader Wolf-Dieter Hasenclever and grass-roots activists in Baden-Württemberg over future midterm rotation, the six Green deputies declined to seek reelection. Ultimately, the state party assembly left rotation up to the district party of each deputy elected in 1984. Only three of nine district parties mandated rotation and one later changed its position to enable parliamentary leader Fritz Kuhn to remain in the parliament throughout the session.

Even though they had differences of opinion regarding the merits of rotation, AL deputies, elected in 1981, after two years gave up seats to those lower on the list, as did AL deputies elected in 1985. The Lower Saxony Greens decided as a compromise to require rotation of only half of their Landtag deputies in 1984. However, after five Green deputies agreed to rotate, the parliamentary majority blocked the partial rotation. Finally, a year later a Lower Saxony high-court decision allowed the deputies to give up their seats; in the interim, the issue disrupted the work of the *Fraktion*. The GAL rotated its eight seats in the Hamburg city-state parliament in 1984 and 1985. Feminists had protested because women were underrepresented among the *Nachrücker* (successors), but the female deputies defused the issue by declining to retain their seats. In 1988 the AL dropped midterm rotation, and in 1991 the GAL did likewise. In contrast to other Green Landtag groups, Hesse Greens integrated the successors into the work of the *Fraktion* as full-time staff assistants with voting rights and salaries comparable to those of the deputies. In a smooth transition, six Green deputies gave up their seats in April 1985 to become the assistants of their successors. After the formation of the "Red-Green" coalition, factionalism undermined the group's solidarity. The sole fundamentalist Green deputy voted against the Green minister and his colleagues in parliament, and the seventh deputy refused to give up his seat because his successor would sabotage the coalition's narrow majority.[17]

Although the Baden-Württemberg Greens created a scene by entering the Landtag in casual dress and with flowers in 1980, their six deputies (and the nine deputies who followed them in 1984) emphasized constructive involvement rather than symbolic media events throughout the term. They cooperated with other deputies in dealing with specific issues. As a small parliamentary opposition, the Greens were disproportionately active in introducing bills, initiating interpellations (*Kleine* and *Grosse Anfragen*), asking questions orally, proposing motions and amendments, and pushing for topical debates. Although other Green parliamentary groups have shown more flair than this group in exploiting opportunities for symbolic politics, all have followed the course of the Baden-Württemberg Greens in actively using parliamentary procedures. For example, from 1982 to 1986, the deputies of the Hamburg GAL—who constituted about 7 percent of the parliamentary membership—generated 37 percent of the proposed bills, 35 percent of the *Grosse Anfragen*, 41 percent of the *Kleine Anfragen*, 47 percent of the motions, and 37 percent of the topical debates.[18] Although the Hesse Greens' deputies also actively used parliamentary procedures, they alone could point to major pieces of legislation regarding waste disposal, decentralized energy, and computer data protection passed by SPD-Green majorities during the period from 1985 to 1987.

An imbalance of resources in favor of Green deputies has marked from the outset the relationship between state parliamentary groups and state party organizations. The party leadership simply has lacked the time and the staff to participate in the decisionmaking of the *Fraktion*. For example, during the mid-1980s the AL executive committee met weekly; the AL delegate council, biweekly; and the AL membership assembly, bimonthly, whereas the AL *Fraktion* operated virtually full-time. The media (and the citizens) tended to treat the *Fraktion* as the AL. It was more reachable, more acquainted with current issues, and more prepared to take the initiative. The Green politicians interviewed between 1985 and 1987 in five states agreed overwhelmingly that Green parliamentary groups have been largely autonomous.[19]

However, within the overall state party, the influence of the Landtag Greens has been limited by their own factional differences, by their sense of obligation to party resolutions, and by the suspicions of many activists (who have tended to be more radical than the Green deputies). On important questions, Landtag Greens must persuade the majorities of party bodies to approve their position. The Hesse Landtag Greens did not carry their Red-Green strategy against the party; they won the support of majorities at a series of party assemblies. Also, Green deputies have had their strategy vetoed by party bodies, as did the AL *Fraktion* when it advocated cooperation with the SPD before the 1985 Berlin elections.

The outcome was quite different when, to the pollsters' surprise, the January 1989 West Berlin elections produced a mathematical majority of seats for the SPD and the AL. In a just a few weeks, the AL had agreed to the SPD's preconditions for negotiations, had dropped its more utopian programmatic demands, and had signed a detailed 150-page coalition agreement, which, following the Hesse Greens' model of the mid-1980s, was hammered out with the SPD by a joint commission of AL deputies and party leaders.

Both parties' memberships overwhelmingly approved a formal coalition. During the 1985–1987 Red-Green coalition in Hesse, the Greens held only one ministerial post: *Realo* leader Joschka Fischer was environment minister. In contrast, the AL received three Senate (cabinet) posts and chose to fill them with experts who were neither members of the *Fraktion* nor of the party. The AL *Fraktion* sent representatives to cabinet meetings in order to facilitate feedback to the movement-party. However, local activists were soon complaining about a lack of grass-roots involvement in decisionmaking. Despite its amicable beginning, the SPD-AL coalition began to unravel over policy differences during 1990. Poor working relationships between the partners had brought the coalition to the brink of collapse. The SPD's unilateral response to the urban rioting of autumn 1990 pushed it over, all to the delight of the CDU, whose campaign equation was Red + Green = Chaos. Yet despite all the frictions, the AL indicated its willingness to renegotiate the coalition if the December 1990 election in Berlin produced a Red-Green majority. It didn't.

In contrast, the Lower Saxony Red-Green coalition, which emerged from the June 1990 state elections, has functioned more smoothly. Although the Greens received two cabinet posts, the SPD denied them the environmental ministry. Both partners endeavored to establish a working relationship that could weather political storms for the duration of the term. The same determination was evident between the SPD and the Greens in Hesse after the two parties received a narrow majority of Landtag seats in the January 1991 elections. The Greens obtained two cabinet posts, including that of environment minister (again held by Joschka Fischer). By spring 1991, all Landtag Greens had either participated in a coalition with the SPD or had expressed a willingness to negotiate one.[20] As state parliamentary strategies, both fundamental opposition to and toleration of a minority SPD government had lost their appeal to Greens.

How about other options? At the local level there have been scattered cases of CDU-Green coalitions. However, only in Baden-Württemberg have prominent Greens spoken out at various times during the 1980s for this option at the state level. The formation of the Ampelkoalition (traffic light) of Red, Yellow, and Green after the October 1990 elections in the new eastern state of Brandenburg provides another model. Its Green coloration has been provided by the Bündnis 90/Grüne, which received a share of ministerial posts. Contrary to predictions, the coalition in Bradenburg has proven stable so far despite the difficult policy circumstances following unification. After the September 1991 Bremen elections, the Greens, who had campaigned for a Red-Green coalition, voted to enter an Ampelkoalition with the FDP and the SPD. They gained two cabinet ministries. It remains to be seen whether such experiments (if successful) might be transferable to the federal level in the mid-1990s.

Bundestag Greens

In March 1983, the Greens won twenty-seven Bundestag seats and with the AL's one Berlin seat qualified (with two seats to spare) for *Fraktion* status. Accordingly, they received seats on all standing committees, the chairmanship of one committee, and institutional support of 7.2 million deutsche marks (DM) per year. However, the established parties denied the "radical" Greens a Bundestag vice-presidency and a seat on the intelligence services control subcommittee. The Bundestag Greens' institutional resources dwarfed those of the Landtag Greens, but there were trade-offs for an antibureaucratic, grass-roots democratic party: The size of the total parliamentary group was large, the legislative workload was heavy in volume and specialized in scope, the distance from the grass roots was psychologically (and physically) greater, and the Green deputies' origins were even more diverse. Compared to the Landtag Greens, the Bundestag Greens seemed to be in perpetual crisis.

The Bundestag Greens settled upon a collective approach to parliamentary leadership, which diverged in several ways from that of the established parties. Instead of a chairperson, the Greens elected three coequal speakers, who along with three parliamentary managers constituted the Vorstand (executive board). Its job was to coordinate (not control) the work of the *Fraktion*. Elections occurred annually and the Greens had a high turnover of parliamentary leaders compared to other parties. For example, discontent with the media profiling of their first executive board (three men, three women) led to its replacement by six less prominent women in 1984. From the outset, women were much more highly represented in the Greens' parliamentary leadership than in those of the established parties. Green deputies who disagreed with the decisions of their executive board could have them reconsidered in the marathon plenary sessions of the *Fraktion*. The SPD, CDU/CSU, and FDP parliamentary groups have operated more hierarchically. And, in contrast to the other parties, the *Fraktion* meetings of the Greens were (with rare exceptions) open to the media and the public.

However, the Bundestag Greens followed closely the pattern of the SPD and the FDP in allocating specialized policy work to six (later nine) Arbeitskreise (working groups of deputies and staff assistants).[21] The Bundestag Greens soon confronted their party's lack of programmatic development in many areas. The authors of the group's first annual report complained, "We can't launch into the particulars of parliamentary work, if we don't know where we really want to go."[22] It was the members of Arbeitskreis I who not only initiated and shaped the Umbauprogramm but also guided it during 1985 and 1986 through the gauntlet of party bodies. Programmatic developments regarding women's issues stemmed from the efforts of the federal policy working group (BAG-Frauen) and feminist movement activists, not from those of the *Fraktion*; however, this was exceptional.[23]

The Green party mandated rotation of seats to prevent the professionalization of its Bundestag deputies. The successors (*Nachrücker*) served as full-time members of the parliamentary group after rotation, as could their predecessors (*Vorrücker*). They received a salary equivalent to the deputies' from the *Fraktion* and had equal voting rights in its decisionmaking. They were supposed to work alongside their deputies and then to switch places after two years. However, there was no close matchup between the policy specialties of deputies and successors, who hardly thought of themselves as assistants to the deputies. Furthermore, the uncertainty over whether some deputies might refuse to rotate strained working relationships between deputies and successors. In contrast to the deputies, the successors had come to Bonn without a legal guarantee for getting their old jobs back. Although only two of the deputies elected in 1983 ultimately refused to rotate, the federal party in 1986 abandoned midterm rotation for Bundestag Greens in the future. However, at this time there was still consensus for limiting the tenure of Green deputies to no more than one or two terms. Otto Schily's defection to the SPD was to be caused in part by his state party's rigidity on this point.

In addition to the current and former deputies, the Bundestag Greens employed in May 1985 over sixty people. In June 1987, they employed over 130; two-thirds of these staff assistants had served during the period from 1983 to 1987.[24] The second *Fraktion*, its majority sensitive to legislative norms of professionalism, voted to reallocate staff so that each deputy had at least two full-time assistants. In comparison, the Green party's federal executive board employed approximately twenty people. Although both sets of figures are complicated by part-timers, one can easily observe that the human resources of the *Fraktion* eclipsed those of the federal executive board. When, following their defeat in the December 1990 all-German elections, the Greens dissolved their *Bundestagsfraktion*, its staff had grown to over 200 in Bonn and 20 more in regional offices.

Projecting themselves as the only real opposition to Kohl's CDU/CSU-FDP government, the Greens entered the Bundestag in 1983. Their opposition strategy involved, first, creatively utilizing the Bundestag as a stage from which to communicate the "new politics." To disrupt the "monoculture" of plenary sessions, Green deputies disregarded the dress code, departed from customary forms of speech, and carried in banners, flowers, and assorted stage props. The symbolic politics of the Greens was unprecedented within the Bundestag and drew heavy media coverage during 1983 and 1984. The other side of the Bundestag Greens' opposition strategy involved actively using all the tools of parliamentary membership to develop proposals and to raise questions pertinent to their party's programmatic goals. During the period from 1983 to 1987, Green deputies introduced almost as many motions to amend bills or to pass resolutions as did SPD deputies.[25] Although the Greens' bills and motions rarely passed, the major parties had no qualms about borrowing ideas from the Greens. In recent decades, the roll call voting cohesion of *Bundestagsfraktionen* has been high compared to that of U.S. congressional parties. Thomas Saalfeld's study found that the Greens were less disciplined in

TABLE 7.1   Parliamentary Activities in the Bundestag by Party Groups, 1987–1990

	CDU/CSU	SPD	FDP	Greens[a]	Independents
Gesetzentwürfe (bills)	88	81	87	71	
Grosse Anfragen (grand interpellations)	19	58	19	68	
Kleine Anfragen (small interpellations)	19	197	17	1,206	
Fragestunde (questions)	4,728	11,865	1,323	2,161	157[b]
Anträge (motions)	105	332	106	373	
Aktuelle Stunden (topical debates)	18	40	10	60	

Note: Subtotals include cosponsored initiatives but exclude all-party initiatives.

[a] October–December 1990 activities of Greens include contributions of Eastern Bündnis 90 deputies as part of an enlarged *Fraktion*.

[b] In addition, the PDS deputies posed seventeen questions after October 1990.

Source: Wissenschaftlicher Dienst des Deutschen Bundestages, July 8, 1991.

their voting behavior than the other parties during the period from 1983 to 1987. However, statistical gaps were not large, and, furthermore, the Greens were more cohesive on roll calls than the FDP had been during some earlier parliamentary terms.[26] To the observer of *Fraktion* meetings, intragroup disputes might seem sharp, but Green deputies generally closed ranks on roll call votes.

The Greens' activism in using interpellation procedures for submitting debatable questions to the government (*Grosse Anfragen*) and for requesting written information about governmental policy (*Kleine Anfragen*) was unprecedented in the history of the Bundestag. For example, during the period from 1983 to 1987, Green deputies initiated 820 *Kleine Anfragen;* SPD deputies, 143; CDU/CSU deputies, 40; and FDP deputies, 40. The small Green opposition also actively posed verbal questions and initiated almost as many "topical hour" debates (*Aktuelle Stunde*) as the large SPD opposition.[27] In quantitative terms, the Green deputies elected in 1987 continued their predecessors' high parliamentary activism (see Table 7.1). The second Green *Fraktion* introduced only slightly fewer bills than did the large SPD *Fraktion*. The Greens introduced more motions (*Anträge*), initiated more topical debates, and submitted more *Grosse Anfragen* and *Kleine Anfragen* than did any other parliamentary group. In fact, the *Kleine Anfragen* of the Green deputies constituted 85 percent of the total submitted by all deputies. A common practice of the Greens was to call press

TABLE 7.2   Parliamentary Questions in the Bundestag by Party Groups, 1987–1990

Departments	CDU/CSU	SPD	FDP	Greens[a]	PDS[b]	Independent
BK/Chancellor	11	146	12	46	0	0
AA/Foreign	642	566	65	235	1	4
BMI/Interior	371	886	148	255	0	29
BMJ/Justice	127	213	30	35	1	6
BMF/Finance	304	2,313	110	78	1	5
BMWi/Economics	365	840	65	190	0	7
BML/Agriculture	360	308	58	63	4	1
BMA/Work	381	912	101	53	3	14
BMVg/Defense	222	1,323	165	236	0	6
BMJFFG/Youth	361	672	132	131	0	9
BMV/Transport	721	1,413	149	236	0	33
BMPT/Post and telecommunications	128	334	41	48	0	3
BMBau/Building	102	418	23	11	3	0
BMB/Education	90	107	5	0	0	1
BMFT/Research	115	276	31	85	0	6
BMBW/Education	101	142	27	23	0	2
BMZ/Economic cooperation	69	131	24	69	0	4
BMU/Environment	258	865	137	367	4	2
Total	4,728	11,865	1,323	2,161	17	157

Note: Oral, written, and "urgent" questions.
[a]After October 1990 includes Bündnis 90 deputies.
[b]PDS parliamentary group, October–December 1990.

Source: Wissenschaftlicher Dienst des Deutschen Bundestages, July 8, 1991.

conferences when they found the government's responses to their inter-pellations to be inadequate (or not forthcoming).

Question hour (*Fragestunde*) statistics allow us to compare the foci of the parliamentary groups' inquiries (see Table 7.2). Clearly the most popular target of the Greens' questions was the environmental ministry, followed by the interior ministry; however, the data also show that the Greens were wide-ranging in their concerns. In absolute terms, the SPD deputies asked more questions of the environmental ministry than did the Greens, but, in relative terms, five other ministries received more SPD attention. CDU/CSU deputies asked large numbers of questions of the transportation ministry and the foreign ministry, whereas FDP deputies seem to have spread their attention more evenly. In sum, the Greens presented an alternative profile in parliamentary statistics.

Yet one should also note the "qualitative" side of the parliamentary activism of Green deputies. As a prime example, Otto Schily's role was crucial in the investigative committee hearings regarding the Flick affair, which entangled politicians from all the major parties in illegal corporate contributions. In the case of the controversy regarding emissions from the new Buschhaus power plant, the Greens showed their tactical skills by utilizing the wording of a FDP party resolution in their own motion and then compromising to get a cosponsored motion. This necessitated a special parliamentary session, where CDU/CSU and FDP deputies, under party discipline, changed sides to defeat the original motion to tighten pollution control, an act that publicly exposed the government's limited environmental commitment. Plenary speeches by Green deputies also at times broke parliamentary taboos, such as Waltraud Schoppe's blunt speech to male deputies about "everyday sexism." In addition, the Greens were aggressive in taking complaints to the Federal Constitutional Court. For example, their legal challenge to the system of public funding for the major parties' "educational" foundations failed, but their criticisms of the federal census administration resulted in partial success.

Despite *Basisdemokratie*, the election of Green deputies to the Bundestag transformed intraparty relationships. The *Fraktion* became the de facto party leadership in terms of media coverage and organizational resources. The federal steering committee had the power to pass resolutions to "bind" the *Fraktion*, but its members were "weekend" politicians who met every four to six weeks. The federal steering committee initially set up a watchdog subcommittee to monitor the work of the *Fraktion* and to participate in its decisionmaking. However, this attempt failed because of strong objections from the deputies and from some state party leaders, who felt that deputies should be directly responsible to the grass roots and not to the federal steering committee.[28] For most policy areas, the full-time working groups (Arbeitskreise) of the *Fraktion* took over the real think-tank role from the two dozen part-time federal party working groups (Bundesarbeitsgemeinschaften) of extraparliamentary experts and activists.

The long-running conflicts between the *Fraktion* and the federal party leadership stemmed more from differing factional balances than from institutional rivalries. Until March 1989, federal party assemblies regularly elected executive boards dominated by advocates of "fundamental opposition" who stressed extraparliamentary activism, shunned governmental responsibility, and opposed coalitions with the SPD. During the mid-1980s, the federal executive board attempted to derail the SPD-Green alliance in Hesse while prominent Bundestag "realists" supported the Landtag Greens.

The first Bundestag Greens included neither a majority of committed fundamentalists nor committed realists, which was reflected in the mixed composition of their elected parliamentary leadership. However, about two-thirds of the Green deputies elected in 1987 were (in some sense of the term) realists; five of six leadership offices went to self-identified moderates or realists. During late 1987, escalating tensions between prominent realists and fundamentalists in Bonn generated open talk of splitting the *Fraktion* until moderate deputies mobilized to ease the tensions. In early 1988, one could identify four camps within the *Fraktion:* fundamentalists, nondogmatic leftists, moderate realists, and superrealists. As discussed in Chapter 5, Antje Vollmer of the third camp launched a national campaign (Grüner Aufbruch) to reintegrate the party by democratizing its structures. Prominent members of the other camps of Green deputies were also actively involved in the debates about the future development of the party.

The *Fraktion* and the federal party executive collided in May 1988 in a manner that was unusual even for the Greens. Favoring a one-year minimum sentence for rape, the majority of the deputies declined to draft a bill with a two-year minimum sentence as demanded by feminists and supported by the March 1988 federal party assembly. Fundamentalists and feminists sought to censure the *Fraktion* by running a large paid ad in the *Frankfurter Rundschau* declaring, "The Green *Bundestagsfraktion* no longer represents its party's base." The published list of 300 supporters included eight of eleven members of the federal executive board.[29] This controversy was significant in the Greens' development because, in effect, a majority of Bundestag Greens declared that they could exercise discretion in implementing party resolutions.

Bündnis 90/Grüne

Despite the premature obituaries, the Green *Fraktion* managed to survive, if not flourish, during the late 1980s. Then suddenly the Western Greens' defeat in the December 1990 all-German elections left the small Bündnis 90/Grüne (B'90/Gr) parliamentary group to carry on alternative politics in the Bundestag. These eight eastern deputies could have hardly expected such early prominence in unified Germany. The grass-roots memberships of their respective movements had steadily ebbed since late 1989. They sorely lacked the organizational base of the Western Greens, but they were not inexperienced.

The Round Table of government and opposition representatives emerged in December 1989 as an outgrowth of informal contacts among East German political groups. The voting scheme of the Round Table equally represented the SED (Sozialistische Einheitspartei Deutschlands; Socialist Unity Party of Germany) and the old bloc parties and the new democratic movements (parties). In a de facto sense, the Round Table was displacing the GDR's political institutions in domestic policymaking. Then on February 5, 1991, the old Volkskammer confirmed a government of national responsibility that included eight ministers-without-portfolio from the opposition, including the Green Party (East). Two of the B'90/Gr deputies elected in December 1990 were among those movement activists on whom ministerial rank had been thrust by the transitional GDR government.

Democracy Now (DJ), New Forum (NF), and Initiative for Peace and Human Rights (IFM) joined forces as Bündnis '90 to contest the March 1990 Volkskammer elections, which were conducted without a 5 percent threshold for parliamentary representation. Otherwise, Bündnis '90 and the electoral alliance of the East German Green party (GP) and the Independent Women's Association (UFV) would not have won any seats. The twenty Bündnis '90/Grüne deputies constituted only the fifth-largest parliamentary group in the Volkskammer. Within the parliamentary opposition to Lothar de Maiziere's grand coalition of Christian Democrats, Social Democrats, and Liberals, B'90/Gr deputies were easily outnumbered by the PDS deputies. Yet as a full-fledged *Fraktion*, B'90/Gr deputies were represented on the Presidium and the standing committees of the Volkskammer. However, the lopsided majority of the governing coalition precluded any power broker role for the alternative politicians, whose majority, in contrast to their Western counterparts, have been pragmatists from day one.

The Volkskammer's traditional function had been to ratify the SED leadership's policies, which meant that institutional support for active parliamentarians, as B'90/Gr deputies aspired to be, was virtually nil. Matthias Platzeck described the work conditions of his *Fraktion:* five deputies per office; no place for staff assistants; no typewriters, computers, or photocopy machines; and inadequate salaries with no legal guarantee of return to previous jobs.[30] The workload was heavy, the pace furious, and the stakes high. For example, B'90/Gr deputy Marianne Birthler (who later became education minister in the new eastern state of Brandenburg) labored as the chair of the special Volkskammer Committee for the Control of the Dissolution of the Ministry for State Security (Stasi). When the *Fraktion* in September 1990 voted against the unification treaty, it did so on grounds that the treaty ignored Volkskammer resolutions, particularly those regarding Stasi files.

After October 3, 1990, 144 Volkskammer deputies, by nomination of their respective parliamentary groups, became members of the Bundestag. Seven B'90/Gr deputies joined the forty-two Bundestag Greens,[31] who to symbolize their desire for partnership changed the name of the *Fraktion* to Die Grünen/Bündnis 90. Three of the eight B'90/Gr deputies elected on December 2, 1990, had been members of the joint *Fraktion* during the period from October to December 1990; two others had served in the Volkskammer during the period from March to October 1990. The heterogeneity of the eight B'90/Gr deputies was diverse even by the standards of the Western Greens: They ranged from an ex-SED leftist lesbian to a male conservative whose traditional values have much in common with those of Christian Democrats. However, the B'90/Gr deputies have shared a fundamental consensus that parliamentary representation at all levels is a precondition for opening politics to grass-roots activism. In contrast to Western Greens, as a result of direct experiences with "real socialism" they have not been inclined to question parliamentarism itself.[32]

The standing orders of the Bundestag require a parliamentary group to include at least 5 percent of the total membership (after 1990 thirty-four deputies) before it can be recognized as a *Fraktion*. Neither the B'90/Gr nor the PDS parliamentary groups qualified for *Fraktion* status. This meant that the B'90/Gr deputies received less financial support from the state budget (3.5 million DM/year[33]) than otherwise would have been the case. However, the Council of Elders granted the B'90/Gr and the PDS representation on standing committees and on the Council of Elders itself. And both groups received the right to introduce bills, to make motions, to submit interpellations, to propose topical debates, and to utilize plenary speaking time proportional to their sizes. There remained some actions that the groups could take only if supported by a number of other parties' deputies, and they were blocked from some subcommittees and boards. Neither group received a vice-presidency or a committee chairmanship.

As a small parliamentary group, the B'90/Gr deputies had no need for a collective executive (Vorstand) to coordinate parliamentary activities. They selected Werner Schulz of the New Forum not as chairman but as parliamentary manager (along with two assistant managers) with the understanding that the leadership role would rotate. Members of the executive (or speaker) councils of those movements or parties represented in the B'90/Gr group were given the right to participate in its meetings. However, in contrast to the meetings of the Bundestag Greens (1983–1990), those of the B'90/Gr group were closed to the public. Given the diversity of the deputies, the group took this decision to prevent intragroup disagreements from becoming the main theme of media coverage. Respecting individual autonomy, the parliamentary group decided to allow a minority the option of introducing in the Bundestag B'90/Gr motions with which a majority had disagreed.[34]

The B'90/Gr parliamentary group could hardly take up the many causes of the defeated Green *Fraktion*. Their small numbers did not even allow for coverage of all the standing committees. The B'90/Gr group's suborganization included a management committee to prepare group meetings and three Arbeitskreise for specialized policy work regarding economic, social, and environmental issues; foreign issues; and legal issues. The group's institutional stipend allowed for twenty-nine staff assistants. Twenty of them were recruited by and worked under individual deputies. More of the staff assistants were *Wessis* (Westerners) than *Ossis* (Easterners). The B'90/Gr's initial staff included prominent veterans of Western Green politics: Lukas Beckmann as *Fraktionsgeschäftsführer* (business manager) and Heinz Suhr (a *Super-Realo*) as press secretary. The B'90/Gr deputies' entry into parliamentary politics has not been marked by the symbolic gestures that initially had provided the first Bundestag Greens with a disproportionate amount of media coverage. The new deputies are a more pragmatic group, not as inclined to seek publicity for its own sake. However industrious the B'90/Gr deputies might be as individuals, from the outset they have recognized the necessity to be selective in their parliamentary efforts. Naturally their common concern is the special interests of the population of the former GDR. For example, the deputies have maintained a focus on the "de-Stasification" process in eastern German political and social life. They have participated in the debate about asylum seekers and immigrants, proposing a quota system as a possible solution. They have raised questions about the rebuilding of the economic infrastructure of eastern Germany in a way that considers, in advance, social and environmental costs. They have spoken out against the revival of racism and the passivity in the face of violence against foreigners. Their challenge—as a small group on the easily overlooked fringe of the parliamentary stage—will be to articulate issues of societal renewal for all of Germany.

The relationship between the B'90/Gr parliamentary group (which includes two eastern Greens) and the Green federal executive has been quite different than it had been between Bundestag Greens and the Green federal executive during the period from 1983 to 1990. Because the parliamentary group is outside the Green party charter, the relationship has been tactical, not institutional. The Greens' federal speakers have the permission to participate in parliamentary group meetings. Yet the B'90/Gr group appears to have a decentralist preference for contacts and cooperation with state parties.

The parliamentary group also has not been an organizational unit of Bündnis 90, which had the standing of an electoral alliance until September 1991. DJ, IFM, and a majority of NF then merged as a party under federal law; the feminist UFV (which includes one B'90/Gr deputy) declined to take the party path. Political constellations vary in the East from state to state. For example, Saxony Greens and citizen movements united as a new state party, Bündnis 90/Grüne, while, in Brandenburg, NF and DJ officially launched Bündnis 90 as a state party. The latter party's collective leadership included the B'90 *Fraktion* chair and two of its staff assistants. Thus, Bündnis 90 appears to be consolidating itself—minus a minority of the NF—without the Greens' historical distrust of parliamentarians.

Greens in Local Government

This chapter has focused on the participation of Green (and allied) parties in the state and federal parliaments of Germany. Because of limitations of space and data, we can only briefly deal with Green parties in local councils. Beginning in the late 1970s, Green local councillors have been elected throughout Germany, even in Länder where the Greens have not been able to win parliamentary seats. As mentioned in Chapter 5, the early successes quickly drained the alternative party's limited pool of activists and undermined its *basisdemokratische* procedures, such as mid-term rotation. In Hesse, for example, one out of every eight party members held a local council seat in 1987. Although Kitschelt argues that the more pragmatic activists have tended to be drawn to the concrete realities of local politics[35], Thomas Scharf maintains that the Greens' involvement in the "everyday compromises demanded of local politics" has reinforced the dynamic of *Realpolitik*, even for fundamentalists.[36] Currently there are around 7,000 Greens in local councils from small rural communities in Baden-Württemberg to major metropolitan areas, such as Frankfurt.

From the outset Green local councillors have had to confront the question of working relationships with the major parties. Between 1979 and 1984, Bielefield Greens cooperated selectively with the minority SPD administration and jointly passed three of five city budgets. Typically the Greens have had greater affinity with the local SPD's policy priorities, though in a few cases there have been alliances with other parties. Some SPD-Green alliances have been transitory, whereas others have lasted an electoral period (for example, Kassel 1981–1985), yet there are many SPD local parties that would prefer to govern with the CDU.

The initial inclination of the local Greens was not to seek executive offices. But soon they discovered that this "shyness" allowed the local SPD to delay policy implementation favored by the Greens and to take public credit for positive contributions by the Greens.[37] Since the mid-1980s, Greens have headed dozens of environmental departments at the local governmental level. Greens have served as deputy mayors, where they are not directly elected, and in at least one case a Green has been directly elected mayor. After the 1989 Frankfurt city elections, as a result of the SPD-Green majority, four Greens became executive department heads. Beyond Hesse, there have been Red-Green alliances or coalitions in Nuremberg, Hanover, Brunswick, Oldenburg, Wuppertal, and Lever-kusen. In other major cities, such as Munich, Cologne, and Düsseldorf, they became a relevant variable in power equations during the 1980s.

German local government is restricted by the many decisionmaking powers that are situated at the higher Land and Bund levels. Scharf's analysis indicates that the outcomes of SPD-Green local coalitions in Hesse were significantly dependent on the balance of power in the Land-tag.[38] Nevertheless, local Greens can point to specific instrumental successes, such as recycling programs, support for women's shelters, traffic controls, as well as symbolic successes, such as nuclear-free zones and multicultural festivities. In general, even where the Greens have failed to win sufficient seats to share power, they can be credited with introducing new politics issues and challenging the all-party cartels found in many local governments.

Conclusion

When parliamentary Greens interviewed in 1985 were asked to assess the major impact of the Greens, the most common response was that the Greens have been changing the political culture by representing new ideas and forcing other parties to respond to them. As a Hesse Green deputy replied, "Because of the Greens, many Germans recognize now the positive role of 'real' opposition, of having 'outsiders' represented in parliament."[39] But how has the public assessed their *parliamentary* activities? Seldom have polls directly asked this question and, furthermore, the public has probably known few particulars about the virtual Green flood of parliamentary initiatives. A review of survey data from the 1980s at the state and federal level shows that many who did not vote for the Greens nevertheless viewed their parliamentary presence positively.[40] Perhaps this sizeable minority of the electorate saw the Greens as thus becoming more integrated into the system or they saw some partisan advantages from having the Greens inside. In any case, an EMNID national survey in 1984 indicates that most voters did not see the Greens as playing a major role at the federal level. An INFAS survey in Baden-Württemberg provides more specific data. When asked to assess the Landtag performance of the Greens, 33 percent indicated that the Greens had brought new ideas and initiatives, 21 percent felt that they had played no important role, and 36 percent expressed negative evaluations. Not only in this state survey but also in several national surveys throughout the decade the Greens received the highest competence rating of all parties in regard to environmental protection.

The Greens quickly settled into the role of an "engaged" opposition in the federal and state parliaments of West Germany. Both counterculture symbolism and an industrious work ethic were pervasive during the 1980s. Although lacking the resources of the large *Fraktionen*, the Greens utilized fully the varied institutional tools of parliamentary membership, forcing the large *Fraktionen* to react to new demands. In most parliaments the

Greens scored no major successes in passing or amending legislation; rather, they energetically performed those functions traditionally attributed to a "responsible" parliamentary opposition, such as seeking fuller information about policy implementation. In general, Green parliamentary parties behaved as a "competitive" opposition not only toward the government but also toward the established opposition. They utilized scandals to distance themselves from the "party cartel" and singularly voted against parliamentary pay increases and public funding increases for party campaign expenses. Yet the major parties' selective borrowing of Green proposals, such as greater representation of women in politics, indicates the positive side of their "outsider" appeal within the system.

In 1983, Hesse Greens assumed the role of a cooperative opposition by tolerating the SPD minority *Land* government. Polls showed throughout the decade that clear majorities of Green voters favored coalitions with the SPD, which first occurred in Hesse (1985–1987, 1991–) and then in Berlin (1989–1990) and Lower Saxony (1990–). Such a strategic reorientation has profound implications for the Greens' triangular relationships among party-in-movement (which initially had highest place), party organization (second place), and party-in-government (third place). When a new party shares power with old parties, complete with its own cabinet ministers and state secretaries, its professionalization seems inevitable.

However, many Green activists have had a negative fixation on the historical experience of the SPD as a movement-party that overaccommodated itself to the parliamentary status quo. Accordingly, the founders of the Greens launched their movement-party with various grass-roots democratic controls on Green deputies. Experience soon made clear that some controls, such as midterm rotation, had dysfunctional side effects. In another sense, the Greens were increasingly "parliamentarized" despite themselves. As early as the mid-1980s, Green deputies and staff assistants were expressing frustrations over the growing tendency for many grass-roots groups to turn the political initiative over to the *Fraktion*. Furthermore, "weak" state and federal party executives clearly lacked the resources to match those of the *Fraktionen*, whose working groups took the lead in programmatic development in most policy areas. Some of the Green deputies interviewed by the authors stated that they would welcome better-informed guidance from the party, whereas others saw no alternative to the wide autonomy of the *Fraktion* given the time constraints of parliamentary work. Green parties, with the possible exception of the pre-1991 GAL, became preoccupied with parliamentary electoral percentages as the indicator of political success.

In short, despite the intentions of its founders, within a decade the Green party had become "semiparliamentarized." We say "semi" because *Basisdemokratie* still provided its "counter legitimacy" (though there was a growing realization of the need for procedural reforms). The Greens' self-identity as an antibureaucratic, grass-roots democratic party had persisted despite power sharing at the local and state levels. Green state and federal parliamentary groups had maintained a distinctive profile: collective leadership, high turnover, open decisionmaking, high representation of women, and full-time work orientation. At times, the Green deputies had ignored parliamentary norms regarding plenary behavior but had followed others, such as policy specialization, in committee behavior.

At the end of the decade, the *Realos'* vision for the future was a fully parliamentarized Green party. In contrast, the nondogmatic Left envisaged a "rationalized" alternative party that would maintain the separation of party office and parliamentary seat. By December 1990, the Greens (West) had evolved from being the antiparty party to being the main alternative parliamentary party. Then suddenly with their stunning defeat, the torch of alternative parliamentarism had to be passed in the Bundestag to the small, diverse eastern Bündnis 90/Grüne group. The "new" newcomers during their first year generally demonstrated a determination to avoid the political mistakes of the Greens (West) and a disinterest in ideological squabbling about grass-roots democracy versus parliamentary democracy.

Notes

1. Frank Sorauf, *Party Politics in America,* 5th ed. (Boston: Little, Brown, 1984), pp. 8–11.

2. Bodo Zeuner, "Parlamentarisierung der Grünen," *Prokla* 61 (1985):13–18.

3. Thomas Saalfeld, "The West German Bundestag After 40 Years: The Role of Parliament in a 'Party Democracy,'" in *Parliaments in Western Europe,* Philip Norton, ed. (London: Frank Cass, 1990), pp. 83–85.

4. Gerhard Loewenberg, *Parliament in the German Political System* (Ithaca: Cornell University Press, 1967).

5. Bernhard Badura and Jürgen Reese, *Jung-parlamentarier in Bonn—Ihre Sozialisation im Deutschen Bundestag* (Stuttgart: Frommann-Holzboog, 1976), pp. 43, 57, 67.

6. Winfried Steffani, "Parties (Parliamentary Groups) and Committees in the Bundestag," in *The U.S. Congress and the German* Bundestag: *Comparisions of Democratic Processes,* Uwe Thaysen, Roger H. Davidson, and Robert Gerald Livingston, eds. (Boulder: Westview Press, 1990), p. 278.

7. William E. Paterson and David Southern, *Governing Germany* (New York: W. W. Norton, 1991), p. 121.

8. Nelson W. Polsby, "Legislatures," in *Handbook of Political Science, Volume 5: Governmental Institutions,* Fred I. Greenstein and Nelson W. Polsby, eds. (Reading, Mass.: Addison-Wesley, 1975), pp. 293, 296–297.

9. Hans-Joachim Veen, *Opposition in Bundestag* (Bonn: Eichholz, 1976), pp. 15–16.

10. Manfred Friedrich, "Parlamentarische Opposition in der Bundesrepublik Deutschland: Wandel und Konstanz," in *Parlamentarische Opposition,* Heinrich Oberreuter, ed. (Hamburg: Hoffmann & Campe, 1975), pp. 260–261.

11. Saalfeld, "The West German Bundestag after 40 Years," p. 78.

12. Klaus von Beyme, "Die ökologische Bewegung zwischen Bürgerinitiativen und Parteiorganisation," in Bernd Guggenberger and Udo Kempf, eds., *Bürgerinitiativen und Räpresentativen System,* 2d ed. (Opladen: Westdeutscher Verlag, 1984), pp. 373–374.

13. West German Greens were later elected to the state parliaments in Bavaria (1986), Rhineland-Palatinate (1987), and North Rhine–Westphalia (1990). East German Greens or their allies were elected to seats in four of five of the new (eastern) Landtage in October 1990.

14. One of the authors posed the comparative question to Hesse, Hamburg, and Baden-Württemberg Greens interviewed in April and May 1985.

15. Interviews with GAL *Fraktion* and executive board members, May 22–25, 1985.

16. During April and May 1985, open-ended interviews were conducted by one of the authors with thirteen present or former Green Landtag deputies in Baden-Württemberg, Hamburg, and Hesse. During June 1987, nine present or former Green (or AL) Landtag deputies were interviewed in Lower Saxony, Berlin, and Hamburg.

17. This deputy had replaced a person who resigned after serving only one year. His decision not to rotate was later supported by the *Realo* majority at the state party assembly.

18. Hamburg parliamentary statistics for June 1982 through November 1986 were provided by Karl-Heinz Stahnke of the Hamburg *Bürgerschaftskanzlei.*

19. In addition to the Landtag deputies (see note 27), fifteen state party leaders or parliamentary staff assistants were interviewed in 1985 and thirteen in 1987 by one of the authors.

20. Saarland Greens and Schleswig-Holstein Greens have never been successful in winning Landtag seats. In October 1990, because of their inability to form an electoral alliance, the Greens and citizen movements in Mecklenburg–West Pomerania failed to enter this new state's parliament.

21. The CDU *Fraktion,* rather than having *Arbeitskreise,* has organized its specialized policy work according to eighteen more focused *Arbeitsgruppen.*

22. Die Grünen im Bundestag, *Bericht zur Lage der Fraktion* (March 1984), p. 19.

23. E. Gene Frankland, "Green Politics and Alternative Economics," *German Studies Review* 11, no. 1 (January 1988):111–132.

24. Interviews with Renate Mohr, the Bundestag Greens' press secretary, Bonn, May 1985 and June 1987.

25. E. Gene Frankland, "The Role of the Greens in West German Parliamentary Politics," *Review of Politics* 50, no. 1 (1988):92–122.

26. Saalfeld, "The West German Bundestag After 40 Years," p. 74.

27. E. Gene Frankland, "The Role of the Greens in West German Parliamentary Politics," pp. 111–112.

28. Gertrud Schrüfer, *Die Grünen im Deutschen Bundestag: Anspruch und Wirklichkeit* (Nürnberg: Pauli-Balleis-Verlag, 1985), p. 61.

29. *Frankfurter Rundschau*, May 27, 1988.

30. "Gespräch mit dem Volkskammer-Abgeordneten der DDR-Grünen, Matthias Platzeck," *Die Grünen* [Wochenzeitung], May 19, 1990, p. 4.

31. Two Green deputies elected in 1987 had resigned from the *Fraktion* but remained in the Bundestag as independents.

32. Matthias Geis, "Potsdamer Aufbruch," *Die Tageszeitung*, September 21, 1991, p. 8.

33. Interview with Lukas Beckmann, B'90/Gr *Fraktionsgeschäftsführer*, Bonn, June 6, 1991.

34. Gerd Nowakowski, "Acht neue Bonner Köpfe bilden (noch) keine Gruppe," *Die Tageszeitung*, March 6, 1991, p. 13.

35. Herbert Kitschelt, *The Logics of Party Formation* (Ithaca, N.Y.: Cornell University Press, 1989), pp. 153–162.

36. Thomas Scharf, "Red-Green Coalitions at Local Level in Hesse," in *The Greens in West Germany: Organization and Policy Making*, Eva Kolinsky, ed. (Oxford: Berg, 1989), p. 173.

37. Scharf, "Red-Green Coalitions," p. 166.

38. Ibid., pp. 180–182.

39. Interview with Hesse Landtag deputy Jochen Vielhauer, Wiesbaden, April 24, 1985.

40. See Frankland, "The Role of the Greens in West German Parliamentary Politics," pp. 116–117, for specific details and citations regarding the surveys summarized in this section.

8

The Impact of the Greens

THE SIMPLEST COMMENT TO BE MADE about the Green party of West Germany from 1977 to 1990 is that they moved the environmental problem to a position on the political agenda where political and economic elites, media power brokers, lobbyists, and bureaucrats could not ignore it. The Greens promoted other issues—disarmament, women's rights, further democratization—but none were so pertinent for the citizenry as the threats to natural and human resources, which the traditional parties seemed to ignore. The heart of the Green critique asked pointed questions about the direction and purpose of economic development, and neither the citizenry nor the major parties could sidestep this debate.[1]

The Greens began their search for votes and supporters on the local level in Lower Saxony in the late 1970s and persisted in electoral competition on all levels—local, state, national, and European—for the next fourteen years. After a decade on the stage of national politics, the electorate in December 1990 pulled the curtain down on the West German Greens while the citizens of the former East Germany elected eight members of the Alliance 90/Greens to the all-German parliament. Did it make any difference to the old Federal Republic of West Germany and now for the new Germany that these Greens strutted and fretted their time upon the political stage?

Gauging the Impact of the Greens

The common wisdom in assessing the influence of minor parties is that they burst on the scene accompanied by citizens dissatisfied with the traditional parties. These parties, after sizing up the popularity of the challenger's programs, skillfully adopt their popular policies, co-opt most of their voters and some of their personnel, and then, by dint of superior organizational skills and powerful interest group connections, simply push the usually amateur group to marginal status.[2] The common wisdom may not adequately explain the unconventional party of the Greens.

We need to point out that in gauging the influence of the Greens in the German political system it is necessary to be aware that influence can be lasting or fleeting, significant or minor. Influence can operate on various levels of government, and closeness to events doesn't always provide the best perspective.

We now need to look for the consequences of this party on the micro (personal) and macro (system) level of politics as well as look at those political organizations that link personal political actions to the larger institutions. We know from earlier chapters that the Greens represented a breakthrough in the party system and in the constellation of pluralism on the local, state, and national levels. But just what were the consequences or effects of the political norms (values) and the forms (organizations) that the Greens brought to the scene in the late 1970s?

And with those new organization forms—the citizen initiatives and social movements—was the traditional power structure affected by the way the Green party amplified its political messages? We also should not neglect the question about the duration or intensity of the possible influence of this minor party. Was it a short-lived gadfly to be swatted away casually by the *Volksparteien* or a more formidable creature, pesky and persistent, with a capacity for renewal and adaptation that changed traditional patterns of competition? Did the Greens shape a new organizational form? Were there policy changes; if so, can they be attributed to the Greens? Did they place new issues on the agenda or block the usual order of business? Were they considered coalition partners with persons of ministerial caliber? And did this party encourage new left parties in other political systems by their breakthrough in the German party system?

To exert influence in a political sense is to change predispositions or actions, and, as we stated a moment ago, relationships of influence are not static but fluid. Consider the following contrast. The Greens of 1987 pulled over 2 million votes and had forty-two members in the Bundestag and 260 staff personnel from 1987 to 1990. The Greens of the West in 1990 received almost 1.8 million votes, received no parliamentary seats, and 260 people sought new jobs. So there is a cycle of impact or influence. In this chapter we speculate on those cycles and the changing nature of that influence that the Greens sought to exert. Because parties work at political socialization, recruit candidates, run campaigns, organize interests, set forth policies, and try to exercise power (or serve as the opposition), we want to know whether the Greens have left any particular mark in these areas. Finally, these same questions apply to the more fledgling Greens and citizen movement-parties of the former East German political system. Their role in the fall of the old regime in 1989 and in the unification process is critical for our understanding of the long-range prospects for an ecological civil rights party in the newly united Germany.

The Greening of a Participatory Political Culture?

Basic questions about a political culture focus on the role of authority in a society: Who should have authority and how should it be exercised? On the Western side, the Federal Republic effected a political miracle to match its economic miracle by moving from a representative democracy in which the political and economic elites were given a wide range of discretion in policymaking to a more participant democratic polity where deference to authority has declined, the boundaries of dissent and criticism have widened, and the repertory of political actions have expanded substantially. The scholars who have documented these developments of the political culture have provided us with a series of societal and political "photographs" that, when assembled, give us a hint of the complicated process of political and cultural change.[3]

A summary of these changes in the political culture is noted by Conradt in a recent essay. Speaking of the late 1960s, he notes that "having learned and accepted democratic norms and values, the Germans were starting to put them into practice. The *Machtwechsel* of 1969, the student movement, the *Bürgerinitiativen*, the Greens and the new social movements—peace movement, environmental groups, women's rights groups—are the most obvious manifestation of this development. By the 1980s millions of Germans were engaging in political activities beyond the simple act of voting."[4]

Conradt sees the Greens "as the products of this cultural change," but it can also be said that the Greens are, albeit in a minor way, agents of political cultural change. In the sphere of the participatory impulses of the 1970s and 1980s, the Greens are both transformers and transformed. The forces that Conradt describes—especially the student movement and the citizen initiatives—certainly are major shaping organizations for the Greens, but a unique aspect of the Greens as a party deserves mention here. From the beginning a clue to the particularity of the Greens has been that they have been as interested in bringing about political cultural change (a new way of thinking about and acting in politics)—by changing the mode from being elite-directed to elite-challenging—as they have been in winning votes. Rarely did the other parties devote themselves to consciousness raising, as did the Greens.

A balanced view of the Greens' accomplishment in changing political values would assert that they accelerated or reinforced the ideals of a more participant citizenry that other organizations in society had initiated.[5]

More specifically, the Greens were successful in helping to shape the political values of the younger, more educated members of the new middle class, especially those pupils and students at the *Gymnasium* and university who were not yet anchored in society. For the older Green activists and voters, the Greens offered an organizational outlet for their political values and a chance to experiment in the electoral arena, which appealed especially to that generational cohort with its mission of democratizing society. The Greens have to be given credit for acting as a safety valve, as they changed some dogmatic radicals to serious reformers. That is, for some of the leftists they changed their idea of "marching through the institutions" to "grappling with the institutions."

The Green project for the polity was one of radical democracy. In addition to wanting more participants, they wanted to extend the sphere of what issues should be accountable to democratic control far beyond the programs of the other parties. For the Greens, concentrations of power, both political and economic, should be subject to democratic control. There should be decentralization of power from the national level to the local level, more experiments with regional authority, and greater use of referenda on important policy and constitutional issues.

It is absolutely essential to call attention to these proposals for a more grass-roots democracy for several reasons. The passage of time, the economic and political stability of the old Bonn republic, and the arguments of the Greens have encouraged not only attitude change but more experimentation with direct democracy than in the first three decades of West German politics. We also note that to many citizens these schemes for deconcentration of power seemed naïve and ill considered, particularly when demands for more specifics of the "Greenprint" for restructuring authority went unanswered. Lastly, the Greens led with their chin by attempting to implement what one Green politician and decade-long activist called the "utopia of equality," or the myth of grass-roots democracy within their party organization. This attempt to transfer the decision-making style of the social movements to the Green party brought perverse and unintended consequences that reduced the overall influence of the party in a number of ways. Trying to reverse the imperatives of oligarchy and bureaucracy led the Greens after a decade-long organization struggle to the realization that party politics exacts a more complex organizational price than the more flexible movement tactics. By that time, the effectiveness of the national Green party organization was badly in need of repair.

In sum, the Greens were shaped by the changes in the postindustrial society, particularly the expansion of educational opportunities, which Inglehart analyzed in *The Silent Revolution*. Their political demands are clearly postmaterialist. An improved quality of life for Green activists and voters included a more participant, less armed, and ecologically sensitive society. But, as we have noted, the Greens saw themselves as the cutting edge of these reforms in the West German polity, and the decision to form a party included the goal of providing an organizational bridge for the social movements, the leftists of the late 1960s (dogmatic and nondogmatic) and a segment of the younger voters whose disenchantment with the traditional parties showed up regularly in the public opinion polls. What organizational structures did the Greens construct to embody their polit-ical values and advance their political views, to convert changed attitudes to party activity and votes, and in what way did this change the constel-lation of pluralism and the party system in the federal republic of Bonn?

The Changing Shape of Pluralism

The opening statement of the Party Constitution, 1980, is "The Greens are the alternative to the traditional parties." To change attitudes is one matter; to transform attitudes into political actions is another. And sus-taining actions on a patterned basis over a period of time with formal rules creates institutions. The variety of political institutions in democratic political systems is exceedingly rich. There are powerful political parties with lines of historical continuity extending far back in time and less durable forms of single-interest citizen action groups that are mobilized to save a park or stop a road and then dissolve. The Greens are not a flash party, as was the Poujade movement party, which Stanley Hoffmann has analyzed, but what are they?

Many of the founders of the Greens and the activists in the party had had experience in the extraparliamentary opposition, the citizen initia-tives, and the social movements that flourished in the 1970s and 1980s. They hoped to combine the flexibility, sense of solidarity, and informal structure of these movements with the power-seeking potential of a political party. It was to be a party unlike any other (*das ganz andere*) and would promote policies that the major parties—tied to powerful interests of labor and capital—neglected. It would aim not just at promoting public issues but would also engage in consciousness raising and political cultural change. Finally, it would try to reach these goals through a party organi-zation whose guiding principles would show a commitment to decentral-ized, grass-roots democracy. The Green optimists stated that the party "corset" prevented spontaneous and positive movement; to be a natural and free party—whatever that might mean—a new party form needed to be invented.

The Greens celebrated their diversity. They had to. Given the span of opinions, which ranged from system-critical Marxists to right-wing con-servative nature-lovers, the party made a virtue of necessity and promoted

the slogans "Unity in diversity," and "Neither right nor left but forward."
Over the course of a decade or more, the party has located—painfully and
with scars from organizational battles—its center of gravity as a moderate
leftist ecological party with strong concern for issues of civil rights,
especially women's equality.[7] Along the way, the Greens have "shed a
number of skins" to bring themselves to the moderate left position. The
very Green conservative ecologists left in the early 1980s as the brighter
Red (Communist League and dogmatic Marxists) piggybacked on this new
party to advance its critique of capitalism.[8] In the late 1980s ecosocialists
and other leftist ideologues quit the party and in spring 1991 Jutta Ditfurth,
a fiery polemical fundamentalist opposed to pragmatic organizational
reforms and the professionalization of the party, walked out. These actions
further signified the move toward the center left and the impact of the
political system, especially electoral competition, on the Greens. In retrospect, the all-German election of 1990 shoved the Greens toward a new
equilibrium.

Diversity turned out to be both a strength and a burden. The Greens
certainly performed the important task of integrating a cranky, angry Left
into the German polity by offering them a role in the party, but they never
successfully integrated this system-critical Left *within* their own party. Ten
years of practical political work helped lower the ideological temperature
of the more inflexible leftists, and the downfall of real existing socialism
in Eastern Europe and unification reduced this political option within the
Greens even more. This "shakeout" process within the party as it sought
a more stable place to stand in terms of its political identity was a difficult
but necessary step to regain lost voters. The Greens of the West may have
solved some of their major problems of diversity, but they face a challenge
of formidable proportions with the prospect of developing a working
relationship with the citizen movements and the Greens of the East, who
currently label themselves Alliance 90/Greens. In short, unification helped
solve one problem yet created another for a national Green party.

The Greens acted as the amplifier for the social movements in the late
1970s and for part of the 1980s, and the type of linkage network that they
organized certainly did influence the pattern of power and influence in
the West German political system. Especially on the local level and
occasionally on the state level, the Green party acted as a clearinghouse
for citizens wanting to slow down the growth machine or, as one Bavarian
Green called it, "the concrete and street building faction." In terms that
Robert Dahl has used in describing the dilemmas of pluralist democracy,
the Green mobilization and coordination of group demands added a
measure of competitiveness to the pressure group battle and thereby
moved West Germany from a skewed pluralism focused narrowly on
economic growth and international competitiveness to a more balanced
pluralism that called attention to the environmental costs exacted by rapid

economic growth. In short, the traditional elites, the crowd of politicians, powerful economic interests, and bureaucrats now had less discretion to call the shots. The Greens provided new players with new critiques and encouraged far from traditional techniques for the political arena.[9]

Forming coalitions in politics is difficult enough, and holding them together in a harmonious manner is even more difficult. For a variety of reasons, the dynamism and energies of these social movements ebbed substantially in the latter part of the 1980s.[10] The peace movement declined when modernized nuclear weapons were put into place and the coalition against nuclear power plants declined as, in many instances, it accomplished its objectives. Quite obviously, the opposition from the citizen action groups and the Greens slowed the nuclear power plant forces considerably.

The movement advocates who opposed the formation of a national Green party attributed the decline of the social movements to the existence of the party, which drained away energies, but the preceding examples of a changed political context suggest that a more complex interrelationship has been at work. Events have undermined the pressing demand of some political changes, the Greens have been less adept at being good brokers with the social movements, and the other political parties have paid more attention to the tensions working between economy and ecology than they did before. In any event, the coalition of forces that the Greens helped orchestrate in the political arena brought a change in the arguments that were heard and in the political tactics—protests, demonstrations, happenings—that were used to influence public decisions. That impact was stronger in the earlier 1980s and waned in the late 1980s. The changing issue agenda, organizational inefficiency, and alert adaptation on certain issues among the major parties reduced the influence of the Greens in the latter half of the 1980s. But the configuration of pluralist forces had been changed. It was now more resilient, more varied, and amenable to new players. An opposition force that refused to go along with the usual crowd of party politicians established a foothold in the electorate. That was a positive influence for the political system of the old federal republic.

Electoral Competition

We have discussed the role of the Greens in electoral competition in an earlier chapter, but perhaps a quick overview of their record will aid us in understanding their impact on the political system. One obvious change with the advent of the Greens on all levels of government was that the citizens' choices were expanded. The Greens' calculation that there was a niche in the party system when the Social Democrats moved to the center, which was widened by a series of environmental disasters and the nuclear threat, proved to be more than correct. In point of fact, the Greens felt that all of the traditional parties ignored critical issues, but their disaffection with the SPD was greatest because of that party's reform profile. There was also a growing segment of new middle-class voters concerned about the practical issues of peace, pollution, and feminist concerns; there were also citizens who felt that democratic renewal was the right medicine for an ailing, unresponsive, and scandal-tinged party system.[11]

From 1977 to 1991, the Greens elected candidates on all levels of government. In many contests in the early 1980s they eliminated the FDP from the local council or state legislature and reduced the vote of the SPD. They changed the usual arithmetic of coalitionmaking that the major parties had mastered, and, as a result of discarding an antipathy to coalition participation, they developed in the late 1980s and the 1990s as a more stable coalition partner. In Lower Saxony, Hesse, Bremen, and Brandenburg, they currently share governmental responsibility and have received cabinet posts. For the fundamentalist Greens, a decreasing force in the party as the 1990s began, this was selling out. For the pragmatic realists of the Greens, this was responsible participation without throwing principles overboard. It was also bringing the party activists closer to the wishes of their electorate. The Greens have representation in thirteen of sixteen state legislatures with an average vote on all levels that approximates 6 to 7 percent. In 1990, *Die Zeit* noted that they had 7,000 elected members on the local government level, 170 on the state level, 8 in the national parliament, and 8 in the European Parliament. The strength on the local level has been the most evenly distributed and stable—discounting the European elections—of the various levels of electoral support. In general (there are exceptions), the Greens have been a competitive and constructive opposition that has done its legislative homework diligently and has contributed legislative ideas the best of which the parties adopted.[12]

Can we say at the end of over a decade of competition for votes that the Greens have a core electorate, that is, all-weather supporters who are not tactical voters? The all-German election of December 1990 put that question to the acid test. Although some scholars determined the core to be 6 to 7 percent, it is more likely 4 to 5 percent on the national level and slightly higher on the state and local levels. This percentage of core voters represents a significant change in the German electorate, out of which protest movements and minor parties have come and gone over the last several decades. For a party that challenged the basis consensus of the party system on domestic and foreign affairs, it is a singular accomplishment. In a comparative sense, the Greens mobilized more voters on more levels over a longer period of time than counterpart parties in other postindustrial democracies.

Policy and the Greens

Imitation may be a sincere form of flattery, but when in electoral competition a minor party loses its profile on certain issues—ecology, women's rights—the results can be fatal. The Greens charge the major parties with *Themenklau* (stealing issues), and that attests to their impact as an innovator in certain policy areas. Although the Greens had passed no major national legislation, they were taken much more seriously by the major political parties, especially the Social Democrats, in the mid-1980s. The SPD was hurt most by the Greens and had the fewest inhibitions in adopting the rhetoric and policy initiatives of the Greens on certain issues. The national legislative period from 1983 to 1987 had a delegation of Greens that was *bienenfleissig* (busy as bees) in its attentiveness to public policy, as our earlier chapter on parliament notes, but this respect gained from their ideas and work habits in the minds of many voters was dissipated through increasingly fractionalized internal quarreling and amateurish media politics.

Most commentators on the Greens agree that the party has shaped policy most effectively on the local level. Whether it was preventing a high-speed highway, offering a critical opinion on the siting of a nuclear plant, or designing a plan for waste disposal, the Greens left their tracks. We do not yet have detailed studies of the current coalitions in Hesse, Lower Saxony, Bremen, and Brandenburg, but we know that in coalition arrangements the Greens usually control the ministries of women's affairs and the environment. It has taken ten years for the party to substantially support coalitional opportunities with the Social Democrats, a sign of increased willingness to share in the risks of exercising power as well as a sign of moving away from dogmatic oppositionalism. A long-range problem for the Greens that has reduced their impact in the policy area is that they are not perceived as competent on subjects the electorate considers important. Our chapter on programs and policy shows that the Greens are hardly a one-issue party, but Raschke's diagnosis of the maladies of the Greens includes the prescription for more attention to issues of practical concern, including guaranteed income, societal control of technology, and the emerging problems of the multicultural society.

Organizational Innovations and Organizational Imperatives

The Greens intended to be a party of a new type. Have they fulfilled that intention and thereby added a new political organizational form to the postindustrial polities? Once again, we need to look at their intentions to answer the question. They sought to create a party with energy flowing from the grass roots to the top. As we noted earlier, the party organization was built to be elite-proof, to be scarce of areas where concentration of power could collect. The allergy to elites, hierarchy, centralization, public relations, bureaucracy, and personal leadership was part of the argument with the fascist past, partly a reaction to what many saw as an authoritarian present, and partly what they hoped for: a future of radical democratic experiments in societal and political forms. As observers have noted after the past decade, the exultation of the amateur democrat fits well with ideas of romantic populism but faces tough problems with the realities of electoral competition.[13] The Greens were being logical—perhaps too logical—in their organizational structure: The form fits their ideals and their boast to create a party "unlike the others."

Our chapter on the organizational development of the Greens has described the mechanisms of rotation in office, the prohibition of holding a party job and a public office at the same time, the provision of the control of the grass roots over the elected official, and the division of responsibility into myriad nooks and crannies. Although in the development pattern of the party of the past decade no oligarchy had a chance, neither did any semblance of cogent leadership. The Greens created a form that no others will use as a model, but their failed experiment on the national level in the West no doubt influenced what party activists are calling a second beginning. Constant invocation of the *Lernprozess* (learning process) by the current activists is testimony for this hope. It may be a sign of a generation taking stock of a failed ideal, recognizing the limits of amateur politics and surveying the damages from ideological and factional infighting. Democracy is a complex form of decisionmaking in which efficiency of leadership—using resources effectively to accomplish goals—is as important as openness and participatory opportunities.[14]

The influence of the Greens diminished not just because of a particular decisionmaking structure. The movement experience cast too heavy a spell on the origins of the party structure. Trying to live up to their theory that imagined a *Standbein* (a stable leg) in the social movements directing a *Spielbein* (a mobile leg) in parliament, they neglected to provide a *Gehirn* (a coordination intelligence) or stable leadership. They also did not anticipate the decline of the social movements, the demands of electoral competition, and the importance of unified and effective leadership in presenting their case to the public. To take this fragile party structure, laden with the leftist ideals of council democracy and other techniques for decentralized policymaking, and populate it with lively and polemical factions created too much ideological baggage for a party of marginal status to bear.

For all that, Green leader Antje Vollmer is right when she writes that it is the privilege of the innovator to make mistakes[15] and that not all of the Greens' innovations were mistakes. The Greens insisted on a greater role for women in their parliamentary and organizational positions, and the other parties have duly observed and followed the tradition. The Greens showed a greater sensitivity toward minority groups in the society and in their party—Eastern Europeans, guest workers, the aged—a practice the other parties have not followed as much. CDU politician Kurt Biedenkopf is partially right. The Greens did pose the right questions, and some of their answers led to positive reforms.

All in all, the Greens' experiment in amateur politics convinced others and themselves that a political party has no staying power in the electoral arena without a measure of professionalization, bureaucratization, personal leadership, and civility or tolerance of diverse viewpoints. It is clear at this juncture that the Greens and the political system have influenced each other. The Greens have added a critical voice to the party chorus, one that refused to blend in but wound up, on certain themes, influencing the chorus. It is equally clear that the organization reforms of the party in 1991, the moderateness of newly elected leaders of the party, and the interest in trying to keep their ideals *and* professionalize are consequences of the feedback that the electorate and the institutional constraints of the polity had given them. The long-term significance of the Greens as a party organization is difficult to speculate about. They may get a second wind from their national defeat of 1990 and develop a professional framework party of highly educated, middle-class party activists and voters who perform both "surrogate politics" (for minorities, the working class, and women) and long-range planning for reform. As a party detached from the powerful and persistent demands of capital and labor—which separates them from the framework party of the FDP—the Greens could increase their impact as the institutionalized gadfly and poser of tough questions for the future.

The Greens brought about no institutional changes of any significance, but their political cultural *Aufklärung* (enlightenment) work on experimenting with more aspects of direct democracy may have an effect in the future. On local and state levels, politicians are less cautious in discussing the merits of using binding or nonbinding referenda on controversial political issues. In an ironic way, the Greens, weighted down with the desire to challenge a difficult past by creating a reformed present, may have given the new Germany the confidence to shape a more flexible and democratic polity. The Weimar shadow made plebiscitarian democratic politics distasteful, but the totalitarian Third Reich experience made decentralized experiments attractive, especially to the successor generation of the late 1960s. Representative democracy with plebiscitarian features is not to be rejected out of hand. It may be the mix for societies in which electorates feel powerless and distant from their government even with regular elections. In short, the Greens convinced many Germans in the 1980s that grass-roots politics has a role to play in the evolving German democracy. On this point, the Greens of the West have solid support from the Alliance 90/Greens of the East, an area of joint agreement that may create a hinge for the future.

Greens and Citizen Movements of the East

The influence of the Western Greens on the activists in the former East Germany who became the leaders in the first democratic revolution from below in German history cannot be called critical. Other than Petra Kelly, Gerd Bastian, Milan Horacek, and Lukas Beckmann, the Greens of the Federal Republic made the usual criticisms of the German Democratic Republic but did not stretch much beyond the traditional parties. Bundestag member Kelly and others took the ecopax (for ecology and peace) theme, tied it to the human rights issue, and confronted the authorities of East Germany with provocative acts while building up a network of contacts with dissidents on the eastern side of the Wall.[16] When the epochal event of unification came, neither the Western Greens nor the citizen movements or Greens of the East were ready for the tempo of events.

The citizen movements and Greens of the East also wanted something other than being incorporated in rapid fashion to the Federal Republic. Their members had played a decisive role in throwing out the Communist rascals, but the alliance they formed in early 1990, a very loose confederation of citizen movements, was perplexed and disturbed by the rapid pace toward unification. After they correctly read the handwriting on the wall in the March 1990 East German national elections (unification, the quicker, the better), they were further perplexed by the Western Greens' inability to accept the reality of unification. Similar on many lines of policy—ecology, women's rights, civil rights, disarmament, democratization via decentralized authority—the citizen movements and Greens of the East had, for a variety of reasons, a skeptical and problematical relationship with the Western Greens. Many in the electronically linked global village were surprised and delighted to see the rapid changes in Eastern Europe that led to the dissolution of the Soviet satellite empire, the breaching of the Wall, and the independence of the East Germans from the double yoke on the Soviet Union and the Communist party of East Germany (Socialist Unity party). Several members of the electoral grouping that ran as the Alliance 90/Greens in the December 1990 election played crucial roles in the events of 1989 and 1990. The Alliance 90 contains the following citizen movements: New Forum, Democracy Now, Initiative for Peace and Human Rights, and the Independent Women's Association. These citizen movements were allied with the Greens of Eastern Germany, and that collection of forces contains political activists who had been in conflict with the East German authoritarian state for over two decades.[17]

These dissidents in the citizen movements challenged the state with their activities in peace groups and human rights groups long before a glimmer of change was in the offing.[18] They took courageous stands against the party state in fall 1989 by directing the demonstrations in Leipzig, Berlin, Dresden, and other large cities. Their leaders pushed for the removal of the party leaders, called for roundtable discussions to prepare for their independence, worked on the treaties linking the two Germanys, and provided leadership for a people in a state of shock as they surveyed the consequences of forty years of political tutelage, economic mismanagement, and widescale spying. When it became clear that unification would occur, and that the East Germans would have a series of three elections within a year, the citizen movements had to confront the same question the Greens of the West—under very difficult circumstances—faced in 1980: to compete in the electoral arena as a party or to remain an active citizen movement. The moment of truth came on March 18, 1990, as the East Germans elected their national legislature. The citizen movements, including the Greens, ran candidates and were completely overwhelmed by the sister parties of the CDU, the FDP, and the SPD. These parties—formerly bloc parties controlled largely by the Communist party—had received massive aid from their Western counterparts, were more highly organized, and conveyed their messages much more effectively. The citizens of East Germany clearly voted for unification as quickly as possible instead of at the more moderate tempo that the citizen groups urged.[19] The Alliance 90/Greens wanted a different, more deliberate path to a union or confederation in which they could negotiate and further define their proposals for the shape of the new Germany. They wanted more evenhanded negotiations with the "Wessies" and not a leveraged buy-out in which the East simply accepted the terms of the West.

The people thought otherwise and expressed that view in this first free election in fifty-three years. The overwhelming majority of citizens honored the courage of the citizen movements by allocating a small percentage of the vote to them but approved the quicker plan to unity held out by Chancellor Helmut Kohl and Foreign Minister Hans Genscher. The movement activists were disconsolate, but they barely had time to recover from the March 18, 1990, election before other decisive choices faced them. Should they run as a party or alliance in the first all-German elections? Should they ally themselves with the Greens of the West or should they sit it out?[20]

After a complicated set of legal maneuvers, the Federal Constitutional Court, at the insistence of the Greens of the West and other minor parties, decided that parties could run separately in the electoral districts of East and West Germany if they wanted to. The Greens of the West correctly refrained from trying to take over the Alliance 90/Greens. They respected the autonomy of their Eastern counterparts and with good reason. Any attempts by the West Greens at steering the Alliance 90/Greens would have ended in disaster. The principle of autonomous organizational control overrode the tactical consideration that a united party might have won more seats. In point of fact, they would have won more seats in a common effort.

For obvious reasons, it is well-nigh impossible to assess the impact of the "Greens" of the East. To begin, we should note emphatically that their political alliance is not called the Greens and that the East German citizen movement activists changed its name from "The Greens/Alliance 90" to "Alliance 90/Greens" to make a very clear point: The overall Green identity may come to have a more significant organizational meaning in the future, but for the present what exists is a loose confederation of citizen movements with the irony of eight parliamentarians from Eastern Germany as the nominal representation of all the Greens of the new Germany.

In short, hardly enough time has passed to judge the influence of these citizen movements and the Greens except to again emphasize their historic role in the democratic revolution from below, their frustrating attempts at defining a separate political identity of East Germany after the Communist dictatorship and before the new Germany, and their policy commitments to civil rights, ecology, women's rights, and disarmament. They have been vocal in demanding that the state security account for its past injustices and in pushing for constitutional reform on state and national levels. In a series of interviews with all eight elected members of the Alliance 90/Greens in June 1990, the question of the future alliance of the two Greens and the other citizen movements 90 was met with cautious judgments that ranged from "we'll wait and see" to "we need to work together to see what we can build."

The Influence of the Green Party from the Bonn Republic (1977–1989) to the Berlin Republic (1990–1991)

According to Kurt Biedenkopf, CDU politician, "the Greens have raised the right questions, but they give the wrong answers." Theo Sommer, editor of *Die Zeit*, says that "the Greens are the soluable fertilizer on the fields of the traditional parties." These comments give a representative sample of how the Greens' influence has been seen by knowledgeable observers of German politics. In the first instance, there would be few who would dispute the significance of the Greens in raising the environmental issue to a position of public concern. Not only do most politicians look more carefully at the cost-benefit analyses and the trade-off inevitably involved in economic development and environmental quality, but bureaucrats must anticipate environmental consequences of public policies and corporations must do the same calculations for their future investments.

The Greens are obviously not *the* pioneers in raising concerns about the environment either in Germany or in the postindustrial democracies. Rachel Carson's book *The Silent Spring* is a ground-breaking analysis of the dangers to the environment, and works like *The Limits to Growth* of the Club of Rome of 1972 and CDU politician Herbert Gruhl's book *The Planet is Plundered* have important historic significance. But the Greens did take the risk of confronting the voters with these problems in the arena of competitive party politics. Theo Sommer sees the effort of the Greens as providing a little fertilizer for plants—the traditional parties—that were well under way. The problem with this metaphor is that the traditional parties do not have deep roots and neither they nor the society would have dealt with the negative consequences of rapid economic growth without the serious challenge of the Greens.

Whatever the Greens accomplished since their start on the local level in the late 1970s, they certainly reduced their effectiveness on the national level with an organizational experiment that went awry. Intent on breaking the tabus of an older generation that they perceived as dismissive or forgetful of the authoritarian historical legacy and oblivious to the harmful consequences of growth-above-all-costs capitalism in an increasingly militarized alliance, the Greens brought their own generational tabus and hang-ups—to use a word of the 1960s—to the political marketplace: Hierarchy demeans human possibility, democracy means thoroughgoing egalitarianism, pluralism means antidotes to possible centers of power, and the folk on the grass roots are the fount of collective wisdom. There is some caricature in these characterizations, but there was a tone of moral uppityness in the dialogue between the generations that the Green activists conducted. Experience has modulated that tone.

Organizationally, the attempt to mate the movement style to the political party environment produced a hybrid that was neither democratic nor very efficient. As Jürgen Maier of the Greens Federal Executive Committee noted in 1990: "However, the party seems to develop a tendency to lose the advantages of a grassroots democratic organization without really gaining at the same time the advantages of a professional organization structure."[21] The Greens' fear of being co-opted by the world of party professionals, media consultants, and bureaucratic elites led them to develop a very weak institutional structure in a universe of very strong party institutions. Dispersed power led to pluralistic stagnations. However brilliant and innovative the ideas for change that the Greens did formulate, the vehicle for delivering it was horse and buggy in an autobahn environment. Beyond their talk about the need for tolerance in the larger society, the Greens' style of organizational guerrilla warfare between persons and factions indicated a want of civility that diminished both internal effectiveness and the image of the party in the mind of potential supporters. Critical dissent has its virtues; conflicting policy statements from a hydra-like organization undermined public confidence.

Despite all these limitations, the Greens are both a product and an agent of a more participant political culture that changed the way many citizens—especially the younger, more educated, urban middle class—saw their civic roles. They helped others conceive of a more critical attitude toward those wielding authority and in so doing continued the antiauthoritarian attitude that issued out of the student movement of the 1960s. By taking up the ecological issue, and in particular the antinuclear protest, the party effectively redirected the energy plans of the public sector and the policy proposals of the major parties to a different track. Because of the Greens and their allies in the social movements, there is less deference in the political culture and a more developed sense of the function of opposition.

The breakthrough of the Greens in the overall structure of pluralism in the old Federal Republic has two notable features. The Greens enlarged the field of competition, widened the choices for the voters, set up a linkage network with social movements that had not had much access, and changed the nature of the debate on certain public policy issues—the changing role of women, Germany's obligations to the Third World, investment in public transportation—in an indisputable way. As many observers have noted, the activity of Greens in local politics added a distinctively different voice to the debates of urban policy. On the national level, the Greens can point to no one piece of legislation upon which they left their stamp of particularity, but they can show their "fingerprints" on a wide range of legislation in their role as a competitive and constructive opposition.

The Greens agonized internally, and quite publicly, about whether they should preserve their principles (and "political chastity") by refusing to share power with any other party in a coalition. That was a major conflict between the pragmatic *Realos* and the purist *Fundis*. The issue was handled on an individual basis: city by city, state by state. The impact of these experiences is mixed. Several coalition negotiations in Hamburg wasted valuable time. Coalitions in Hesse and West Berlin were not successful partnerships for the Greens and the SPD, but the more recent coalitions of Lower Saxony, Hesse, Bremen, and Brandenburg show that however devastating the loss of the Greens of the West on the national level was, Green politics on local and state levels is a force with which other parties must reckon. It is increasingly clear that coalition opportunities will be looked at in a more professional and pragmatic way in the future.

The Greens and allied citizen movements of Eastern Germany had a critical role to play in the fall of the German Democratic Republic and in the rise of the East German political system, but the problems of the day in Eastern Germany are economic restructuring, large-scale unemployment, and rebuilding the infrastructure—not the constitutional, ecological, and human rights issues with which the Alliance 90/Greens have shaped their profile. The agenda in Germany, especially Eastern Germany, is presently materialist and not postmaterialist, and the future impact of the parties, East and West, will depend on their abilities to adapt their principles to the present problems.

How these two parties of East and West will work together in the next several years is as much an open question as is whether they will compete together as a party in the next national election of 1994. They have had very little experience in working with each other, but the imperatives of electoral competition suggest that separately neither party would make it in the 1994 national election, in which all of Germany will be the electoral district. Whether Green can remain a force of color in the party system of the new Germany will depend on a restructuring of the organization of the old Greens and a workable partnership with their Eastern counterparts.

Finally, we should note that the Green experiment in formation and development from the movement stage to the party stage and from the antiparty stage to the quasiprofessionalized stage has been watched with great interest in other postindustrial democracies. Although this party and its message of radical reform caused right-of-center politicians in other countries to inveigh against the Green "sickness" and caused left-of-center parties to worry about their left flank, it also encouraged a number of political activists in other democracies to give voice to a critique of thoughtless economic growth that threatened their sense of careful stewardship. The Greens of Germany have clearly been pioneers. Whether they can sustain their experiment into the 1990s will be our focus in the final chapter.

Notes

1. "The Greens didn't invent the ecology and women's questions, but they did the most to make these issues central themes of German domestic politics." Joachim Raschke, *Krise der Grünen* (Schüren: Marburg, 1991), p. 187.

2. Stephen Fisher, "The Decline-of-Parties Thesis and the Role of Minor Parties," in *Western European Party Systems*, Peter Merkl, ed. (New York: Free Press, 1980), pp. 609–613.

3. Gabriel Almond and Sidney Verba, eds., *The Civic Culture Revisited* (Boston: Little, Brown, 1980), pp. 212–272.

4. David Conradt, "German Unification and the Remade Political Culture." Paper presented at the American Political Science Association, San Francisco, August 1990.

5. In *Krise der Grünen*, p. 189, Raschke writes, "The alliance between an extraparliamentary left and ecology [forces], which solidified in the late 1970s and the early 1980s is, in its intensity, a German singularity among the west European nation-states."

6. Hans-Joachim Veen, "The Greens as a Milieu Party," in *The Greens of West Germany*, Eva Kolinsky, ed. (Oxford: Berg, 1989), pp. 31–60.

7. Michael Schrören, ed., *Die Grünen: 10 bewegte Jahre* (Wien: Überreuter, 1990); Ralf Fücks, ed., *Sind die Grünen noch zu retten?* (Hamburg: Rowolt, 1991).

8. Raschke, *Krise der Grünen*, p. 178.

9. Peter Katzenstein, *Policy and Politics in West Germany: The Growth of the Semisovereign State* (Philadelphia: Temple University Press, 1987), pp. 356–359; Robert Dahl, *Dilemmas of Pluralist Democracy: Autonomy Versus Control* (New Haven: Yale University Press, 1982).

10. Claus Offe, "Reflections on the Institutional Self-Transformation of Movement Politics; A Tentative Stage Model," in *Challenging the Political Order*, Russell Dalton and Manfred Küchler, eds. (New York: Oxford University Press, 1990), pp. 232–250.

11. Gerard Braunthal, *The West German Social Democrats, 1969–1982: Profile of a Party in Power* (Boulder: Westview Press, 1983).

12. Frank Drieschner, Wolfgang Gehrmann, Thomas Kleine-Brockhoff, Norbert Kostede, Klaus Pilatzky, Ulrich Stock, and Christian Wernicke, "Wie die Zukunft aus dem Parlament verschwand," *Die Zeit*, December 14, 1990.

13. Samuel Beer, *Britain Against Itself: The Political Contradictions of Collectivism* (New York: Norton, 1982). Speaking of a change in the political cultures in Western polities, Beer states: "The thrust has been twofold. On the one hand, a powerful, indeed, an exaggerated and unbalanced assertion of the values of scientific rationalism engendered a trend toward technocracy. At the same time, a romantic revolt in politics gave rise to a new populism that embodied a hardly less exaggerated expression of democratic values" (p. 111).

14. Raschke, *Krise der Grünen*; Robert Dahl, *Democracy and Its Critics* (New Haven: Yale University Press, 1989).

15. Antje Vollmer, "Das Privileg der ersten, viele Fehler zu machen: Gründe für den Nidergang," in *Sind die Grünen noch zu retten?* Ralf Fücks, ed. (Reinbek: Rowolt, 1991), pp. 10–17.

16. Interview with Petra Kelly, June 1991, Bonn, West Germany.

17. In addition to the interviews with the eight members of the Alliance 90/ Greens Bundestag delegation, there are various interviews in print by these party members.

18. Hubertus Knabe, ed., *Aufbruch in eine andere DDR* (Reinbek: Rowolt, 1989).

19. Daniel Hamilton, *After the Revolution: The New Political Landscape in East Germany* (Washington, D.C.: American Institute for Contemporary German Studies, 1990).

20. Interviews with five members of citizen movements associated with Alliance 90/Greens in Rostock, June 16, 1991, focused on this topic.

21. Jürgen Maier, "The Green Parties in Western Europe," *Die Grünen: Monatszeitung* (Bonn: Die Grünen, 1990).

9

The "Greening" of Europe?

OVER THE PAST DECADE, Green parties have become the rule and not the exception in West European party systems. They have emerged though the odds are typically stacked against the success of new parties. They have been new in more than the chronological sense: They have raised new issues and have reflected new organizational forms. The international effect of their example was apparent by the late 1980s as ecology clubs and movements launched Green parties in Eastern Europe as the Communist party-states crumbled.

Although the German Greens were not the first national Green party in Europe, they quickly became the most conspicuous member of this new "family" of political parties. Given Germany's historic importance in European and world politics, antiestablishment parties emerging there are bound to receive wide media coverage. Furthermore, the Federal Republic's generous provision of public funding for political parties made the Greens the wealthiest member of the new family. During their first decade, the Greens won significant numbers of parliamentary seats at all levels of West German government, demonstrating sufficient support to influence the programmatic development of the major parties. Even after losing their *Bundestagsfraktion* in December 1990, because of persisting votes and power sharing at the local and state levels, the Greens have remained a relevant force in the party system of united Germany. Although Green parties have not yet made the transition from "protest" to "contender" status elsewhere in Western Europe, they are represented in the national parliaments of Switzerland, Belgium, the Netherlands, Luxembourg, Ireland, Finland, Austria, Italy, Greece, Portugal, and Malta. French Greens are represented at the local, regional, and European levels, whereas British and Swedish (since September 1991) Greens are only represented in local councils. Small Green parties also exist in Denmark, Norway, Iceland, and Spain but have had little electoral significance. Ferdinand Müller-Rommel's comparative study of West European Green parties during the period from 1978 to 1989 ranked the German Greens as the most politically successful Green party, followed by the Belgian Green parties.[1]

The results of the June 1989 European Parliament elections provide a synchronic perspective on the relative strength of the Green parties of European Community member states. Green parties won 8.1 percent of the Euro-votes, which Wolfgang Rüdig assesses as "quite an achievement for a new type of party that hardly existed 10 years ago."[2] The Greens did only slightly better by winning 8.4 percent of Euro-votes in West Germany. However, the British Greens (14.9 percent), the Belgian Green parties (13.9 percent), the Luxembourg Green parties (11.3 percent), and the French Greens (10.6 percent) demonstrated more strength. The low turn-out for the 1989 European Parliament elections in Britain (36 percent) and France (49 percent) exaggerates their Green parties' voter appeal when one presumes that Green supporters tend to be more motivated to vote than the supporters of the major parties. Yet the high (legally obligatory) turnout in Luxembourg (88 percent) and Belgium (91 percent) does not lend itself to such facile deflating of the electoral strength of their Green parties.

Thus some of the members of the new family of political parties in Western Europe have made progress in establishing themselves in their respective party systems; however, most are unlikely to be contenders for national power in the near future. Some observers argue that in the early 1990s this family had already begun to fade, as major parties have taken up environmental issues. They overlook the fact that while German and Swedish Greens have suffered national setbacks, other Green parties, for example, Swiss, Finnish, Austrian, and Belgian, have recently scored gains at the national or provincial levels. Although the German Greens have been the most important model of Green party politics (its strengths *and* weaknesses), one should be aware of the diversities within this new growing family of parties. In the following sections, we will focus on the contrasting development of the British Green Party, survey other West European Green parties, outline the characteristics of the European Parliament's Green group, and consider the uncertain prospects of East European Green parties.

British Greens

In January 1986, the obscure British Ecology Party (then 5,700 members, whereas West German Greens numbered 38,000) relaunched itself as the Green party of the U.K. It hoped to make explicit the association with the more successful West European Green parties and to prevent other British parties from "poaching" the identity. The party traces its roots back to

1973, which gives it the distinction of being Europe's oldest nationally organized Green party. However, its level of electoral success (except for its surprising protest vote in the 1989 Euro-elections) contrasts negatively with that of the West German and Belgian Greens. In national elections for the House of Commons, the British Greens have never won more than 0.3 percent of the total votes. Eighteen years after their founding, the British Greens hold only about 200 local council seats (mostly at the parish level); the German Greens hold 7,000.

The political opportunity structure that the British Greens confront has been anything but encouraging. Britain's plurality (first-past-the-post) electoral system precludes any parliamentary role for a small party that lacks geographical strongholds. British electoral law also hinders small parties in parliamentary elections (though not in local elections) by requiring constituency deposits (currently 500£) to get on the ballot. Only once (in a 1989 by-election) has the British Green party won sufficient votes in a Westminster election to save its deposit. In contrast to Germany, Britain has no public funding for party campaign expenses. Furthermore, the British Greens did not spring from a widespread grass-roots base of citizen action groups. The passionately fought direct action campaigns against nuclear power, which set the stage for the Greens in West Germany, were largely missing in Britain during the 1970s. Also, unlike in West Germany, feminist groups did not link up with the British Green party. Although British Greens took positions similar to those of West German Greens regarding nuclear disarmament, they were overshadowed by the antimilitarist left wing of the Labour Party and the revived nonpartisan Campaign for Nuclear Disarmament (CND) in the early 1980s. West German Greens could build up resources, experience, and visibility by winning seats in the Landtage, but under Britain's centralized unitary system, the isolated wins of local council seats by British Greens translated into no real advantage for national politics.

The party's 1979 manifesto advocated fundamental changes toward a stable economy with basic security and prosperity through self-sufficiency, a decentralized way of life, long-term vision, and an emphasis on non-material values. According to Müller-Rommel's classification, the British Greens are one of the "pure green reformist parties" whereas the West German Greens are one of the "alternative green radical parties."[3] Yet the British Greens have perceived themselves as a radical party in the sense that they are addressing the causes and not just the symptoms of the sicknesses of industrial society. As the West German Greens did in the early 1980s, the British Greens have portrayed themselves as neither a party of the left nor the right. During the 1980s, the majority of British Green activists maintained that the conventional ideological distinction has little relevance to current policy dilemmas whereas many West German Green activists saw themselves, in varied ways, as ecosocialists. At the European level, British Greens clashed at times with West German Greens over political strategy. The latter favored alliances with small radical and leftist parties, which in the case of the Netherlands in the 1984 Euro-election campaign meant cooperation with the Communists. The former doubted the ecological conversion experience of such leftist parties. During the 1980s, prominent British Greens, for example, Sara Parkin, were critical of the role of Marxist-oriented activists within the West German Greens and alert against leftist "entryism" within their own party.

The formidable challenge for British Greens has been to apply their policies of decentralization, devolution (for example, Scottish and Welsh Greens are separately organized), and democratic electoral reform to their own party organization and still survive the harsh realities of the British political opportunity structure. The party constitution emphasized the wide autonomy of local parties but also set up an annual conference of members as "the supreme policy-making forum of the Party."[4] Complaints about overloaded conference agendas have been as common as among the German Greens. The Party Council of twenty-five members had no policymaking powers between conferences; instead its role was policy interpretation. The participation of many area representatives in council meetings tended to be irregular. Party Council tenure was limited to three consecutive years. Yet given the frustrations of the work, the real problem was not preventing competent leaders from entrenching themselves but getting them to stay. Collective leadership was provided by three coequal chairs elected annually by the Party Council. Women have been well represented as party officers and as parliamentary and council candidates, without the party's resorting to the formal quotas enacted by the German Greens. In the late 1980s, the British Green party employed only two full-time and two part-time workers and operated on a national budget of 48,000£, organizational resources roughly comparable to those of Lower Saxony Greens.

Although one could read realist-fundamentalist cleavages into the intraparty politics of the British Greens, a better case can be made that their persisting cleavage has been between a larger camp of "electoralists" and a smaller camp of "anarchists."[5] The electoralists aim to win seats at all levels of government and see no inherent evils in political parties. The anarchists oppose anything that strengthens the national party organization. They emphasize involvement in direct action campaigns. However, electoralists have seen in even nonviolent protest the danger of alienating voters, given Britain's lack of a revolutionary tradition.[6] The evidence indicates that Green local councillors have been pragmatic idealists willing to cooperate with other parties in effecting concrete changes.

By winning 14.9 percent of the Euro-votes in June 1989, the British Greens surprised the pundits *and* themselves. However, the party was not able to follow up on its long-awaited electoral breakthrough. Soon its third-place standing in the national polls faded and its membership (which had surged to 18,000) plunged by a third, putting a party heavily dependent on membership dues again on the verge of bankruptcy. In the 1990 and 1991 district elections, where the Greens contested seats, they averaged about 5 to 6 percent of the votes.[7] This outcome represents an improvement over the results of the 1980s, but still trails far behind the Liberal Democrats, who in recent years have projected themselves as the practical Green alternative. Both the Labour and Conservative parties also have spoken more about environmental protection since the 1989 Euro-results.

As in the case of the German Greens, structural reform rose to the top of the British Green party's agenda in the early 1990s. A national group of veteran electoralists launched the Green 2000 initiative, which succeeded in winning majority support for constitutional changes to strip away cumbersome antiparty features. The Green 2000 motion declared, "The party recognizes the existence of, and need for a formal, open, and accountable leadership."[8] Specifically, the September 1991 annual conference voted to abolish the Green Party Council and replace it with a Regional Council (representing area parties) and a Party Executive (nine voting members and two nonvoting speakers) with all officers elected to specific posts by postal ballot of the membership. The Party Executive is responsible for day-to-day direction of the party but is also to review the party's election and campaign strategy. Furthermore, the annual conference is to be recast as a delegate (not membership) assembly so as to be more representative of local parties. Despite divergent circumstances and characteristics, majorities of both the British and German Greens thus voted in 1991 to increase the political efficacy of their party organizations for the long haul. In the case of the British Green party, its power prospects are remote without major electoral reform; however, Rüdig's membership survey found a "core of long-term activists who are not discouraged by this prospect."[9]

Other West European Greens

Although the British Green party is one of Western Europe's larger Green parties in terms of dues-paying membership (in 1989–1990 second only to West Germans), it is clearly less well established electorally and governmentally than Green parties in a number of other West European countries. As in Britain, political ecology has had a long and frustrating history in France. However, in 1989 the French Greens (Les Verts) scored their dual breakthrough at the local and European levels, which proportional electoral provisions (not available to the British Greens) facilitated. Although the French Greens, who have about 5,000 members[10] still rank behind the British Greens in size of membership, their prospects appear more promising in the 1990s.

In France, ecological candidates have contested local elections since 1973 and national elections since 1974. In 1977 ecological lists won thirty or so local council seats; twelve years later the Greens won 1,369 seats. In 1986 they won three seats in the new elected regional councils. Green candidates gained media attention with their credible 1.3, 3.9, and 3.8 percent of first-round votes in the presidential elections of 1974, 1981, and 1988. In the 1979 European elections, the candidate list of Europe-Ecologie won 4.4 percent of the French votes (missing seats by only 0.6 percent). The Greens slipped to 3.4 percent in the 1984 European elections—because of a competing list headed by former presidential candidate Brice Lalonde—but then surged to 10.6 percent in the 1989 European elections, thus electing the largest number of parliamentary representatives (nine MEPs) of any Green party. However, the French Greens have not enjoyed success in national parliamentary elections. Even when France departed from the two-rounds plurality system to employ a proportional electoral scheme in 1986, the Greens won only 1.2 percent of the votes.

Because of strong aversions to the party format and strong decentralist views among ecological activists, the Green organizational pattern into the early 1980s was one of ad hoc electoral alliances of groups that between elections pursued goals by lobbying and demonstrating. Electoral alliances were loosely knit and soon torn apart by philosophical, tactical, and personality issues. Frustrations with this organizational experience paved the way for the formation of two Green parties in 1981 and 1982. Then in 1984 they merged as Les Verts with 700 members.

As in the cases of the German and British Greens, the French Greens have emphasized intraparty democracy, decentralization, and collegial leadership. The Annual General Meeting and the party regions together elect the sixty-member National Council, which annually elects the twenty-member Executive Council, which is headed by four cospeakers. Despite the Greens' institutional procedures and cultural predispositions, in recent years Antoine Waechter has emerged as the de facto national leader, particularly in terms of media coverage. During the 1980s, the French Greens encountered severe financial difficulties and at times had to turn to German and Belgian Greens for aid. The French electoral system provides public funding as campaign reimbursement for parties receiving 5.0 percent, in contrast to 0.5 percent under the German electoral law.

According to Müller-Rommel's classification, the French Greens, like British Greens, are a "pure green reformist" party.[11] John Ely observes, "The purist 'moss green' tendency is purest in France, where it has been strong ever since the French ecologists split over the issue in 1978."[12] The majority of Green activists have opposed electoral alliances with small radical leftist parties in national and European campaigns and have prioritized environmental (naturalist) themes higher than socioeconomic themes. Waechter has worked to keep the party independent from the Left and the Right in elections. Yet the party membership includes prominents, such as Yves Cochet, who have advocated a "Red-Green" strategy like that of the West German Greens. However, recent electoral successes have reinforced the party's "Green-Green" majority. In late 1991, when the polls indicated 15 percent support for the Greens, both prominent French conservatives (Rally for the Republic [RPR]) and socialists (Socialist party [PS]) were publicly raising the prospect of national coalition building with the Greens. Already there have been local government alliances between the Greens and other parties, mainly on the left, in several large cities (for example, Lille, Dunkirk, Aix, Avignon).[13] Thus, in comparison to German Greens the French Greens are more centrist, but one should not ignore the survey, electoral, and programmatic evidence, which indicates that they tend both to question the meaningfulness of the left-right continuum in reference to contemporary problems and to sympathize more with the Left.

The successes of the French ecologists in the 1977 local elections encouraged their Belgian (and West German) counterparts to move toward party formation. Agalev is the Flemish Green party and Ecolo is the Walloon Green party. They are sister parties that do not compete against each other in elections but instead work together in Belgian and European parliamentary politics. Agalev stems from an alternative life-style movement founded in 1970, whose "catacomb" Christianity set it apart from the established Catholic church (and the Christian People's Party). Agalev evolved from being the alternative movement's electoral committee to becoming a party in 1982, a year after it won two seats in the Belgian Chamber of Deputies. Ecolo grew out of the political linkage of Walloon regionalists and ecologists. In the late 1970s, Ecolo faced competition from other Green lists, which were more open to the left. In 1980 Ecolo launched itself as a new kind of party and in 1981 won two seats in the Chamber of Deputies. Thus the two Belgian Green parties were represented at the national level two years before the West German Greens entered the Bundestag. In 1982 Agalev and Ecolo won 120 seats on local councils and in 1984 both won seats in the European Parliament.

The Belgian system of proportional representation does not handicap small parties whose votes are geographically spread. Agalev and Ecolo's combined share of the national votes increased in the 1985 and 1987 parliamentary elections. In the 1991 parliamentary elections, the Belgian Greens together received 10.0 percent of the votes; Agalev won seven seats and Ecolo (which doubled its electoral percentage) won ten seats. Although their share of the votes appears to be less than it was in the 1989 European Parliament elections, one must remember that the Belgian parliamentary election was a "first-order election" with a national government at stake. West German Greens in a "first-order election" have never won more than 8.3 percent of the votes. The November 1991 results may mark the transition of Belgian Greens from a protest party to a contender party if in its aftermath they become a relevant variable in the major parties' national coalition calculations. Both Green parties have already participated in local coalitions with other parties. Most noteworthy is that during the period from 1983 to 1988, Ecolo in coalition with the socialists held three of eleven seats in Liege's governing committee. Fundamentalists have constituted the minority within the Belgian Greens.[14]

The Belgian Green parties are both structured to be more democratic organizations than the established parties. According to Kitschelt, "participatory openness, decisional decentralization, and the rotation of party leaders [and members of Parliament] are meant to protect Agalev and Ecolo from oligarchical tendencies."[15] In the mid-1980s, Agalev was the more pluralist and nonhierarchical party, in which strong personalities turned up in the parliamentary group, and Ecolo was the more centralized, hierarchical party, in which strong personalities turned up in the party executive. Yet compared to the other parties, both Green parties have operated as "more open, fluid organizations"[16] with party militants committed to defending local party autonomy. Agalev and Ecolo each have about 1,000 members, but evidence indicates that their high level of activism, compared with the established parties, helps to make up for their relatively small memberships.

Müller-Rommel categorized the Belgian Green parties as "pure green reformist parties."[17] Both Agalev and Ecolo have been opposed to alliances with radical leftist parties. Eurobarometer data indicate that Belgian Green voters include significantly lower percentages of left and moderate left self-identifiers than do French or West German Greens. However, Kitschelt and Hellemans's activist study found that over two-thirds of Belgian Greens classified themselves as left or center-left. On closer analysis, their responses reflect a blending of "post-material, ecological, leftist, and libertarian demands."[18] One could say the same for the views of West German Green activists except that their leftist component was generally stronger during the 1980s.

Green party politics has been more complex in neighboring Netherlands. Supported by European Greens (except the West Germans), a small

Dutch Green party (De Grönen) emerged in 1983. Although Dutch electoral law is based on strict proportionality with only 0.7 percent required to obtain seats in the lower house of the national parliament, De Grönen has failed to win seats. Preexisting small radical and leftist parties, which already claimed to represent new social movements, have revised their programs to appeal to the presumably growing Green electorate. Radicals (PPR), Pacifist Socialists (PSP), and the Communists (CPN), running jointly as the Green Progressive Accord in the 1984 European Parliament elections, won two seats with 5.6 percent of the votes. (One should note that running separately the three parties won a higher percentage of the votes in the 1982 parliamentary elections.) During 1989, this Red-Green alliance won two seats (7.0 percent) in the Euro-election and later six seats (4.1 percent) in the Dutch parliamentary elections.

In the following year, the PPR, PSP, CPN, and the small Evangelical People's Party (EVP) agreed to merge as a new party, the Green Left (Groen Links). The combined membership of over 18,000 makes it the second largest Green party (after the German Greens) in Western Europe. In the 1991 regional elections, Groen Links won 5.2 percent of the votes, in contrast to only 0.6 percent for the pure Green De Groenen. Paul Lucardie's study concludes that "the purpose of the merger was not only the preservation of parliamentary seats but also an ideological renewal. . . . [However,] the 'greening' of the Communists may have started only recently and remained rather spotty."[19] Nevertheless, his survey data indicate that the activists of the PPR, PSP, and EVP also see themselves as on the left, if not far left. Müller-Rommel's mid-1980s classification of Dutch Greens under the "alternative green radical" heading[20] seems even more appropriate in the early 1990s. The future role for the new Green Left party in Dutch multiparty politics seems to be that of a "Red-Green" permanent opposition party with perhaps indirect influence on the policy agenda.

Of the remaining Green parties in the European Community (EC) member states, only the Luxembourg Greens (Dei Greng Alternative) have since 1984 independently won and maintained seats in the national parliament, despite splits and competing lists. Founded in 1983, this tiny party (which had 120 dues-paying members) modeled its organization and program on the neighboring West German Greens. Although the Luxembourg Greens have raised public consciousness on Green issues, their chances of government participation appear slim.[21] Such also would seem to be the case for the small Green parties represented in the national parliaments of Ireland (one seat) and Greece (one seat).

Generally, public concern about environmental problems has lagged in the less developed southern European countries. In 1981, the Portuguese Greens (Os Verdes) emerged. This party has claimed to have about 1,000 members. Since 1987 they have won a couple of national parliamentary seats by standing on the candidate lists sponsored by Portugal's Communist party, which is dominated by the old guard. Initially discounted by some observers as a Communist front, Os Verdes eventually became a full-fledged member of the international organization of European Greens. In neighboring Spain, the Greens have run as multiple lists (including right-wing groups) with meager results in national and European elections. The largest Spanish Green party, Los Verdes, claimed in 1987 to have at least 800 members and to have elected two local councillors.[22] The Italian Greens have not coalesced as a national party and possibly may never, given the tactical advantage of their antiparty appeal for those voters alienated from established minor as well as major parties in Italy. After electing 141 local councillors in 1985, Italian Greens formed a federation of Green and Alternative Lists. In 1987 their parliamentary candidates won 2.5 percent of the votes and thirteen deputies and two senators were elected. Two competing lists contested the 1989 European Parliament elections. The (red-green) Rainbow List won two seats (2.4 percent) while the Green List won three seats (3.8 percent). In recent years the Italian Communist party, by changing its program, logo, and name, has sought to adapt to new political realities, including the appeal of political ecology.

Beyond the EC countries, we find Green parties represented in the national parliaments of three countries of the European Free Trade Association (EFTA). Austrian Greens have been represented since 1984 at the provincial level and since 1986 at the national level. Their electoral breakthrough was the result of an alliance of two ecology parties both formed in 1982—a moderate environmentalist party (VGÖ [Vereinte Grüne Österreichs]; United Greens) and an alternative left party. Their small parliamentary group, Die Grüne Alternative, has functioned as a constructive opposition. Yet in view of recent trends, one can no longer rule out a working relationship with the Social Democrats (SPÖ) at some point in the future. Finnish Greens have seen their share of the national parliamentary votes increase from 1.5 percent in 1983 to 6.8 percent in 1991. However, their small group of MPs has been neither a power factor nor an active opposition. At the local level, where the Greens held over eighty council seats in 1986, there has been a tendency for their councillors to support the Communists on local issues.[23] Swiss Greens also have seen their parliamentary representation increase since 1979, when a regionalist Green party elected Europe's first Green national MP. In 1991 Swiss Greens won fourteen seats in the national parliament. Two Green federations of local and regional parties, one moderate and one radical, emerged in 1983. In 1987 the moderate federation gave birth to the Swiss Green party (GPS), which continued to face competition from alternative left groups. The GPS, which has about 4,500 members, has become well rooted in the regional parliaments and has even held a few regional executive offices.[24]

During the period from 1988 to 1991, the Swedish Green party (Miljöpartiet) was represented in the Rikstag (national parliament) by twenty deputies. Founded in 1981, the Swedish Greens' membership had grown to 6,500 in the late 1980s. In the parliamentary arena, the Greens took a purist stance by refusing to associate with either the socialist or the nonsocialist bloc of parties. In contrast to 1988, environmental issues were not at the top of the policy agenda during the 1991 campaign. This, coupled with the Greens' disorganization, brought their share of the national vote down from 5.5 percent to 3.4 percent (0.6 percent short of the parliamentary threshold for seats). Despite the national setback, they managed to hold onto hundreds of local council seats and to be a power factor in several cities.

In sum, our West European survey reveals the prevalence and the diversity of the Greens. Although virtually all West European Green parties have been represented at the subnational level of government and a majority have been represented at the national level of government, they have typically played marginal roles in national politics. Some have suffered recent setbacks, but others—ignored by the media—have seen their support persist in less favorable materialist times and even increase, as in the case of Ecolo in Belgium.

Europe: Rainbow and Green Politics

The European Greens Coordination dates from 1983. It is the successor organization of the Coordination of European and Radical Parties, which was launched in the aftermath of the 1979 Euro-elections. Its current membership includes two dozen parties from Western and Eastern Europe. The European Greens' Joint Declaration of January 23, 1984, outlines the common viewpoint: "Europe should no longer be governed, or misgoverned, by central authorities. The diversity of its culture, of its peoples and regions . . . [must] be conserved and developed for the benefit of every European." The European Greens advocate a "truly democratic Europe" with a "federal structure based on regions rather than nation states"[25] and embrace the notion of a third ecological path between Western liberal capitalism and Eastern state socialism.

In their 1984 European election program, the West German Greens contrast postwar hopes for European unity with the realities of West European integration. To put it simply, the German Greens are for (all) Europe but against the European Community, whose bloated, costly, and complex bureaucracy they portray as beyond democratic controls. The EC Commission and Council of Ministers are criticized for encouraging the environmentally destructive forces of industrial capitalism. According to the Greens, the directly elected but essentially powerless European Parliament functions primarily to legitimize movement toward West European union. The 1984 European program of the Greens attempts to have it both ways regarding the European Parliament. First, the EC is criticized because of the subordinate role of its parliament. Second, the major West German parties' support for more powers for the Parliament is criticized as part of a plan to develop the EC as a superpower complete with its own military forces. As their alternative, the Greens advocate "the decentralization of political-economic decision making structures and the decartelization of existing European institutions."[26]

On the basis of "our common commitment for a new Europe, neutral and decentralized, with autonomous regions," EC Green parties formed a "technical alliance" to contest the 1984 Euro-elections—and hopefully to qualify for campaign reimbursements.[27] Although German, Belgian, and Dutch Greens won sufficient seats to form a European parliamentary group, the German Greens put together a wider alliance of Greens, radicals, regionalists, and the Danish anti-EC movement. The resulting Rainbow Group had twenty MEPs, who shared little more than their opposition to existing EC institutions and policy priorities. The Rainbow Group included three organized subgroups: the Green Alternative European Link (GRAEL), the regionalist European Free Alliance (EVA), and the Danish anti-EC movement. The Rainbow Group rarely met in plenary sessions. Its three subgroups, which had little to do with each other, were represented in the executive bodies of the European Parliament by a rotating president (who was one of the four Rainbow vice-presidents).

Only the GRAEL subgroup was preoccupied with international Green issues of ecology, peace, and human rights (especially of women). Its parliamentary membership included seven Germans, two Dutch, one Belgian (Agalev), and one Italian. The Belgian Ecolo MEP chose to be a member of the regionalist EVA subgroup. The MEPs and their alternates had equal rights and duties in the GRAEL subgroup. As in the Bundestag, the German Greens were supposed to rotate by giving up their seats at midterm to their alternates. However, three of the seven refused. This action should not have come as a surprise: In putting together their MEP candidates list, the Greens had nominated conspicuous nonmembers, who had their own personal agendas, to favorable positions. One of the Dutch MEPs was also obliged to rotate and did so. The other parties represented in GRAEL did not mandate rotation for their MEPs. The GRAEL employed a staff of eighteen members, who, according to one critical observer, "gradually gained more power and importance than the disparate and mostly inexperienced MEPs."[28]

Yet one must remember that during the period from 1984 to 1989 the Rainbow Group held a small minority of the seats as the seventh largest parliamentary group within the European Parliament, which has been little more than a large consultative assembly. The parliamentary dilemma was balancing two approaches: "to adopt strong positions of principle, knowing the Council of Ministers will totally disregard the opinions of the European Parliament . . . or . . . to compromise, in the hope that the Council will be prepared to take the opinion of the European Parliament into account in its discussions."[29] Nevertheless, GRAEL MEPs made full use of parliamentary devices (reports, resolutions, and questions) to try to influence public opinion and to build up contacts with movement groups. In retrospect, Jakob von Uexkull, a GRAEL MEP, maintains that the Greens, in trying to prove themselves good parliamentarians, spread themselves too thin. And like the Bundestag Greens, and in contrast to other parliamentary groups, GRAEL also emphasized their members' involvement in nonparliamentary activities. As evidence of overachiever behavior, von Uexkull points out that the eleven GRAEL MEPs' postage bill was larger than that of the Socialist Group's 165 MEPs.[30] From the outset, it was apparent that the institutional constraints of the GRAEL subgroup guaranteed that it could have no more than a (rare) limited impact on EC policies. GRAEL's impact was even further diminished by the lack of a coherent strategy on European issues not only among its MEPs but also, more basically, among their national Green parties.[31]

The West German Greens in their 1989 Euro-election program declare their objective to be the ecological, social, and feminist reconstruction (Umbau) of the "Common House of Europe."[32] They look beyond the EC to see promising signs of a unifying Europe in recent activities of the Council of Europe and the Conference on Security and Cooperation in Europe (CSCE). As in 1984, they oppose the development of the EC as a superpower and the predominance in EC policymaking of powerful industrial interests. Compared to 1984, the German Greens are less ambivalent regarding the European Parliament. They support giving it not only codecision powers in legislation and budget control but also the power to elect and remove European commissioners. In contrast to other supporters of institutional reforms, the German Greens also emphasize the importance of direct democratic elements as a counterweight to the behind-the-scenes influence of the EC bureaucracy. According to their 1989 Euro-program, the presence of the Greens in the European Parliament is vital to amplify the voices of grass-roots movements, to obtain information for them, and to utilize parliamentary resources to support and to draw them together.

West German Green MEPs elected in 1989 sought to renew the Rainbow Group by putting together an even larger Green alternative alliance, including again small antiestablishment parties. However, Belgian and French Greens as well as the European Greens Coordination favored a smaller, more coherent Green Group in the European Parliament. The majority view was that to embrace radical leftists and right-wing regionalists would obscure the separate Green identity. Because one German Green MEP and one French MEP chose to join regionalists and another Rainbow Group, the Green Group ended up with twenty-nine members. The Greens are thus the fifth largest Euro-parliamentary group; they hold one seat more than the Communist European United Left. The Green Group is represented on all committees (chairing the Regional Policy and Planning Committee) and holds a vice-presidency of the European Parliament.[33]

The Bureau of the Green Group consists of two copresidents, two vice-presidents, and a treasurer who coordinate the workings of the Group. This time the German Greens have not obliged their MEPs to rotate; only the French Greens have. The Group includes seven Italian MEPs from several Green, Red-Green, and radical lists or parties. A couple of them have appeared more committed to the strategy of the Radical party than to that of the Green Group. MEPs from Belgium (3), the Netherlands (2), Spain (1 Basque), and Portugal (1) round out the Group, which has the highest proportion of women (41 percent) of any Euro-parliamentary group. Within the Green Group, each MEP has two votes, except for French MEPs, who have one vote because their alternates also have one vote. Although Britain's plurality electoral system prevented the election of British Green MEPs, the British Green party has a voting representative in the Group (because one of the MEPs loaned his second vote). The European Greens Coordination sends a nonvoting representative to meetings of the Bureau and the Group. The Green Group employs a staff of about forty, whose recruitment was laborious because of the need to achieve gender and nationality balance.[34] The Green Group has taken its parliamentary work seriously. For example, in its first year, the Group introduced 114 *urgences* motions with about a fourth of them being adopted by the Parliament. Also the Group has been involved with sixty-seven parliamentary reports, several of which have received favorable reactions from the Parliament.[35] The Greens' strategy in the Parliament has been to work to build up issue-related alliances, not just with left parties. Outside of Parliament, Green MEPs have worked to provide information and assistance to Green and alternative movements in Eastern and Western Europe. For example, in June 1990 they organized the first Parliament of Greens, which brought 116 representatives to Strasbourg from over twenty European countries, including the USSR.

The impact of the Greens within the Commission/Council-dominated EC policymaking process is hard to assess in the short run, but in the long run the Green Group appears to be well positioned to raise public awareness about the ecological and social costs of the Single European Market. Already, for example, the Greens have protested the advantages to be reaped by agroindustrial firms at the expense of small family farms.

East European Greens

During the 1980s, local groups protesting environmental dangers began to spring up in Eastern Europe. Although some Communist governments had allowed naturalist clubs to operate, all had repressed those who sought to expose the environmental costs of industrialization. Although the USSR and several Eastern European countries had tough water and air quality standards on the books, given the Communist party leadership's fixation on industrial production, the implementation of these standards had been poor.[36] Despite frequent harassment, local protest groups in some countries had managed by the late 1980s to establish national networks, which contributed to mobilizing public discontent with the overall policy performance of the Communist leaderships. Against the historic backdrop of Mikhail Gorbachev's promotion of *glasnost* (openness), *perestroika* (restructuring), and new thinking in foreign policy, East European environmentalists helped to set the stage for broad-based democratic opposition movements.

As Communist regimes began to crumble, in some places top-down Green parties emerged overnight (the evidence suggests that they were Communist fronts) and in other places ex-Communist activists joined existing (bottom-up) Green movements. As in Western Europe a decade earlier, some Green activists favored remaining movements while others favored legal organization as Green parties. Despite the supporting role that Green activists had played in the transformation of East European politics, Green movements and parties did poorly (compared to what the polls had predicted) in the first round of free elections (1989–1990). With the fall of communism, nationalist themes resurged in public debate. And as the euphoria faded, the public's anxieties about the personal sacrifices involved in the transition to a free market economy quickly overshadowed long-run environmental threats.

Generalizations are precarious, but as a rule East European Green parties tend to be liberal-democratic rather than left-alternative. As fledgling party organizations, they have been vulnerable to schisms over personality, strategy, and ideology. Activists from the Polish Ecology Club (associated with Solidarity) launched East Europe's first Green party in

December 1988. However, Polish Greens soon splintered into competing parties that have not become individually or collectively a contending force in post-Communist national politics. In late 1991, Green parties (some of which label themselves movements) could be found in every East European country (except Albania), in each of the Baltic states, and in at least five former Soviet republics.[37]

In Eastern Europe, Greens are represented in the national parliaments of Bulgaria and Romania. In Bulgaria, the Ecoglasnost movement, which played an important role in the overthrow of the Stalinist regime of Zhivkov, and a Green party participated in the 1990 national elections as part of a united democratic coalition and together won thirty-two seats. The Ecological Movement of Romania (EMR), which claims over 60,000 members and operates as both an environmental group and a Green party, holds twelve parliamentary seats, whereas the Romanian Ecology Party holds eight seats. Their combined share of the votes is 4.3 percent. In Czechoslovakia, Greens won six seats in the Slovakian parliament but failed to clear the 5 percent threshold to win seats in the Czech parliament and in the federal parliament. The rise of the Czech Greens was complicated by the involvement of Communist security agents in the party formation process. In the breakaway Yugoslav republic of Slovenia, Greens won 8.8 percent of the votes, ending up with not only parliamentary deputies but also three cabinet ministries. Hungarian Greens date back to the campaign by environmentalists ("Blues") to protect the Danube River from a megahydropower project. Misha Glenny credits the Hungarian Greens with helping to move the Communist party in a reformist direction during the 1980s.[38] However, they fizzled in the spring 1990 elections and have continued to splinter.

In the Baltic states, the Greens are relatively well rooted, typically receiving 6 to 10 percent of the votes. The Lithuanian Green party, which claims to be Eastern Europe's second oldest Green party organization, has nine MPs. The Estonian Green Movement, which became the first full-fledged Eastern member of the European Greens Coordination, has seven MPs. Estonian Green leader Thomas Frey became his country's environment minister. Latvian Greens have six MPs.[39] In short, Baltic Greens have functioned as integral components of their respective national independence movements.

During the late 1980s, umbrella organizations emerged in the USSR, but they failed to link together local and republican groups as an all-union Green movement. Subsequently Green parties have sprung up in various republics. In these unsettled times, information on their development is scarce. In a number of republics, for example, Georgia, Greens claim to already hold parliamentary seats and in at least one case, for example, Ukraine, they claim to head a cabinet ministry. Whether these Greens are opportunists, independents, or indeed members of organized Green parties is at present impossible to discern. One can conclude that the backlog of environmental disasters in the former USSR and in Eastern Europe guarantees environmental protection a long-term place on the policy agenda. However, it is too early to say whether Green parties will become enduring, let alone major, phenomena in the post-Communist political systems of the so-called Second World.

Conclusion

In this chapter we have attempted to put into context the German Greens by surveying the development of Green party politics within other Western European countries, at the supranational level of the European Community, and within Eastern European countries. During the 1980s, the German Greens were the vanguard of the European Green party movement. Their name, program, and organization have been widely emulated. Yet it is often overlooked that a number of West European Green parties such as in Belgium have also become well established in their party systems. Because of harsh political opportunity structures, others, such as the British, have survived as minor protest parties. Most West European Green parties have experienced intense infighting over structural reform, strategy, and program. Some splintering has been inevitable. The West German Greens (in contrast to the East German Greens) have been on the alternative left side of the European Green spectrum. Our survey has revealed that there are also important West European Green parties on the more moderate reformist side. The West German Greens, in contrast to the others, have faced the challenge of sharing governmental power above the local level. So far, others have had at best an indirect impact on national policies by threatening to attract votes away from the major parties. As in the case of the West German Greens, one can find signs of a cross-national trend toward more pragmatic strategies and more professional organization among West European Greens.

The process of European integration in the aftermath of the December 1991 European Summit at Maastricht should provide new opportunities for the Greens as a creative opposition force. The results of the 1989 European Parliament elections indicated that a growing number of voters see environmental problems as belonging on the policy agenda of the European Community. The Green Group is externally constrained in its impact by the institutional weaknesses of the European Parliament and internally constrained by the wide diversities of its members. Yet by avoiding the "Rainbow" approach, the Group has increased the odds in favor of communicating a Green identity.

The development of East European Green parties contrasts in significant ways with that of the West German Greens. The more successful East European Green parties have arisen out of grass-roots movements, protesting the policy performance of socialist systems, whereas the West German Greens arose from protests about the performance of capitalist systems. West and East German Greens have viewed German nationalism as a negative repressive force. East European Greens have seen their own nationalism as basically a positive liberating force. West German Greens have been a feminist party, whereas East European Greens have reflected more traditional values. West German Greens have struggled with competing protest and power imperatives. East European Greens have had fewer qualms about sharing governmental power. In the current unsettled times, East European electorates want above all an improved material standard of living. Economy policy has never been the strong card of West German Greens; thus one wonders how the new Green parties of Eastern Europe will cope with public demands for quantitative economic growth. The prospects for the nascent Green parties of Russia, Ukraine, Byelorussia, Georgia, and Azerbaijan are even more uncertain.

Notes

1. Ferdinand Müller-Rommel, "Political Success of Green Parties in Western Europe." Paper presented at the 1990 annual meeting of the American Political Science Association, San Francisco, August–September 1990, p. 15.

2. Wolfgang Rüdig, "Green Party Politics Around the World," *Environment* 33, no. 8 (October 1991):9.

3. Ferdinand Müller-Rommel, "The Greens in Western Europe: Similar but Different," *International Political Science Review* 6, no. 4 (1985):491–492.

4. The Green party constitution as adopted at the 1986 annual conference meeting, Newcastle, England.

5. Wolfgang Rüdig and Philip D. Lowe, "The Withered 'Greening' of British Politics: A Study of the Ecology Party," *Political Studies* 34 (1986):262–284.

6. Interview with party council member Brian Kingzelt, Wandsworth, March 27, 1982.

7. Chris Rose, "Lessons of the 1991 Local Election," *Econews* [British Green Party], no. 57 (August 1991):5–6.

8. *Green Activist* [Newsletter of the British Green Party], October 1991, p. 1.

9. Rüdig, "Green Party Politics," p. 27.

10. Paul Hainsworth, "Breaking the Mould: The Greens in the French Party System," in *French Political Parties in Transition*, Alister Cole, ed. (Aldershot: Dartmouth, 1990), p. 98.

11. Müller-Rommel, "The Greens in Western Europe," pp. 491–492.

12. John Ely, "Beyond Germany: Green Politics in Europe and the United States." Unpublished manuscript, 1991, p. 8.

13. Hainsworth, "Breaking the Mould," p. 96.

14. See Kris Deschouwer, "Belgium: The 'Ecologists' and 'Agalev,'" in *New Politics in Western Europe*, Müller-Rommel, ed. (Boulder: Westview Press, 1989), pp. 39–53 (especially p. 50).

15. Herbert Kitschelt, "Democracy and Oligarchy in Belgian Ecology Parties," in *Green Politics One*, Wolfgang Rüdig, ed. (Edinburgh: Edinburgh University Press, 1990), pp. 82–114 (especially p. 94).

16. Ibid., p. 108.

17. Müller-Rommel, "The Greens in Western Europe," p. 491.

18. Herbert Kitschelt and Staf Hellemans, *Beyond the European Left: Ideology and Political Action in the Belgian Ecology Parties* (Durham, N.C.: Duke University Press, 1990), pp. 54–55, 91–92.

19. Paul Lucardie, Jelle van der Knopp, Wijbrandt van Schuur, and Gernt Voerman, "Greening the Reds or Reddening the Greens? The Case of the Green Left in the Netherlands." Paper presented at the 1991 annual meeting of the American Political Science Association, Washington, D.C., August–September 1991.

20. Müller-Rommel, "The Greens in Western Europe," pp. 491–492.

21. Thomas Koelble, "Luxemburg: The 'Green Alternative,'" in *New Politics in Western Europe*, Müller-Rommel, ed., pp. 136–137.

22. Sara Parkin, *Green Parties: An International Guide* (London: Heretic Press, 1989), pp. 243–249.

23. Jukka Paastela, "Finland: The 'Vihreät,'" in Müller-Rommel, ed., *New Politics in Western Europe*, pp. 82, 85.

24. Andreas Ladner, "Switzerland: The 'Green' and 'Alternative Parties,'" in *New Politics in Western Europe*, Müller-Rommel, ed., pp. 159, 161.

25. Joint Declaration of the European Green Parties, January 23, 1984, Brussels, reprinted in Parkin, *Green Parties*, pp. 327–329.

26. Bundesvorstand der Grünen, *Global denken—vor Ort handeln! Erklärung der Grünenzur Europawahl am 17. Juni 1984* (Bonn: Bundesvorstand der Grünen, 1984), pp. 5–6.

27. "The Paris Declaration," reprinted in Parkin, *Green Parties*, pp. 329–330.

28. Parkin, *Green Parties*, p. 262.

29. Rainbow Group, *Rainbow Politics: Green Alternative Politics in the European Parliament* (Brussels: Rainbow Group, 1988), p. 18.

30. Jakob von Uexkull, "Reflections on Parliament and Government," in *Green Light on Europe*, Sara Parkin, ed. (London: Heretic Press, 1991), pp. 346–352.

31. Karl H. Buck, "Europe: The 'Greens' and the 'Rainbow Group,'" in *New Politics in Western Europe*, Müller-Rommel, ed., pp. 167–172.

32. *Europa Braucht Grün: Kurzprogramm der Grünen zur Europawahl '89* (Bonn: Bundesvorstand der Grünen, 1989), pp. 6–7.

33. Jean Lambert, "The Impact of the Green Group in the European Parliament." Paper presented to the workshop entitled "The Greens: The European Challenge" at the Joint Sessions of the European Consortium for Political Research, University of Essex, Colchester, March 1991, pp. 1–2, 4.

34. Ibid, p. 5.

35. Ibid., pp. 5, 13.

36. Hilary F. French, "Green Revolutions: Environmental Reconstruction in Eastern Europe and the Soviet Union," *Worldwatch Paper 99* (November 1990):34–35.

37. Based on recent information from Rüdig, "Green Party Politics"; Carlo Jordan, "Greenway 1989–90: The Foundation of the East European Green Parties," in *Green Light on Europe*, Parkin, ed., pp. 76–83; and European Green Coordination data provided by Sara Parkin, November 1991.

38. Misha Glenny, *The Rebirth of History: Eastern Europe in the Age of Democracy* (London: Penguin, 1990), pp. 94, 203.

39. Jordan, "Greenway 1989–90," p. 81; Rüdig, "Green Party Politics," p. 27; and French, "Green Revolutions," p. 33.

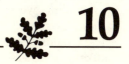

10

Conclusion: Future Prospects for the Greens in the New Germany

As a result of the West German Greens' failure to gain representation in the Bundestag on December 2, 1990, the future prospects of the Greens and the allied citizen movements of the East in united Germany are problematic. Without a superior organization effort from party activists who have been disdainful of the "organizational imperative," the Green party project could go down in history as a one-generational effort that brought new issues onto the policy agenda and then lost its focus, and eventually its influence, through intraparty wrangling, improved inter-party competition from the SPD, and ineffective coordination with the Eastern Alliance 90/Greens. Furthermore, it may be noted that the New Left postmaterialist Greens lost some of their appeal in the 1990s in their core group of the new middle class when the material issues relating to the reconstruction of Eastern Germany came to the fore. Postmaterialist parties, as organizations, appear to be precarious vehicles for "New Politics" issues especially when the political space to the left of a reform-oriented social democratic party gets smaller and when economic issues dominate the policy agenda.[1] A key question for the future is how the party reacts to its defeat in the national election of 1990. The state elections of 1991 and 1992 give grounds for cautious optimism that the Green project still has momentum.

To get an overview of the prospects for the Greens and their Eastern counterparts, let us start with some impressions of the night of the all-German elections on December 2, 1990. Then we will look back to the pattern of party development of the Greens in the 1980s and the Alliance 90/Greens in the late 1980s before moving forward to more recent events: the election campaign of 1990, the results of the election and the consequences for the party, the attempt at reform suggested by the state elections of 1991 and 1992, and the outcome at the party conference in April 1991. In concluding, we shall comment on the future prospects of the Greens in a united Germany.

The Greens began the decade of the 1980s with the founding of a party "unlike the others" in Karlsruhe after often chaotic and tumultuous debates. At the end of a decade in early December 1990 the voters in the Western part of Germany told them that their experiment on the national level was to be halted. In one fell swoop, a lively New Left opposition party with over forty deputies—the largest parliamentary representation of all such parties in the industrial democracies—and its over 200-member staff was eliminated as an alternative political force in Bonn. The interpretations by Green activists and other political commentators of this debacle were candid and direct. Hubert Kleinert of the Federal Steering Committee complained that the Greens had used up their political credit, that they had tried to defy the laws of political physics, and that the time for a housecleaning (party reforms) among the Greens was at hand.[2] Wolfgang Ullmann, a newly elected Bundestag deputy from the Alliance 90 (East) noted that, though he regretted it, the *Kasperltheatre* (Punch and Judy show) antics of the Western Greens had not served them well. The *Frankfurter Rundschau* lamented the demise of the Western Greens and the degeneration of a party of great creativity and innovation to self-absorbed factionalists who lost their way in a paper chase (*Schnitzeljagd*). Walter Momper of the Berlin SPD, in a comment reflecting his disgust with the Alternative List (Green) party in West Berlin, said that the Greens were an *auslaufendes Modell*, a phased-out model. Are reports of the death of the Greens greatly exaggerated? Although most political analysts attributed the defeat of the Greens of the West to their ambivalence or *Sprachlosigkeit* (silence) on the issue of German unity, the reasons for defeat had long-term causes as well as short-term precipitating effects, and both factors must be assessed in order to comment on the future of the Greens.

The Development of the Green Party

A flashback to the developmental dilemmas of the Greens in the 1980s gives us ample evidence that there were significant problems long before the dramatic events of 1989 and the election campaign of 1990. One can sketch the pattern of party development in the 1980s in quick brush strokes as follows. Riding piggyback on the extraparliamentary movements and the wave of unconventional political actions of the 1970s, especially of the antinuclear protestors, a gadfly party emerged in 1980. New Left activists joined forces with ecologists, feminists, antiwar peaceniks, antinukers (plants and weapons), Third Worlders, socialists of all colors, and counterculture alternative life-stylists to campaign for votes on the national level after minor successes on the local, Land, and European level. Ecology and democratization were the key aims of a grass-roots movement-party in which organizational norms and forms were to complement one another. A consensus on antipathy to elites, hierarchy, and market rationality was also part of the glue holding this unusual coalition together. With the exception of a poor showing in the national election of 1980, the Green party during the first two-thirds of the 1980s scored many electoral successes, whereas the Social Democratic Party, its large rival, had trouble finding its bearings. Events gave credence to the Green critique. Acid rain, dying forests, toxic chemical spills, nuclear fallout from Chernobyl, modernization of nuclear weapons, Flick financial scandals, and the numerous protests over proposed nuclear plants aided the party as it offered a lively opposition, untied to powerful interests, to challenge sluggish *Volksparteien* (people's parties).

But even with the electoral successes on all levels of government and the support for Green criticisms in the public opinion polls, there were problems with what Tocqueville would have called the origins or point of departure of the movement-party. What Green activist Joschka Fischer has called the errors of the original construction—its organizational style—eventually reduced the political influence of the party. That the movement-party had an identity crisis was obvious from the start. Even after the early departure of conservative ecologists, the left-ecological party was composed of a very diverse coalition of pragmatic reformers and ideological radicals. The pragmatists envisioned a constructive opposition practicing sound parliamentary work with the long-term goal of exercising power whereas the radicals saw themselves as tribunes of the citizen initiatives and new social movements not wanting to legitimate the system by constructive opposition and certainly not interested in sharing power with the dreadful opportunistic SPD. In the movement-party, the antiorganizational allergies of the movement activists, whose mandate supposedly emanated from the grass roots (*Basisdemokratie*), collided with the pragmatic *Realos*, who accepted the inevitabilities of parliamentarization, professionalization, and the role of *Promis* (prominent personalities) as political leaders.

In the language of one scholar, the logic of constituency representation (fidelity to the grass roots) was in unhealthy tension with the logic of electoral competition ("adjustment of the internal organization, program, and strategy to the conditions of the political marketplace to maximize electoral support").[3] Or, as Joachim Raschke notes in *Krise der Grünen*, "Wer um Stimmen wirbt, verändert sich selbst" (When you compete for votes, you even change yourself).

The problem with the Greens over a long period was that "power is neither vested in an entrenched unified elite nor in the grassroots. Party advocates have been successful in preventing the emergence of a power center, but rather than shifting to the rank and file, power—the ability to bring about collective action—evaporates in a stratarchal organization riddled by group pluralism."[4] In other words, the party structure dispersed and fragmented power. What began as a celebration of variety, diversity, and pluralism wound up as pluralistic stagnation. Instead of *e pluribus unum*, the party got *e pluribus plures* (from many, rather too many). We have noted earlier how Jürgen Maier of the Federal Executive Committee of the Greens summed up the dilemma: The party seemed to develop a tendency to lose the advantages of a grass-roots democratic organization without really gaining at the same time the advantages of a professional organizational structure.[5]

Besides the continuous wrangling of factions within the party that left the Greens with little organizational discipline, hierarchy, or cohesiveness, other problems that accumulated through the 1980s can be briefly listed:

1. Disunity on policy pronouncements undermined the appeal of the party to potential supporters.
2. The Greens experienced membership problems. Recruitment was poor, and a large percentage of members were officeholders who had little time for party affairs.
3. The social movements that provided so much energy in the early part of the 1980s also declined in activity. The party couldn't attract and hold members, and the causes that mobilized the party activists in the early days declined in importance for a variety of reasons.
4. The party lost popular and experienced candidates with its practice of rotation. In an age of media politics with its focus on personalities, the Greens stuck to their early principles—issues over personalities—and soon reaped the negative consequences.
5. The age composition of the Green electorate began to shift in the latter third of the 1980s on the Land and Bund levels. The party held an increasingly smaller percentage of younger voters, had a solid number of voters in the thirty to forty-five age cohort, and was invariably unsuccessful with older age groups.
6. Demographically the Greens' center of gravity was the new middle class, a none-too-stable electoral base of party-switchers.
7. In the mid-1980s the Greens were pleased to see that some of their issues were catching on with the other parties, and yet this meant that the clear profile of the Greens was becoming indistinct to the voters, especially the tactical voters or shifters. All of the parties "Greened," at least in terms of rhetoric, discovered the talents of

female party members for office, and talked about balancing ecology and economics, each in accents attuned to the auditory sensibilities of independent voters or party loyalists wanting an up-to-date party.

8. The decreasing novelty of the party reduced its overall media exposure, and intraparty infighting tended to crowd out positive policy achievements at the local and state levels in media reports.

9. Finally, the gap between what the Green electorate wanted and what the Green party activists were doing grew quite wide for a party that advocated popular accountability.

The East German Revolt and the Greens' Response

The citizen groups of East Germany that showed such courage in challenging the dictatorial, well-armed state had several aims. They wanted to stop their fellow East Germans from emigrating and they wanted constitutional and democratic reforms. The crowds that gathered in early November 1989 in numbers up to a half-million shouted, "We are the people." That phrase asserted their right to self-determination, to real elections, to civil liberties. The most influential citizen group, New Forum, embodied this nonviolent, democratic, and constitutional program. It believed in reforming East Germany toward an ideal of democratic socialism, neither capitalist nor SED-socialist. New Forum clearly espoused a two-German state position.

When the crowds in late November cried, "We are one people" the citizen movement groups were thrown off balance. They envisaged a transitional period of some duration in which East Germany would formulate a new constitution based on extensive participation, after which some type of arrangement would be worked out with West Germany. They had not expected the train for German unity to move at the tempo that it did. They had been on the cutting edge as the true heroes in overthrowing the old regime, but they were not to be the shapers of the new regime: "Faced with the relentless exodus of tens of thousands of fellow citizens, a crumbling economy, and a catastrophic health care situation, confronted daily with revelations of the Old Guard's systematic abuse of power, and casting an apprehensive glance at the economic disaster afflicting other reformist states in Eastern Europe, the East German people looked quickly for a short-cut to prosperity and democracy. That short-cut became unification."[6]

The citizen movement groups, especially New Forum, Democracy Now, Initiative for Peace and Human Rights, the Greens, and the Independent Women's Association (all eventually members of Alliance 90/Greens and partners of the Western Greens)[7] had to learn the democratic game of hardball politics in short order. They participated actively in the roundtable discussions[8] with Hans Modrow's government and with the front parties that the Communist regime had propped up since 1950. But as soon as the date for free elections of the East German Parliament was in sight, another factor came into play. In *Federalist* Number 10, James Madison says that liberty is to faction what air is to fire, an indispensable element. Capitalizing on the liberty of this new public space in East Germany, the major West German parties hustled to "empower" their sister parties. The citizen movements cried foul and cursed the "colonizers" for contaminating their politics with mass advertising, public relations hoopla, and organized "spontaneous" demonstrations, but they were drowned out by the tumult and hurly-burly of modern West German campaigning techniques.[9]

In between the March elections to the East German Parliament and the May local elections, which returned roughly the same proportions for the parties—with the citizen movements doing better locally—the Greens in West Germany met for an extraordinary conference in Hagen in which they acknowledged that the March 18 electoral outcome pointed to rapid unification yet set out a number of caveats that indicated little enthusiasm for this timetable. They also passed a resolution calling for cooperation with the citizen movements of East Germany for the national election that would come later in the year.[10] Even with this bow toward political reality, the Greens were soon to be left at the station. They did not want the fast train to unity, but it was well under way. They had inhibitions, based on their principles, of not forcing an alliance with a counterpart party—the citizen movements—of East Germany but that "train" had been boarded by the other parties months ago. It was not until September that a formal arrangement with the citizen movements of the East had been accomplished, and it pointed to very little cooperation for the December election. In June, a longtime observer of the Greens summed up their plight: "The German-German union, in principle accepted unwillingly, in its constitutional form rejected, brings the Greens to the all-German election in the dangerous proximity of not jumping the 5% electoral hurdle. A Green-Green alliance would help out in this dilemma, but the Eastern Greens are far from this. Many West German positions and styles of doing things don't suit them."[11]

Bieber was incorrect on the second part. A marriage of convenience was worked out for the December election, but his instincts were correct on the question of the survival of the Western Greens.

The All-German Election Campaign

The prospect of German unification caught many, inside and outside Germany, off balance. The fragmentation of the Soviet empire in Eastern

Europe, the breaching of the Wall, and the rapid psychological transition from "Wir sind das Volk" ("We are the people") to "Wir sind ein Volk" ("We are one people") left the Greens (West) on the wrong side of history. They had earlier pushed to remove the clause for unification from the preamble of the Basic Law, and their position over the years had been for two Germanys independent of the major blocs. The Greens were many things to many people during the 1980s, but they were *not* pro-unification nationalists. They feared the consequences of unification. The issue left the party confused, ambivalent, and discordant. All at once, the Greens' policy positions on demilitarization, bloc dissolution, and the reduction and withdrawal of troops lost much of their edge. The ground beneath the feet of ecosocialists (the Green faction that takes socioeconomic structural changes seriously) began to give way when the full disasters of real existing socialism became more widely known. Thus the all-German election campaign began with the Greens having very little to say on an issue that dwarfed all the others. As the Mannheim Group noted: "The rejection of German unity by the Greens had no majority in its own electorate. On the contrary, 66 percent of the Green electorate were for it even if its enthusiasm was not that of the flag-waving CDU."[12]

Substituting the endangered climate of the planet and fears of the ozone hole (the thrust of the Green electoral campaign) for the concerns about the dynamics and mechanics of unification left the Greens in a hole of their own. The Greens' chances for success were further reduced when their major competitor, the SPD, chose Oskar LaFontaine as its chancellor candidate. LaFontaine aimed right at the new middle-class, educated constituency with issues that the Greens had popularized since the early 1980s. In other words, he moved the SPD to the left, reducing "the hunting ground"[13] of the Greens. Finally, as we noted earlier, the Greens remained constant to their principles and recognized the autonomy of the citizen movements, other Green parties, and related electoral groups in Eastern Germany. They refrained from the organizational takeovers that the major parties had engineered. They promoted a petition to the Federal Constitutional Court that allowed for smaller parties to get representation by jumping the 5 percent hurdle in either East or West Germany instead of the new Germany being the single electoral district. Running apart from their Eastern German counterparts showed them as true decentralists but not very farsighted strategists.

The party activists knew that the election would be close. In September, one of the reliable public opinion polls had the West German Greens at 5.3 percent, but the October and November polls were somewhat more encouraging. The feeling that the "Perils of Pauline" (the silent film star always rescued from a doomed fate at the last minute) would end with Green Pauline once again being rescued by some deus ex machina still

TABLE 10.1   Results of the 1990 Bundestag Election

| | Votes | | | Number |
	West	East	Total	of Seats
Christian Democrats (CDU/CSU)	44.3	41.8	43.8	319
Social Democrats (SPD)	35.7	24.3	33.5	239
Free Democrats (FDP)	10.6	12.9	11.0	79
Greens	4.8[a]	6.0[b]	5.1[c]	8
Party of Democratic Socialism (PDS)	.3[d]	11.1	2.4	17
Republicans	2.3	1.3	2.1	0
Other parties	2.0	2.6	2.1	0
Total	100	100	100	662

[a]Without 5 percent, the Greens of the West received no seats.

[b]With 6.0 percent, Alliance 90/Greens of the East received eight seats.

[c]This 5.1 percent vote means that if the Greens of the West and the Alliance 90/Greens of the East had run in coalition they would have received around forty seats in the Bundestag.

[d]This vote in the West for the PDS suggests that it would not do well in 1994 when all of Germany will be the electoral district.

Source: Adapted from Mannheim Forschungsgruppe Report No. 61 (Dec. 2, 1990), pp. 7–9.

held sway. This time the "machina" was the unification train and Pauline was under the wheels.

Election Results, December 2, 1990

The pollsters were wrong on the Greens, as the final numbers showed that with 4.8 percent of the vote in Western Germany, they had failed to jump the 5 percent hurdle and therefore received no seats (see Table 10.1). They were wrong for several reasons. Almost a quarter million former Green voters did not vote at all, and nonvoters don't show up in many polls. Also, the Greens' core electorate is probably no more than about 3 to 4 percent,[14] which means that many Green voters are floating voters who may change their votes at the last minute—mostly from Green to SPD. In point of fact, although the SPD lost badly in the election, especially in Eastern Germany, they did pull 600,000 votes away from former Green voters. In the complicated tag-team wrestling match of electoral competition, the FDP did best overall, the SPD lost marginally to the CDU in the West and massively in the East, the CSU held their own, and the Greens got thrown out of the ring in the West while the Alliance 90/Greens managed 6 percent of the vote in the East. The successor to the SED party of East Germany, the PDS (Party of Democratic Socialism) benefited from the constitutional interpretation of the electoral law in Eastern Germany and pulled voters away from the Greens in marginal fashion in the city-states of Bremen, Hamburg, and Berlin.

TABLE 10.2 Electoral Coalitions of the Parties in the 1990 Federal Elections (in percentages)

	CDU/CSU	SPD	FDP	Greens	PDS	Total Public
Region						
East	20.6	14.6	21.0	31.9	80.9	20.6
Northwest	26.8	26.7	24.8	28.2	5.2	25.5
Rhineland	24.5	33.4	27.0	22.4	0.0	28.0
Southern	28.1	25.3	27.2	17.5	13.9	25.9
Occupation						
Worker	17.7	24.8	11.7	12.8	21.5	19.5
Self-employed	10.8	4.4	13.8	7.5	4.9	8.6
White collar/government	42.1	44.7	48.9	48.7	50.5	44.2
Student	4.1	5.6	5.9	18.6	10.7	5.7
Other	25.3	20.5	19.7	12.4	12.4	22.0
Religion						
Catholic	48.2	32.7	40.1	30.5	8.3	40.0
Protestant	35.0	42.4	36.6	29.3	5.2	36.6
Other, none	16.8	24.9	23.3	40.2	86.5	23.4
Size of town						
Less than 5,000	25.1	17.8	16.4	20.4	12.4	21.6
5,000–20,000	26.2	25.8	16.8	18.2	13.3	23.0
20,000–100,000	24.5	25.3	28.7	23.2	39.0	25.9
More than 100,000	24.0	29.9	38.1	37.9	35.3	28.8
Age						
Under 40	27.8	43.9	39.9	66.0	61.9	39.8
40–59	38.5	33.1	32.8	25.9	19.1	33.6
60 and over	33.8	23.0	27.3	8.1	19.0	26.9
Gender						
Male	46.4	45.4	59.9	47.8	60.6	46.7
Female	53.6	54.5	40.1	52.2	39.4	53.3

Source: November 1990 German Election Study, conducted by Forschungsgruppe Wahlen, Mannheim.

An overview of what occurred in the election on the Western side is that the Greens lost votes in all age categories. They got a decreasing share of the younger and first voters (one-third less from the eighteen to twenty-four age cohort of 1987 but an even greater loss in the twenty-five to forty group to the SPD). They continued to do very poorly with voters over fifty. Table 10.2 shows the Greens of the West to be primarily a party of the educated new middle class of younger voter living in urban areas. On the Eastern side, the distribution of the Alliance 90/Greens votes by age showed a very high percentage in the younger age categories but with one-third of their voters over fifty. In terms of occupation and education, both Alliance 90/Greens and Greens (West) parties drew heavily from the more educated, salaried, white-collar class in the public sector. Very few votes came from workers and independent businesspeople. Both parties had the highest percentage of voters who are currently studying (which means that, disproportionately, pupils and students still favor this party), but it is also clear that the SPD and the other parties cut into this traditional category.

In the early 1980s there were slightly more male Green voters than female Green voters. This imbalance has reversed itself over the years with the percentage of females continually increasing over that of the males in Western Germany and the gap between female and male being considerably greater in Eastern Germany. In Western Germany, the Greens lost most decisively in their urban, university strongholds of the past. It is here that massive hemorrhaging drained the life from the party.

The West German Greens lost more than seats in the Bundestag. A corps of over 200 staff people in Bonn lost their positions. As *Die Zeit* pointed out,[15] this *Denkfabrik* (think tank) had offered high-quality research and analysis on a wide variety of public policy issues from the innovations of the ecotax to how the West Germans (and the Greens) should adapt to the changing role of NATO, the European Community, and the Conference on Security and Cooperation in Europe. Furthermore, the severe reduction of public financing for the party foundations will undercut support for traditional Green projects, and that in turn will put a further damper on the declining importance of the Green networks in many urban areas.

Postlude: State Elections of 1991 and the Conference on Party Reform

Whether the election was the coup de grace that SPD politician Walter Momper of Berlin wanted it to be or whether it was the shock therapy that would galvanize the party is difficult to say. There were a series of challenges in state elections in the next two years that tested the adaptability of the Greens, and these results showed the party on the rebound. One of the first tests was the Land election in Hesse on January 20, 1991. What can one say about the meaning of the Hesse election?

Joschka Fischer in late November 1990 made it clear in an interview[16] that the upcoming Land election was more on his mind than the national election of December 2. The Hesse Greens were putting their *Realo* approach on the line, and there is ample evidence to suggest that the defeat on the national level merely reinforced the tactics that the Land party was planning. This technique included a very disciplined and structured campaign plan, special attention given to getting out the first voters and youth vote, more care given to media policy, including placards and posters that also played up the personality of the party leader, Fischer, and particular concern directed toward policy positions that showed the contribution of the Greens as thoughtful reformers. Fischer and his party cohorts used the December debacle to make the state election one in which the future destiny of the party was at stake and one in which Hesse would set the style for the party reforms that needed to be implemented by the Greens at large.

The campaign strategy succeeded for a variety of complex and unexpected reasons. The Greens were aided by the interjection of the Gulf War issue into the campaign, which allowed them to mobilize younger voters in demonstrations and protests about the possible role of Germany in the conflict. Although their overall vote was down from the previous 1987 Land election in which they achieved 9.4 percent of the vote, the 8.8 percent that they did garner was a considerable improvement over the 5.6 percent vote in the all-German election of December. The most significant factor in the demographics of the vote was the increase in the youngest age cohort vote from the last Land election.

This trend reversal reflected both the voter mobilization campaign and the appeal of the centrist reforming stance as opposed to the polemical fundamentalist style. The bravado pose with which the Hesse Greens had talked about possible coalitions with the SPD in the past was gone and was replaced by a more moderate approach. Otherwise, there were no major differences in the socioeconomic profile of those who voted for the Greens in Hesse and of those who voted for the Greens (West) on December 2, but the strategy was clear: to build upon the generational core and to make the special effort necessary to broaden the traditional constituency.

There are caveats to this analysis and they include the fact that Hesse voters were voting against Walter Wallmann and his party for the scandals and problems that gave the CDU a low rating among the electorate. The Mannheim polls show that Hessens rated the Green Land party higher than the national Greens and the Land CDU lower than the national CDU. For its part, the Hesse SPD ran a well-organized campaign and followed its Lower Saxony and Schleswig-Holstein sister parties by promoting ecological and feminist themes.

The reformist impetus was reinforced by the results of the Rhineland-Palatinate election of April 21, 1991, where a low-profile, moderate Green party did better than anticipated by winning 6.4 percent of the Land votes. This result represented a higher portion of the votes than the Greens managed there in December 1990 (4 percent) and in the 1987 Land election (5.9 percent). The Mannheim Report attributes these gains mainly to pro-SPD tactical voters who favored a Red-Green coalition; however, the victorious SPD opted for the FDP as its junior partner.[17]

Although the Hesse victory was seen as an important turning point, especially for the pragmatic forces in the party that looked forward to the organizational reforms that Fischer and others had spoken of, it was still an open question whether the Greens could change those marks of origin that many had come to see as a burden for the party. The reforms accepted at the Neumünster party conference on April 27–28, 1991, did eliminate rotation completely, reduced the size of the Federal Executive Committee, increased the role of elected state party leaders and parliamentarians in federal decisionmaking, and set up dual chairs with a Green from the East and a Green from the West. However, the two-thirds majority did not materialize, and they did not change the rule on forbidding the holding of a party office and an elected office. It is very likely that individual Land organizations will soon accomplish that with their own reforms.

The series of Land elections in 1991 ended on a positive note with the Hamburg election of June and the Bremen elections later in the fall. In Hamburg the Greens (GAL) had completely broken down over the past several years as a result of factional infighting. In the aftermath of the Greens' December 1990 debacle, local party activists did a remarkable job of piecing the coalition together (minus radical ecologists and far leftists) to contest the state elections. Although the Greens' share of the Hamburg votes in 1991 (7.2 percent) was about the same as in the 1987 state election, it represented an improvement over the 5.8 percent of Hamburg votes won by the Greens in December 1990. A rival Alternative List, made up of supporters of the fundamentalist views of Jutta Ditfurth (who had resigned from the Green party after the Neumünster reform conference), won a mere 0.5 percent, the same percentage as did the PDS's left list. Although most of their votes in earlier years would have gone to the Greens, the departure of the far leftists clarified the political profile of the Hamburg Greens. The Bremen election in September continued the electoral successes of the Greens on the state level. The Greens increased their vote to 11.4 percent (1.2 percent more than 1987), became part of the governing Ampelkoalition (traffic light coalition) with the SPD (red) and the FDP (yellow), and received the important ministries of Environmental Protection, Energy, and City Planning and Culture, Youth, and Integration of Foreigners. This was the first coalition of these three parties in Western Germany, and it corresponds to a similar coalition in the state of Brandenburg on the Eastern side. The analysis of the election by the Electoral Research Group of Mannheim stated that a good share of the voters saw the Greens as a constructive opposition in the past with a track record of realistic and diligent political work.[18]

Two trends are worth underscoring in the Bremen election. The Greens improved their vote in the youngest age category slightly, but their increases in the twenty-five to thirty-five cohort were greater and even greater in the thirty-five to forty-five group. The generational core is definitely there—the platform upon which the Greens must build—and reform politics appears to pay better dividends across the board than radical demands. The impact of this type of politics is clear. In Bremen, the Greens' suggestion that the inner city be free from cars was accepted in the coalition negotiations. And the critical issue of the widening of the Weser River will be discussed with an eye on environmental consequences.[19] In sum, the state elections of 1991 showed the Greens in a diverse number of locales—Hesse, Rhineland Palatinate, Hamburg, and Bremen—making a good showing. Their core voters were being mobilized more successfully and recruitment for young voters was having minimal success. Campaigns were more organized, media politics and personalities were used, coalitions were sought and in some cases obtained, and policy initiatives were well framed. The old factional wrangling was definitely curtailed. Thus our preliminary overview of the Greens on this level of government at the end of 1991 is that they are alive, well, and reacting positively to past problems.

Less than a year later, in early April 1992, the Green party of the West continued rebounding from its defeat in the first all-German election of December 1990 by making notable advances in the state elections of Baden-Württemberg and Schleswig-Holstein. In Baden-Württemberg, the most moderate of the Green state parties of the West increased its share of the popular vote from 7.9 percent to 9.5 percent. The share of first-time and younger, educated voters for the Greens was quite high, and although the issue of asylum seekers was uppermost in the minds of the voters, the continued importance of the environmental issue and the perception of the Greens as a moderate and constructive opposition party helped it to its biggest vote ever in this relatively prosperous state.[20]

In Schleswig-Holstein, the Greens came within 397 votes of jumping the 5 percent hurdle in this Land. They increased their vote from 2.9 percent in the 1988 state election to 4.97 percent. With the additional votes, they would have had five seats in the state parliament and a likely coalition with the Social Democrats. The near success in this Land of few university towns, relatively low urbanization, and fewer younger new middle-class intelligentsia resulted from an improved organizational effort, a distancing from a fundamentalist (more dogmatic) political identity, and the continued importance of the environmental issue.[21]

The state elections of 1991 and 1992 show largely positive results for the long-term Green project, but we must add a note of caution. The radical leftist wing has decreased in importance in the Greens of the West, and the move from radical to reform politics has been accomplished by better organization, improved campaign techniques, a recovering of some of the younger votes, and a diversification of the occupational backgrounds of Green voters. But the percentage of floating voters is still quite high, and the party still gets votes from citizens more interested in sending a message of dissatisfaction to the traditional parties (CDU and SPD) than in settling in with a permanent link to the Greens.

Speculations on the Future of the Greens in the New Germany

Students of politics are not good at hitting things on the wing, and the pace of change in Eastern Germany and central Europe—including the uncertain reform prospects in the former Soviet Union—should make any would-be Cassandra cautious. When one considers how few experts anticipated the historic changes that have occurred since 1989, then there are double reasons to be modest about peering into the crystal ball. In addition to not knowing the future of the Green party in the Western part of Germany, where there is a track record of about fourteen years of electoral competition and forty years of an extraparliamentary tradition, we also do not know the future of the movement-parties of Eastern Germany, which are in a very fluid and quasi-institutionalized state and for which the track record is very scant. We can organize these speculations by returning to some of the major problems of the party in the 1980s that were discussed earlier.

The Green party will go nowhere if it cannot recruit active members and hold a core electorate that keeps electoral contests from being exercises in survival training. Both of these tasks are difficult. A number of scholars have noted the inhibitions to organizational work that characterizes supporters of left-libertarian parties. Left-libertarian individuals show more loyalty to ideas and issues than to specific parties,[22] and their intellectual sophistication predisposes them to vote strategically rather than to identify with a single party. Inglehart's terminology for the New Politics voters is "cognitively mobilized nonpartisans." He observes: "While electorates are becoming more politicized, their behavior is becoming less constrained by established organizations. . . . The rise of the West German Greens, for example, reflects both the emergence of a post-materialist constituency whose outlook is not captured by the existing political parties and the emergence of a growing pool of voters who are politicized but do not feel tied to established parties."[23] The problem is that these educated nonpartisans do not feel attached to parties in general. In searching for the countermodel to the traditional parties, the Greens found themselves awash in spontaneity, self-emancipation, amateurism, and a type of free-wheeling individualism that made collective action difficult. Building up party activists and maintaining a loyal core in the electorate are two different tasks, but for both of these jobs the independent-minded educated new middle class is the key target.

On the Eastern side of Germany, the organizational problems of the groups that are more movements than parties are formidable, and the chances that they could be largely absorbed by the major parties in the socioeconomic turmoil of the next several years cannot be ignored. The active memberships of these movement-parties have already receded, the financial resources are strapped, and the appeal of a civil rights, feminist, and ecological message during an economic *Wiederaufbau* (rebuilding) period may not have much resonance.

A plus for the Greens at least in the Western part of Germany is their clearly defined generational core of voters, which is now between thirty-five and fifty years old. These individuals are the 68ers, who were socialized in the heady days of the late 1960s and during the expansion of the participatory repertoire in the 1970s. But though this cohort has continued to define itself as loyal, it is still open to poaching by the SPD and the FDP, and it is overshadowed on both sides—younger and older voters—by uncertain and dismal prospects respectively. One possible conclusion to this is that the Greens may represent something quite unusual: a generational party that could not extend its convictions to a wide share of the electorate. On the Eastern side, it is premature to talk of any core voters. Much will depend on how the SPD reorganizes itself in the East, where the PDS voters go, and how the very fragile movement-parties will define themselves differently from the large *Volksparteien*.

As we noted earlier, the networks for the Greens in the West have declined in strength since the early 1980s.[24] Because many of these grass-roots groups provided the shock troops for the Greens,[25] the consequences of reduced support are clear. These informal semi-institutionalized groups just do not provide the same support as the trade unions or the church did for the mass parties at an earlier period of their development. As we noted in an earlier chapter, movement politics is cyclical and episodic; party politics is constant. There is an expanded middle class as a result of greater educational opportunities, but neither the Greens nor the other parties can count these new middle-class voters as "captured" loyalists.

And yet the mobilizable constituency for the Greens of the West still looks sizable in comparison to the problems that the citizen movement-parties (Alliance 90/Greens) may face in holding their supporters and gaining new adherents in the East. If one looks at the background of the citizen movements in the West and compares it with that of the East, one sees an extensive network of groups outside the traditional pressure group system supported by educated, fairly well-to-do middle-class types with a vast array of political skills. The movement experience in the West before the Green party was founded came after a sustained period of economic growth and affluence unparalleled in modern history. In contrast, the movements of the East developed in an atmosphere of fear and anxiety, protected by the church, where the opportunity to expand on styles of opposition and dissent was definitely limited. Forty years of the Communist party in East Germany gave little basis for a "silent revolution" of the type that Inglehart has described.

Given the hard times expected in the coming years, several possibilities are open for the Alliance 90/Greens. Protest on the left may well expand, and the citizen movements may develop a mix of materialist and postmaterialist positions that expand their ranks. However, if the counterpart of the Greens in the East overemphasizes the issues of a new constitution, democratization, and civil rights at a time when economic goals are pressing, they may further diminish their appeal.

This point about the role of the grass roots in energizing the Green party obviously turns on the issues that will be prominent in the new Germany in the next several years. The environmental issue is likely to stay very much in the picture, but it will probably be secondary to the issue of economic development and jobs. It will be a major challenge for the Greens and citizen movements of both sides of Germany to be able to offer policy positions sufficiently different from the SPD in order to attract members and voters. A variation of the question of which issues will be on the public agenda is how the party system will develop, and our guess is that the competition from the SPD could endanger the existence of both East and West Greens. The new generation of SPD leaders—LaFontaine, Engholm, Schröder, and Klose—favor a postmaterialist/materialist mix of policies that is quite different from that of the older generation. Engholm, Klose, and Schröder are not as bold as LaFontaine but they would be just as content to absorb the Greens as to be in coalition with them if they can manage it. Yet the SPD's room for maneuver is limited, caught as it is in a difficult squeeze between the workers and the new middle class. This situation will remain a problem, even with the decreasing power of the unions and the increased size of the new middle class. As we noted earlier, the outcome of the competition for the PDS voters is not easy to describe. The Alliance 90/Greens could attract the younger educated generation but the older voters could easily go to center and right parties.

The road ahead for New Politics in the decade of the 1990s is uphill. Can the Greens' shaky confederation of East and West forces change its spots organizationally and approach the styles and techniques of the other parties while establishing its own positive identity? Can they find a public space in the electorate in the face of the clear capacities for adaptability of the major parties? Can the Greens of the West survive out of Bundestag for four years? Can they develop good working arrangements with the newcomers of the East? Can they change from pouting to thinking more constructively about the problems of the new Germany? The prospects are a bit daunting. One possible scenario is the shrinkage and absorption of the Greens of the West, first on the national level, then after a longer period time in some of the states, and then even still longer in local politics. And on the Eastern side, there is a scenario of courageous neophytes bucking well-heeled and well-organized party machines and articulating issues that will be secondary in importance until economic stability and regular employment is restored.

The scenario of Rainer-Olaf Schultze of Augsburg University is quite different. He sees a party system of some differentiation with strong left- and right-wing voices, reactions against central control and the market, and a series of policy problems where the *Volksparteien* are given plenty of competition. He sees throughout Germany decreasing party loyalty and increased issue voting with a vigorous debate between Left and Right.[26] There is much to Schultze's argument. We do see lively competition between catch-all parties and framework parties with a range of alliances that suggest that the waxing and not the waning of opposition will likely occur.

Conclusion

The catalog of needed repairs for a party looking for a new beginning does not have to be spelled out in detail, but at the top of this list is establishing a clear identity. There are indications that the Greens have worked through their dogmatic phase from the antisystem leftists of the late 1960s. They should now go forward as a party of the reform left that concentrates on ecological and civil rights issues while continuing to push for democratization in society and polity.[27] The latter two issues are crucially important in working out a long-term relationship with the Alliance 90/Greens of the East. The special problems of the East also suggest that ecological concerns must be rethought in relation to scarce resources. The West German Greens' perspective had presumed a post-materialist affluent society. The balance between ecology and economic development—between materialist and postmaterialist demands—obviously needs adjustment given the problems in the new Germany. Are the marks of origin so decisive—as Tocqueville and Panebianco seem to suggest—that adaptation is not possible?[28] We think not. As we have stated, the emerging party system of the new Germany may well have two powerful catch-all parties, CDU and SPD, contending with *two* different types of framework parties in the future. The evidence of the past several decades strongly indicts the lethargy of the *Volksparteien* on their responsiveness to new issues. It is not just the formal, bureaucratized structures that limit flexibility on new demands. Attentiveness to new policies, especially those that rub against the dominant paradigm of international competition, high rates of economic growth, and often-cozy state-labor-capital networks, is often slow. The FDP is a framework party with a looser organizational structure, a smaller membership, and a brokering ability that allows it to move left and right, but its elites are also tied in to powerful clients in the marketplace. In contrast, the Greens are really a different type of framework party. Their activists and voters do not identify with capital or labor in a consistent sense. They issue to a large degree from the new middle class and their critical detachment from the production process enables them to promote radical change or pragmatic reform.

Our investigation has charted that bumpy road between those poles for the Greens in the 1980s. Octavio Paz says that "one of the most incontrovertible glories of the bourgeoisie" is that they assert power with the "weapon of critical thought . . . to analyze itself and its works."[29] The Greens are part of this adversarial company. What they have sought with their experiment in decentralized power was a postindustrial framework party of the middle-class intelligentsia. Their contribution to the West German, and now German, polity has been to add that plasticity, daring, and moral stubbornness that semi-institutionalized political formations often give to overinstitutionalized, state-supported parties. Insulation from powerful economic forces and an almost missionary zeal born of generational conflict allowed the Greens to raise important questions about Germany's brand of capitalism and democracy, but they did not always bring forth convincing solutions. This postindustrial framework party provided a dash of color, unconventionality, and high principle, but its ambiguity—and at times, hostility—toward pragmatic incremental reform through the laborious process of coalition building defined its limits and may mark its demise.

In a way quite different from the FDP, this framework party gave the German political system an innovative shove to help wean it from a rather staid model of representative democracy that reflected on Weimar so intently that it looked askance at more participatory, even plebiscitary, forms of political action. The expansion of the democratic repertoire that influenced the political culture was nurtured by the extraparliamentary opposition of the 1950s, broadened by the student movement of the 1960s, and semi-institutionalized by the citizen action groups, new social movements, and Greens of the 1970s and 1980s. The Greens and these other New Politics forces helped engender public acceptance of a wider degree of dissent, opposition, and civil rights and thereby aided in developing a more resilient and tolerant German polity. Whether that resilience holds up in the face of hard economic times, refugees seeking asylum, powerful supranational organizations, and a Germany defining a new international role will be the challenge for the future.

We note further that the odds are even that the Greens can make the transition from a movement-party to a framework party that accepts a measure of professionalism, the politics of media personalities, and governmental power without jettisoning principles. In the United States, radicals quite often become moderate and conservative Rotarians; in Germany, Green radicals may continue to be persistent reformers. We see signs that the Greens are revising their act. A 1989 study of the Greens' organizational dilemma in the mid-1980s detected a movement from recruiting by ideological reflex to professional criteria.[30] In many ways the factional problems of the Greens have been reduced by the early attrition of right-wing activists and the more recent departure of left-wing activists. The skeptics about the Green party experiment—and they have some solid arguments—tended to see it as a generational flash in the pan because of the inability to renew itself beyond its core of '68ers. The results of the state elections of 1991 and 1992, especially those of Hesse, Bremen, Baden-Württemberg, and Schleswig-Holstein, suggest that organizational work can remobilize young voters, but this work is a different type of party work than in the previous decade. These elections also showed that the Greens' policy agenda is distinct enough to garner sufficient votes, especially if the economic issues of everyday life are addressed. Working out a healthy and mutually sustaining relationship with the Eastern Alliance 90/Greens will be the litmus test for the long-range success of the Greens. With representation in thirteen of sixteen state parliaments, coalition participation in three, thousands of seats in local councils, and access to a sizable amount of funds,[31] the Greens and their allies have the potential to offer the constructive criticism and long-range suggestions on policy alternatives that the new Germany needs.

Despite all their problems, there seems to be a niche for the Greens in the party system in Germany. As we have emphasized, massive overinstitutionalized parties, often tied in, cheek by jowl, to powerful economic interests, need a less institutionalized and more cheeky adversary that has some autonomy from the dominant economic interests. In a recent magisterial work on democracy, Dahl notes that the "prospects for democracy hinge on the diversity of view among policy specialists and the relative weakness of their common interests as a 'class.'"[32] Following this line of analysis, Raschke notes that the big parties are like the massive tankers (of which Peter Glotz has written) and that although they have the power, they need the tugboat to help them change course.[33] The Greens did "tugboat activity" for the SPD in the 1980s and the FDP did it for the CDU. Perhaps if the Greens and Alliance 90/Greens can promote the civility in their party organization that they seek for German society as a whole, they will develop a more stable organization and a more loyal electorate. The domestic and foreign policy challenges for Germany in the 1990s will be formidable, and an elected government needs a lively and constructive opposition.

Finally, we would advance the argument that the Greens have antici-pated problems of democratic governance in the twenty-first century. The domain of democracy has been the nation-state for some centuries now, but the problems ahead include more *supranational* power with institutions such as the European Community, *and* the concerns of many citizens— given voice by the Greens—of democratizing *subnational* institutions. These two problems are related. As one preeminent theorist of democracy has written: "The larger scale of decisions need not lead inevitably to a *wielding* sense of powerlessness provided citizens can exercise significant control over decisions on the smaller scale of matters important in their daily lives: education, public health, town and city planning, the supply and quality of the local public sector, from streets and lighting to parks and playgrounds, and the like."[34] That is a fair summary of the Green political experiment: The antidote to feelings of powerlessness is to con-tinue revitalizing local and regional democracy. Meanwhile, the historical problem is helping give German nationalism—and its development is inevitable—a European and cosmopolitan accent. The Greens have always talked about *Lernprozess* (the learning process). Now it is up to them to apply the lesson before school is out.

Notes

1. Franz Urban Pappi, "Wahrgenommenes Parteiensystem und Wahlentschei-dung in Ost-und Westdeutschland: Zur Interpretation der ersten gesamtdeutschen Bundestagswahl," in *Aus Politik und Zeitgeschichte*, B44/91, October 25, 1991, pp. 15–26.

2. Hubert Kleinert, "Die Grünen 1990/91: Vom Wahldebakel zum Neuanfang," in *Aus Politik und Zeitgeschichte*, pp. 27–37.

3. Herbert Kitschelt, *The Logics of Party Formation: Ecological Politics in Belgium and West Germany* (Ithaca: Cornell University Press, 1989), p. 41.

4. Ibid., p. 165.

5. Jürgen Maier, "Die Grüne Parteien in Westeuropa," *Die Grünen: Monatszei-tung* (Bonn: Die Grünen, 1990).

6. Daniel Hamilton, *After the Revolution: The New Political Landscape in East Germany* (Washington, D.C.: American Institute for Contemporary German Stud-ies, 1990), p. 13.

7. Interviews with citizen movement activists in Rostock in June 1991 give evidence that the pace of change in order to satisfy electoral law was frantic. The hurried tempo prevented an electoral coalition of citizen movements, so they ran

separately and received no seats in Mecklenburg–West Pomerania. In coalition they would have received 8 to 9 percent of the Landtag seats.

8. Uwe Thaysen, "Der Runde Tisch. Oder: Wer war das Volk? Teil II," *Zeitschrift für Parlamentsfragen* 21 (June 1990):257–308.

9. Jane Kramer, "Letter from Germany," *New Yorker* (June 18, 1990). This long essay discussed the politics of a family of several generations in Mecklenburg–West Pomerania.

10. Protocol of the Extraordinary Conference of the Greens, Hagen, April 30–May 1, 1990.

11. Horst Bieber, "Grüne am Abgrund," *Die Zeit*, June 22, 1990.

12. Mannheim Berichte der Forschungsgruppe, "Bundestagswahl 1990: Eine Analyse Der Ersten Gesamtdeutschen Bundestagswahl am 2. Dezember 1990," no. 61 (Mannheim: Forschungsgruppe Wahlen e.V. 1990).

13. Angelo Panebianco, *Political Parties: Organization and Power* (translated by Marc Silver; published in Italian in 1982) (Cambridge: Cambridge University Press, 1988).

14. Helmut Wiesenthal, "Die Wähler und 'ihre' Partei: Notizen über eine Beziehungskrise," in *Sind die Grünen noch zu retten?* Ralf Fücks, ed. (Reinbek: Rowolt, 1991), p. 157.

15. Frank Drieschner, Wolfgang Gehrmann, Thomas Kleine-Brockhoff, Norbert Kostede, Klaus Pokatzky, Ulrich Stock, and Christian Wernicke, "Wie die Zukunft aus dem Parlament verschwand," *Die Zeit* (Hamburg, December 14, 1990).

16. Interview with Joschka Fischer, Wiesbaden, November 1990.

17. Mannheim Berichte der Forschungsgruppe Wahlen e.V. 1991. "Wahl in Rheinland-Pfalz: Eine Analyse der Landtagswahl vom 21. April 1991," no. 64 (Mannheim: Forschungsgruppe Wahlen e.V., 1991).

18. Mannheim Berichte der Forschungsgruppe Wahlen e.V. 1990. "Wahl in Bremen: Eine Analyse der Bürgerschaftswahl vom 29. September 1991," no. 66 (Mannheim: Forschungsgruppe Wahlen e.V., 1991).

19. *Die tageszeitung*, December 10, 1991.

20. Mannheim Berichte der Forschungsgruppe Wahlen e.V. 1992. "Wahl in Baden-Württemberg: Eine Analyse der Landtagswahl vom 5. April 1992," no. 67 (Mannheim: Forschungsgruppe Wahlen e.V., 1992).

21. Mannheim Berichte der Forschungsgruppe Wahlen e.V. 1992. "Wahl in Schleswig-Holstein: Eine Analyse der Landtagswahl vom 5. April 1992," no. 68 (Mannheim: Forschungsgruppe Wahlen e.V., 1992).

22. Kitschelt, *The Logics of Party Formation.*

23. Ronald Inglehart, *Culture Shift in Advanced Industrial Society* (Princeton: Princeton University Press, 1990), p. 369.

24. Bodo Zeuner, "Die Partei der Grünen: Zwischen Bewegung und Staat," in *Die Bundesrepublik in den achtziger Jahren*, Werner Süss, ed. (Opladen: Leske and Budrich, 1991).

25. Franz Urban Pappi, "Die Anhänger der neuen sozialen Bewegungen im Parteiensystem der Bundesrepublik" in *Aus Politik und Zeitgeschichte* (Bonn: Bundeszentrale für politische Bildung, June 23, 1989).

26. Rainer-Olaf Schultze, "Wahlverhalten und Parteiensystem," in *Der Bürger im Staat*, Heft 3, Landeszentrale für politische Bildung, ed. (Stuttgart: Landeszentrale für politische Bildung, 1990), p. 147.

27. Tine Stein and Bernd Ulrich, "Die Kohorte frisst ihr Kind: Die 68er und der Niedergang der Grünen," in *Sind die Grünen noch zu retten?* Ralf Fücks, ed. Also Ralf Fücks, "Ökologie und Bürgerrechte: Plädoyer für eine neue Allianz," in *Sind die Grünen noch zu retten?* Ralf Fücks, ed.

28. Angelo Panebianco, *Political Parties: Organization and Power.*

29. Octavio Paz, *The Other Voice* (New York: Harcourt, Brace, Jovanovich, 1991), pp. 149–150.

30. Kitschelt, *The Logics of Party Formation.*

31. Ferdinand Müller-Rommel, "Stabilität Durch Wandel: Die Grünen vor und nach der Bundestagswahl 1990," in *Neue Soziale Bewegungen in der Bundesrepublik Deutschland*, 2d expanded ed., Roland Roth and Dieter Rucht, eds. (Frankfurt: Campus Verlag, 1991).

32. Robert Dahl, *Democracy and Its Critics* (New Haven: Yale University Press, 1989). p. 339.

33. Joachim Raschke, *Krise der Grünen: Bilanz und Neubeginn* (Marburg: Schüren Presseverlag, 1991).

34. Robert Dahl, *Democracy and Its Critics*, p. 321.

Select Bibliography

THE FOLLOWING BOOKS AND ARTICLES are selected from the English-language literature on the Greens and related topics.

Those students with a German-language competence should see the numerous endnotes in this book referring to the German-language literature.

Baker, Kendall, Russell Dalton, and Kai Hildebrandt. *Germany Transformed*. Cambridge: Harvard University Press, 1981.

Barnes, Samuel, and Max Kaase. *Political Action: Mass Participation in Five Western Democracies*. Beverly Hills: Sage Publications, 1979.

Betz, Hans-Georg. "Strange Love? How the Greens Began to Love NATO." *German Studies Review* 12, no. 3 (October 1989):487–505.

Blondel, Jean. *Political Parties: A Genuine Case for Discontent?* London: Wildwood House, 1978.

Bürklin, Wilhelm P. "Governing Left Parties Frustrating the Radical Non-Established Left: The Rise and Inevitable Decline of the Greens." *European Sociological Review* 3, no. 2 (September 1987):109–126.

Conradt, David, and Russell Dalton. "The West German Electorate and the Party System: Continuity and Change in the 1980s." *Review of Politics* 50, no. 1 (Winter 1988):3–29.

Dahl, Robert. *Dilemmas of Pluralist Democracy: Autonomy Versus Control*. New Haven: Yale University Press, 1982.

———. *Political Oppositions in Western Democracies*. New Haven: Yale University Press, 1966.

Dalton, Russell, and Manfred Kuechler, eds. *New Social and Political Movements in Western Democracies*. New York: Oxford University Press, 1990.

Eckersley, Robyn. "Green Politics and the New Class: Selfishness or Virtue?" *Political Studies* 37, no. 2 (June 1989):205–223.

Hainsworth, Paul. "Breaking the Mould: The Greens in the French Party System." In *French Political Parties in Transition*, Alister Cole, ed., pp. 91–105. Aldershot: Dartmouth, 1990.

Hamilton, Daniel. *After the Revolution: The New Political Landscape in East Germany*. Washington, D.C.: American Institute for Contemporary German Studies, 1990.

Helm, Jutta. "Citizen Lobbies in West Germany." In *Western European Party Systems*, Peter M. Merkl, ed., pp. 576–596. New York: Free Press, 1980.

Hülsberg, Werner. *The German Greens: A Social and Political Profile*. London: Verso, 1988.

Inglehart, Ronald. *Culture Shift in Advanced Industrial Society*. Princeton: Princeton University Press, 1990.

———. *The Silent Revolution: Changing Values and Political Styles Among Western Publics*. Princeton: Princeton University Press, 1977.

Jarausch, Konrad. *Students, Society, and Politics in Imperial Germany: The Rise of Academic Illiberalism*. Princeton: Princeton University Press, 1982.

Kitschelt, Herbert. "Left Libertarian Parties: Explaining Innovation in Competitive Party Systems." *World Politics* 40, no. 2 (January 1988):194–234.

———. *The Logics of Party Formation: Ecological Politics in Belgium and West Germany*. Ithaca, N.Y.: Cornell University Press, 1989.

———. "Political Opportunity Structures and Political Protest: Anti-Nuclear Movements in Four Democracies." *British Journal of Political Science* 16, no. 1 (January 1986):57–83.

Kitschelt, Herbert, and Staf Hellemans. *Beyond the European Left: Ideology and Political Action in the Belgian Ecology Parties*. Durham, N.C.: Duke University Press, 1990.

Kolinsky, Eva. *Parties, Opposition, and Society*. London: Croom Helm, 1984.

———., ed. *The Greens in West Germany: Organisation and Policy Making*. Oxford: Berg, 1989.

Langguth, Gerd. *The Green Factor in German Politics*. Boulder: Westview Press, 1984.

Lawson, Kay. *The Comparative Study of Political Parties*. New York: St. Martin's Press, 1967.

Müller-Rommel, Ferdinand. "The Greens in Western Europe: Similar but Different." *International Political Science Review* 6, no. 4 (1985):483–499.

———., ed. *New Politics in Western Europe: The Rise and Successes of Green Parties and Alternative Lists*. Boulder: Westview Press, 1989.

Nelkin, Dorothy, and Michael Pollak. *The Atom Besieged: Extraparliamentary Dissent in France and Germany*. Cambridge: MIT Press, 1983.

Offe, Claus. "New Social Movements: Challenging the Boundaries of Institutional Politics." *Social Research* 52, no. 4, (Winter 1985):817–868.

Panebianco, Angelo. *Political Parties: Organization and Power*. Cambridge: Cambridge University Press, 1988.

Papadakis, Elim. *The Green Movement in West Germany*. London: Croom Helm, 1984.

Parkin, Frank. *Middle Class Radicalism: The Social Bases of the British Campaign for Nuclear Disarmament*. New York: Praeger, 1968.

Parkin, Sara. *Green Parties: An International Guide*. London: Heretic Books, 1989.

Paterson, William E., and Douglas Webber. "The Federal Republic of Germany: The Re-emergent Opposition." In *Opposition in Western Europe*, Eva Kolinsky, ed., pp. 139–163. New York: St. Martin's Press, 1987,

Raschke, Joachim. "Political Parties in Western Democracies," *European Journal of Political Research* 11, (1983):111–114.

Rüdig, Wolfgang. "Green Party Politics Around the World." *Environment* 33, no. 8 (October 1991):7–9, 25–31.

———. "The Greens in Europe: Ecological Parties and the European Elections of 1984." *Parliamentary Affairs* 38, no. 1 (Winter 1984–85):56–72.

————., ed. *Green Politics One*. Edinburgh: Edinburgh University Press, 1990.

Rüdig, Wolfgang, and Philip D. Lowe. "The Withered 'Greening' of British Politics: A Study of the Ecology Party." *Political Studies* 34 (1986):262–284.

Saalfeld, Thomas. "The West German Bundestag After 40 Years: The Role of Parliament in a 'Party Democracy.'" In *Parliaments in Western Europe*, Philip Norton, ed., pp. 68–89. London: Frank Cass, 1990.

Veen, Han-Joachim. "The Coloration of the Greens: Profiling the Affluent Society's New Left." *German Comments*, no. 5 (April 1985):19–32.

————. "The Greens as a Milieu Party." In *The Greens of West Germany*, Eva Kolinsky, ed. Oxford: Berg, 1989.

von Beyme, Klaus. *Political Parties in Western Democracies*. New York: St. Martin's Press, 1985.

von Uexkull, Jakob. "Reflections on Parliament and Government." In *Green Light on Europe*, Sara Parkin, ed., pp. 343–351. London: Heretic Press, 1991.

About the Book and Authors

D URING THE 1980S, postmaterialist issues of ecology, peace, and human rights were championed by the West German Greens, enabling their party to overcome institutional obstacles and win representation at all levels of government in the Federal Republic of Germany. As Europe's most successful green party, its unique dilemma has been to balance the clashing imperatives of protest and power in Germany's advanced industrial society.

This is the first book to explore the evolution of this gadfly ecological party from its roots in the movements of the late 1960s to the structural reforms initiated following the party's unexpected defeat in the December 1990 all-German election to its rebound in the 1991 and 1992 state elections. Often characterized by intense infighting, the Greens evolved in the 1980s from an electoral alliance of protest movements to a "semi-parliamentarized" party. The authors argue that despite the Greens' self-righteousness, ritualized unconventionality, and ferocious factionalism, the party has had a net positive influence on German political culture and institutions and on international awareness of environmental issues.

However, in the Europe of the 1990s, the prospects are more uncertain for a postmaterialist leftist party. The challenge for the Greens—West and East—will be to adapt to a transformed political arena without renouncing their radical reformist program.

E. Gene Frankland is professor of political science at Ball State University. **Donald Schoonmaker** is professor of politics at Wake Forest University.

Index